The Toll *of* War

CHRIST COLLEGE, BRECON
1914 - 1918

Dr Glenn Horridge
with Felicity Kilpatrick

To my wife Christine, without whose encouragement
and advice this book would not have been completed.

Cover picture:
*1913 school photograph and 1916 Cadet Corps photograph. Nine of the
boys in the 1913 photograph were to die in the First World War.*

ISBN: 978-1-909196-19-3

Abernant Publishing
Alltmawr Fach Builth Wells Powys LD2 3LJ

Contents

Acknowledgements

Help with confirming or providing information has come from a variety of sources. It was tremendously encouraging that people were so willing to assist. In particular, Christ College archivist Felicity Kilpatrick has been central to the shape and format of this book, advising and supporting over a very long period. Her predecessor, Anna Lang, also helped in encouraging this project.

My grateful thanks go to Old Breconian and now history master at Bloxham, Simon Batten, along with Alderman Peter Barwell M.B.E. and resident secretary of the old Bloxhamist society, Roger Stein. Detailed answers to queries were also thankfully received from the editor of the Clifton College register, Dr C.S. Knighton; Louise Smith, Assistant Archivist Clayesmore school; Brenda Waksel and R. Wilson, both Archivists at St. Michaels University School, Victoria, BC, Canada; Major M. Everett, Celia Green and Lucy Jones of The Regimental Museum of The Royal Welsh, Brecon. Staff at The National Archives and The British Library were also always ready to advise on where to find information.

The majority of photographs have come from the Christ College Brecon Archives and I am grateful for the help in sourcing them and for permission to use them. Also to Paul Edgley for taking specific pictures at Christ College for this book. The photograph of Cecil Hoyle Broadbent is reproduced by permission of Oundle School Archivist Mrs E Langsdale, and that of Harold Blakeney Davies in uniform by kind permission of the Warden and Fellows of Keble College, Oxford.

I am grateful to Edmund Fitzwilliams for his support and permission to quote from family memoirs, Nia Griffiths for help with Titho Glynne Jones, Elizabeth Imlay of Parapress Limited and Professor Arthur Stockwin for allowing me to use quotations and poems from the published and unpublished correspondence between his mother and Geoffrey Boothby. I am also grateful to Richard and Catherine Hartnell for permission to use their material on Henry Norman Grant, to Kevin and Debbi Shapland for permission to use the photograph of Geoffrey Shapland, and to West Wales War Memorial Project for the photograph of Harold Madoc Jones. Finally, thank you to Doreen McConnell for proof reading, and Adam Hathaway for formatting the book.

Epigraph

The Last Night At School

"Look in my face; my name is Might-have-been;
I am also called No-more, Too-late, Farewell". - *Rossetti.*

I sat at my study window,
I looked to the western sky,
And I watched the saffron sunset
Deepen and darken and die,
While the old church bells in the distance
Were ringing 'Good-bye, Good-bye'.

Wreathed in the blue of the twilight,
Dimly I saw through my tears
The ghosts of a vanished boyhood,
The faces of by-gone years;
And the sound of reproachful voices
Fell on my shrinking ears.

And out of the gathering darkness
Rose the regretful refrain-
"To-morrow, To-morrow, To-morrow,"
While a sob that I could not restrain,
A sob from a heart overladen,
Went echoing back again.

Written by Harold Blakeney Davies and published in
The Breconian of July 1911, at the end of his last term at Christ College.
Harold was killed in action on 23rd April 1916.

Foreword

Every year during the Summer Term, 13- and 14-year olds from the current generation of pupils at Christ College, Brecon head as a group to visit the battlefields of the First World War around Ypres. Before they depart they have a study day at school in which they are introduced personally to some of the characters who were transplanted from the familiar environment of house, library, chapel, dining hall and games fields to the heart of the dreadful conflict that would claim the lives of so many. The pupils identify strongly with the individuals they study, and their experience in Belgium is greatly enhanced by this identification.

I very much hope that current pupils, as well as many others associated with Christ College past and present, will want to read this book and to understand more about these ordinary young men who occupied the same physical space that they do now at a historical remove of a hundred years, and who made such extraordinary sacrifices when called upon to do so. The rate of attrition is arresting, especially when illustrated visually, such as by the 1st XI cricket photo of 1915, a team of which all but two enlisted (a medic and a cleric) and among whom were two of the youngest casualties, Euan Edward Arnott and David John Thomas, both killed in France at the age of 19. It is fashionable these days to challenge the existence of what used to be called 'public schools', seeing us as bastions of elitism and enemies of social mobility. In practice, schools like Christ College not only provide rich and exciting educational opportunities to thousands of children from widely varying backgrounds, but they also continue to promote the idea of service to others and to society, that antidote to self-interest that acted as a spur to so many of those whose stories are told within this book.

These days, of course, Christ College encourages these qualities not only in boys but also in girls; I am not sure how the characters who people these pages would have reacted to that development. However, I am confident they would have approved of the way in which they are still remembered in Chapel services that would not feel strikingly different from those in which they sat; and of the enthusiasm of our pupils for sport, music, theatrical productions, debating and getting stuck into hearty meals in the school dining hall, as well as sleeping in the same dormitories which they inhabited, albeit now equipped with such luxuries as curtains, carpets and central heating.

There is still room for the evergreen debate about whether society learns from history; today as refugees wash around Europe in flight from totalitarianism and terror it remains a hard question to answer. One thing is certain, though, without encountering history in the unavoidably personal and insistent stories such as those contained within this book, the chances of such learning would be sadly diminished and the chances of the next generation of Old Breconians and other young people being both well-informed and wise as they set out into the world would be much reduced.

Emma Taylor
Head
Christ College Brecon
September 2015

1915 Cricket XI

Back row: Rev. A.E. Donaldson, E.J. Morgan, D.J. Thomas, W.D.G. Wilkinson
Middle row: M.G. Thomas, T.Ll. Evans, D.W. Saunders Jones, D.L. Jones
Seated: R.J. Parry, J.V. Evans, A.G. Henshaw
On ground: H.E. Thomas
Absent: E.E. Arnott and E.T. Akrill Jones, both of whom had enlisted during the season.

Preface

Teaching history at Christ College Brecon, one cannot but have a sense of the history of the school and the town. When time allowed, it seemed only natural to explore this history further and I would occasionally leaf through *The Breconian* in the R. J. Boulton Archive Room, situated on the mezzanine floor of Big School. The then librarian/archivist, Anna Lang, and my daughter Fiona, a pupil at the school, became used to me regaling them with interesting stories culled from the magazine and subsequent research.

Perhaps because of having held a commission in the Army and also accompanying the annual First World War battlefields trips run by the dynamic Head of History, Mrs Ruth Allen, my thoughts came to focus on the 57 Old Boys who were known to have died in the First World War. When I first started looking at them some five years ago, there was not a great deal of information on the internet, some names were not on the Commonwealth War Graves website, some information seemed contradictory and needed research to see if it was indeed the right person, and some Old Boys seemed to have disappeared entirely.

This has therefore been something of a detective story. As more information about the Old Boys has been revealed on the World Wide Web (although not always accurate), so further material has come to light. Conversations with archivists in Great Britain and various parts of the Commonwealth have revealed details or confirmed facts. Regimental Museums, especially the Regimental Museum of The Welsh Regiment, have invariably been helpful. Visits to the National Archives at Kew, the British Library and local heritage centres have all contributed information. In addition, the unflagging support and great interest of Christ College's current Archivist, Felicity Kilpatrick, whose undimmed enthusiasm for patiently reviewing and suggesting changes in the manuscript, has meant an infinitely more authentic tone to school life in particular.

After I moved from Christ College, the evolving story of the 57 resurfaced from time-to-time, especially when August 2014 and the centenary of the start of the First World War drew nearer. The 57 on the original list grew in number to 64 and indeed, it could be argued that one of the greatest ever artillery officers, Major General Charles Budworth (page 13) who died in India on 15th July 1921, should also have been added although his death of heart failure in India was not attributed to his incredible service throughout the First World War.

For those who wish, there are still details to discover. Although many enlistment documents were destroyed by enemy bombing in World War Two, individual men can still perhaps be tracked as more records become freely available. It might be possible to find out more about what some of the boys did between leaving school and enlisting, or about their military career. I hope that the Commonwealth War Graves Commission will be encouraged to add those Old Boys who fall within their criteria but who are not listed by them.

However, this book is both a memorial to those often very young men who died and a commemoration of their life in general and time at Christ College in particular. What struck me of their life and times was how similar, in so many ways, were their lives at school and the life of Christ College today. None more so than when in the Staff Common Room, hearing colleagues talk about the condition of the Chapel Choir's cassocks, only to read a few hours later almost exactly the same words in *The Breconian* of a century earlier. Hymn singing was also enjoyed then as it still is today with the uplifting strains of *Guide Me O Thou Great Redeemer* and *Calon Lân* still wonderful to hear. Following the Chapel theme further, it was and is fitting that life at Christ College is centred on the spiritual. So many boys were sons of the cloth and with the school led by clergy Headmasters in the pre-war years, its message was one of Christ's teaching. Christ College boys were imbued with a sense of Christ-like service for others. The majority of Old Boys joining up in World War One became officers and alongside their Public School contemporaries, carried this sense into the trenches. It was what marked out the British Army from any other Army. Even after the supply of Public School educated boys exhausted itself, the idea of 'Public School values', centred on the spiritual, was taught in officer training.

I hope that this memorial commemoration serves as a fitting remembrance of all the Old Boys who did their duty in the First World War, in particular those who died but also those who returned, mentally and physically scarred, and for whom life would never return to normality.

Glenn Horridge
September 2015

School House 1908

Introduction

The early twentieth century witnessed the great European powers subconsciously yearning to flex their military muscles. The cousins ruling Russia, Great Britain and Germany were to become involved in a family squabble that ultimately led to over 35 million deaths. Czar Nicholas II of Russia, somewhat dominated by his German wife, wanted to expunge from memory the debacle of losing to Japan in the 1904-1905 Russo-Japanese War. Germany, created as a new nation in January 1871 after speedily defeating the French in the 1870 Franco-Prussian War, was jealous of the British Empire and frequently encouraged those causing trouble for it. In return, Britain felt that Germany needed to be taught not to interfere in her sphere of influence. France, although busily building up trade with Germany, never forgot that Germany had stripped the territories of Alsace and Lorraine from her and looked to regain them. Thus a system of Alliances built up, with the key players of Great Britain, Russia and France facing Germany, Austria-Hungary and the tottering Ottoman Empire. In 1914, the thought of a quick European war, perhaps for some justifying the ever more expensive arms race, was not unwelcome in the psyche of many nations.

Whilst the European countries were building their alliances in the decades before the First World War, Great Britain remained the dominant world power. Boys from all the British public schools entered into the political, commercial, spiritual and military life of the Empire and Christ College Brecon certainly contributed its share. Old Breconians annually won scholarships to Oxford and Cambridge Universities, and many followed their fathers into the Church. In addition, a good number studied medicine at the 'hospitals', such as Guy's, perhaps not surprising from a school that was one of the first in England and Wales to include science in its curriculum. Other occupations which were well subscribed included the military, law and the civil service.

Christ College: a modern public school

Christ College had a well-deserved reputation for top quality education (and low fees), and was considered to be amongst the best public schools in 1889. Roughly two-thirds of boys were boarders and family backgrounds ranged from the clergy, medical and legal professions to the military, trade and industry. This success was due to the inspirational work of the Reverend Daniel Lewis Lloyd, Headmaster from 1879-1890 before becoming Bishop of Bangor. His predecessor, the scholarly Reverend J.D. Williams, had never quite fulfilled the promise that was anticipated with his appointment in 1856. Though it has been argued by one of his former pupils that the Reverend Williams was the headmaster who laid the foundations for the future success of the school, it is a fact that in 1878 numbers dwindled to so few that Christ College closed its doors to boarders for a term.

The new headmaster, the Reverend Daniel Lewis Lloyd, had been carefully selected by the governing body to repeat the success he had achieved at Friar's School, Bangor which had been closed for several years before he "made it the first school in the Principality". In January 1879 Christ College re-opened its doors to boarders and, partly due to the reputation of the new headmaster and the loyalty shown by boys who followed him from Bangor to Brecon, numbers increased very rapidly from fewer than a dozen in the previous year.

In December 1879 the Reverend Daniel Lewis Lloyd was accepted as a member of the Headmasters' Conference and under his headmastership Christ College evolved into a modern public school. At the Speech Day of 1881 he was able to announce, no doubt with some pride, that numbers had risen to 130. The new headmaster encouraged many reforms and developments. Among these was the gathering of "a phalanx of teaching power" in the form of new "scholastic staff", a combination of young men and experienced teachers who had been educated at Oxford or Cambridge. This certainly seems to have been a successful initiative and the list of scholarships gained by pupils in 1881 was said to be "the best and largest that a Welsh school has ever produced". In 1882 Big School was opened; the commodious new classrooms, big schoolroom and science

Big School

laboratory provided much needed modern teaching accommodation. Essential additional boarding accommodation was also built on the main school site and 'The Hostel' (now Donaldson's House) was opened in 1890.

In an intelligent blend of tradition and modernity, the Reverend Lloyd reinvigorated the old school seal as a school emblem, the original design of which had inspired the stained glass window in the east window of the school chapel, and in 1888 he introduced an instant 'tradition' in the form of a school song, "The Song of the River", which promoted public school values of loyalty and valour, not least in its final chorus: "be worthy of Brecon, be brave, be strong".

The Reverend Lloyd also encouraged many reforms and developments, including the establishment in 1884 of the school magazine, *The Breconian*. At the time it was much enjoyed by boys and former pupils but its real achievement was its endurance as a record of school events. There is a genuine flavour of the school in all its pages, no more so than in its match reports and letter pages. Victories in rugby football and cricket are recorded in matches against other schools and clubs. Losses sometimes led to anguished reports, such as in the Editorial of the Michaelmas 1889 edition which stated "How are the mighty fallen" after the first defeat in living memory in cricket against Llandovery in the previous summer term. Detailed sport reporting occupies the greater section

The Library

in each of the three publications per year and these reports are peppered with honest comments such as in the annual critiques of the main teams. The letter pages were not devoid of criticisms: despair was reported concerning the state of the choir's cassocks and the infrequency of granting the choir the traditional two half holidays per term; complaints were made about the cricket pitch - where trees got in the way of the bowler - and the lack of practice nets; and a long-standing grievance about the purchase of a display case for the library (which led to the resignation of the Librarian) spanned no fewer than nine separate numbers.

During the Reverend Lloyd's time activities and sport thrived. A debating society flourished and a reading room was established - works of fiction even arrived into the library! Lectures, spelling bees and entertainments were popular and kept boys amused on long winter evenings. In 1886 the Rugby Football XV won its matches against Llandovery, Monmouth and Hereford and the school cricket team toured North Wales on several occasions over the following years. 'Letters from Oxford' and 'Letters from Cambridge' published in *The Breconian* sent news of the "doings" of the Old Breconian societies at the Varsities. The first Old Boys' dinner was held on 13th December 1888 and the Old Breconian Association was inaugurated in 1890.

On the Reverend Lloyd's succession to the see of Bangor in 1890, a new headmaster was appointed. The Reverend M.A. Bayfield continued his predecessor's work and made further improvements to the school fabric and the lives of the boys. There were renovations to the Chapel which resulted in better seating and lighting but which (according to several disgruntled correspondents to *The Breconian*) failed to address the discordant squeaks made by the organ bellows while the organist was "getting up steam". The Reverend Bayfield instigated the building of a tuck shop and fives courts and presented a new school song, *Carmen Breconiense*, to the school. He also introduced "Compulsory Games" (although not entirely successfully), perhaps as an antidote to the deliberate absenteeism from the games field noted on a number of occasions, especially but not exclusively, by Day Boys. A Literary Society and a Natural History Society were added to the range of activities available and, under the supervision of Percy Morton (Master 1885-1909) who saw the importance of keeping boys busy, a workshop was set up. A keen and able photographer himself, Percy Morton was also in charge of the Photographic Club which, though short-lived, saw its members range far and wide around the Brecon area. There were few areas of school life in which Percy Morton was not involved and, as well as enthusing the boys to study science, he also created elaborate sets for the Christmas theatricals that were much enjoyed each year.

One of the most significant innovations of the Reverend Bayfield, though, was the establishment of a school Cadet Corps. In 1894 Christ College was given permission to establish the first school cadet force in Wales. The Corps, affiliated to 1st Brecknockshire Volunteer Rifle Battalion of the South Wales Borderers, was known as

The Tuck Shop

1 C.C. 1 V.B. S.W.B. (1st Christ College, 1st Volunteer Battalion, South Wales Borderers). Their smart uniform consisted of scarlet tunic, blue trousers with red piping, field service cap and white belt and they were armed with the Martini Henry rifle and bayonet. Stirring words in *The Breconian* of 1894 accompanied their foundation:

> We have the honour to be attached to a most illustrious regiment. What boy in Christ College has not read of the heroes of Rorke's Drift and Isandlwana! What heart does not warm within him at the recollections of the exploits of Lieuts Chard and Bromhead! Shall we not then henceforward hold it our chiefest pride to wear the uniform, badge and motto of the gallant S.W.B?

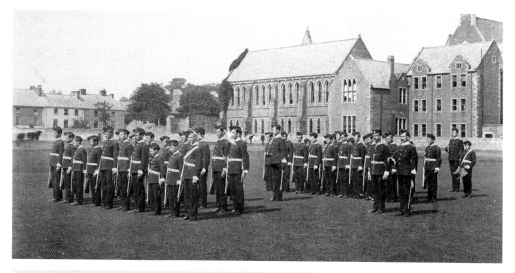

1C.C. 1V.B. S.W.B. 1898

The Cadets were regularly drilled and fortunate in having a close connection with the town's garrison. They joined in a number of events such as church parades and medal awarding ceremonies held at Brecon Town Cricket ground, even having a band sent to escort them there on one occasion. The Cadets enjoyed Annual Inspections and Field Days, especially when they were 'fighting' other school cadet forces. In 1896 Sections, based on houses, were introduced to inspire rivalry: Sections I and III being School House, Section II being Hostel and Section IV being Day Boys together with the boys from two small boarding houses on Bridge Street which were under the supervision of masters Morton and Rubie.

The Boer War 1899-1902: a foreshadowing

Three years after the formation of the Corps, many Old Breconians found themselves fighting in the Boer War of 1899-1902, in a cross section of famous regiments including the Connaught Rangers, the Northumberland Fusiliers, the Devonshires, the Shropshires, the Welsh Regiment, the Norfolk

Regiment, and the Argyll and Sutherland Highlanders. Others served with the various Imperial Yeomanry contingents or, as in the case of Captain H.J.V. Phillips (Christ College 1879-1886), with the Breconshire Militia. Medical representatives were there too such as Dr. P.C.P. Ingram (School House 1890-1892).

In a format that would be repeated within less than two decades, 'Letters from the Front' published in *The Breconian* brought details of life in camp as well as news of battles and old boys at the Front. Writing from Ladybrand in May 1900, future rugby football Welsh international A.F. Harding (Morton's 1890-1897) whose medal clasps read 'Transvaal', 'Cape Colony' and 'Wittenburg', noted that at one place they encamped they ate everything they could lay their hands on, "it seemed like a house supper over again"! G.S. Seaton (School House, dates unknown) writing from Bloemfontein earlier in the same year describes a scene that would seem all too familiar to the next generation of Old Breconians to fight in conflict: "Our trenches had been pushed to within 200 yards of their position. About two o'clock the most fearful fire I have seen or heard began. It lasted a few hours. It was really beyond description".

George Seaton of the thousand strong City (of London) Imperial Volunteers (formed 1st January 1900 from the various London Volunteer Corps) would later receive his medal with seven clasps on it from the King. Seaton was a member of 'the Devil's Own', the nickname of the Inns of Court, which furnished a contingent of mounted infantry and the cyclists detachment and so George Seaton became a member of The Lord Mayor's Mounted Infantry. George Seaton later stated that it was the school Cadet Corps which had "stimulated his martial ardour". He had the honour to be one of Lord Roberts' orderlies and part of Lord Roberts' force which captured Pretoria from the Boers on 5th June 1900, freeing many prisoners including fellow Old Breconian E.V. Jones. Seaton returned home to sit and pass his final law examinations in 1901, eventually becoming a legal advisor to the Siamese government.

The school Cadet Corps' best marksman in 1897, Lieutenant A.G. L'Estrange Le Gallais (School House 1895-1898) of the 'Fighting Fifth', stirringly reported in *The Breconian* having being woken at 3 am by a Boer attack and having to fight in his pyjamas throughout the battle which lasted until 6 pm. He also mentions having marched 43 miles in 32 hours "in awful dust" and later having to exist on what Kipling called 'Khaki Wafer' - similar, he says, to what the domestic dog would be fed. Le Gallais deserves a special mention. Not only did he and fellow officer and Old Breconian G. Le Huquet (School House 1897-1900) survive the Boer War but Captain Le Gallais (Royal Scots Fusiliers) and Le Huquet (Wiltshire Regiment) were, in fact, taken prisoner at Ypres in October 1914. Both survived this war after which Le Gallais became *aide de camp* (ADC) to King George V. He was also Colonel of the Jersey Militia and Deputy Governor of Jersey. Ironically though, now engaged in his third war, Colonel Le Gallais was killed in the Second World War during a German air raid in Sept 1940.

Other Old Breconians who served in the Boer War include J. Walters (Groundsman), and E.D. Browne (Hostel 1897-1900) who joined the Protectorate Regiment and was placed in charge of a section of South African Police. Edward Davies Browne would later take a very active part as a Political Officer in the First World War. Also serving was Captain H.J.V. Phillips of the 3rd Battalion South Wales Borderers who was awarded the DSO for his actions in battle. Along with fellow Old Breconian Lieutenant H. Miers (School House 1894-1896), he returned home with the Battalion reaching Brecon on 25th March 1902.

Several old boys were taken prisoner including Second Lieutenants E.V. Jones (Harding's 1890-1897) of the

1st Battalion, Connaught Rangers who was gazetted First Lieutenant in 1901, and F.F. Rynd (School House 1895-1896) of the Royal Garrison Artillery. Amongst those wounded was Lieutenant Henry Lloyd (Christ College 1890) who was the son of the Reverend D.L. Lloyd (Headmaster 1879-1890); serving with the First Welsh Regiment, H.C.L. Lloyd was severely injured in the arm at Drietfontein and evacuated home. Also wounded were Lieutenant A.A. Lloyd DSO (Christ College 1881) when fighting in a rear-guard defence of a British column, H.A. Hincks (Christ College 1896-1898) and Lance-Corporal L.S. Skeels (School House 1891-1895). The latter was on a troop-carrying train of 500 men which was attacked by the Boers, and from which £20,000 worth of stores and provisions were looted. Fortunately the Boers were not interested in taking prisoners that day.

Captain C.E.D. Budworth (Simmons and School House 1881-1885) of the City (of London) Imperial Volunteers Battery, was personally commended in a speech by the Prince of Wales: "Captain Budworth deserves special recognition for his most gallant conduct on a most trying occasion, when he showed such great qualities of pluck and cool-headedness". Captain Budworth became one of the best and most senior artillery officers in the First World War, directing the artillery fire for the fourth Army during the Somme fighting and the later Ypres Campaign of 1917. He received ten Mentions in Despatches, the CB, CMG and Legion of Honour, ending the war by distinguishing himself "at the storming of the Hindenburgh line and the famous crossing of the St. Quentin Canal". Major General Budworth was sent, via England, to India where he died of heart-failure on 15th July 1921.

Two Old Breconians died in the Boer War, and are remembered by a plaque in the College Chapel: Captain Rhys Price (Christ College 1879-1884) of the Welsh Regiment died at Modder River in March 1900; W. Logie Lloyd Fitzwilliams (Christ College 1892-?) of the Volunteer Company Arygll and Sutherland Highlanders, who marched with Lord Roberts' force to Pretoria, died from enteric fever contracted at De Aar. Logie Fitzwillaims was one of five brothers at Christ College. His brother Major John Kenrick Fitzwilliams MC (Christ College 1896-1898) was killed in action in the First World War.

On the termination of the Boer War, the boys at Christ College were given a holiday after break, and the Cadet Force fired a celebratory *feu de joie* on the cricket field. At the Speech Day of 29th July 1902 the

The Cadet Corps. December 1914

Headmaster, Canon Robert Halley Chambers (Headmaster 1895-1921), spoke volumes in praise of the Cadet Corps, and emphasised that the Cadet Corps was more than "playing at soldiers". He noted that three boys had recently left school and gained commissions, one directly from the school itself. This led him to extol the virtue of having a Cadet Force which required discipline and self-sacrifice, where cadets gained "the advantage that they had learned to shoot tolerably straight and (acquired) the elements of drill, a knowledge that someday might be of service to their country". With some prescience, Canon Chambers also expressed his belief that boys who had been in the Cadet Corps might go on to offer themselves as officers in the Militia or Volunteers and that, if every school had a Cadet Corps, it "would go a very long way towards averting in the future the danger of conscription".

After the Boer War there was much enthusiasm for the new uniform of khaki and puttees but in 1908 Christ College did not apply to become part of the Junior Division of the Officer Training Corps and the Corps officially ceased to exist on 14th July 1910. This may well have been due to a lack of anyone willing to take on the leadership. A letter to *The Breconian* in April 1913 states that "I presume this is the cause of our apparently defective patriotism (which is really not a lack of patriotism on the part of the boys at all). I refer to the fact that there seems no-one to command us". At the outbreak of the First World War the Corps was unofficially reformed through the work of Mr. G. H. Isitt, Mr. Robinson and Sergeant Cryer and on 7th April 1916 it was officially affiliated to the Brecknockshire Territorial Battalion of the South Wales Borderers.

Schoolboy Heroes

Boys at school were often reminded of the academic successes of Old Breconians who had preceded them. In 1887 Honours Boards were hung in Big School showing university scholarships gained and distinctions earned by former pupils. Further successes were reported in *The Breconian* and mention was made of present and past successes in the distribution of prizes each summer. Writing to his parents in July 1908, 15 year old Basil Biggerton-Evans (Hostel 1907-1912) described the excitement at school when A.F.S. Sladden (Hostel 1895-1903) gained a double first in Mathematics at Oxford: "The school is very excited and the old man is so pleased, hopping about and smiling all day long". In his letter he also refers to the only other Old Breconian to have achieved this "about 25 years ago".

The student to whom he referred was D.P. Richards (Christ College 1879-1882) who later took Holy Orders and became a Naval Chaplain. Also a Welsh scholar, the Reverend Richards wrote a detailed but controversial report on the Welsh settlement in Patagonia in 1901. D.P. Richards was a direct contemporary of Maurice Jones (Christ College 1879-1882). An exhibitioner to Jesus College, Oxford, Jones was an educationalist who became a Military Chaplain and later principal of St David's University College, Lampeter which, during his time, flourished and grew considerably in numbers and reputation. Also a contemporary, and another of those who came to Brecon from Friar's, Bangor, was J. Morris Jones (Christ College 1881-1885). He won a scholarship to Jesus College, Oxford to study Mathematics but later gained renown as an eminent Welsh scholar and the first Professor of Welsh at the University of Wales, Bangor.

Perhaps known best in the years immediately before the war was C.T. Davis (Day Boy 1884-1892). Having won the first open Classical scholarship at Balliol to great acclaim, he gained First Class honours and went on to a remarkable public career in the Colonial Office which culminated in the distinction of KCMG and his appointment to the post of permanent under-secretary for the Crown Dominions. C.T. Davis was not the only OB in the Colonial Service to gain distinction: A.J. Harding (Christ College 1894-1897), who won an open scholarship to St John's Cambridge, achieved a First in the Science Tripos in 1901 and went on to be first in the science examinations for the Home and Indian Civil Service, eventually becoming Sir Alfred Harding KCMG in 1935; W.H.H. Vincent (School House 1880-1883) Secretary to the Government of India, Legislative department, who had gained 17th place in the Indian Civil Service examination in 1885, was knighted in the New Year's Honours of 1913.

In the same year a knighthood was bestowed on J.R. Atkin (School House 1879-1885), another of the group of boys who had come to Brecon from Bangor and who came to be known as 'Bishop Lloyd's boys'. A founder of the Old Breconian Association and great supporter of his former school, the career of J.R. Atkin defined an era at Christ College. Made King's Counsel in 1907, he was elevated to the King's Bench and knighted in 1913. He later became Lord Atkin of Aberdovey, a man whose Christian faith instilled, he said, from family and school, led him to make several famous judgements protecting the rights of the ordinary man against the State or unfair business practices.

Perhaps more important in the life of a schoolboy was that a half-holiday would be given to honour those gaining a significant promotion or distinction. All those who gained university scholarships or public recognition were honoured with a half-holiday at their former school. The successes of J.R. Atkin alone were responsible for two half-holidays and a whole holiday, the latter allowing boys to travel to Llandovery to watch the annual cricket match in 1913. However, it was his batting partnership with R.T.D. 'Dick' Budworth (School House 1879-1886) against Llandovery in the summer of 1885 that was the stuff of legend. On returning to school, Atkin and Budworth (who had scored 63 runs) were carried through the town by the boys. Atkin's record (94) for the highest number of runs scored in a Llandovery match held for 44 years until 1929 and Budworth went on to become Brecon's first rugby football blue (Oxford) in 1887. Chosen as reserve for Wales, he later won his three rugby football caps for England.

Indeed, though headmasters openly promoted the academic and scholarly successes of individuals, it was sporting success that created schoolboy heroes. Among those who followed the Reverend Lloyd from Bangor to Brecon, were future Welsh association football internationals: W.P. Owen (Christ College 1879-1880) who made 12 appearances for Wales between 1880 and 1884; and Humphrey

Four Old Breconians played for Wales against New Zealand in 1905. Left to right: J.F. (Jack) Williams, A.F. (Boxer) Harding, W. (Spider) Llewellyn and E. (Teddy) Morgan.

Jones (Christ College 1879-1882) who played 14 times for Wales between 1885 and 1891, including as captain in four matches. Their success on the football field was enthusiastically congratulated in *The Breconian* but it was rugby football that was most meaningful in the lives of boys at Christ College.

The rugby seasons of the pre-war years between 1899 and 1911 comprised one of the "golden eras" of Welsh rugby and Christ College contributed more to their success than any other school: W. 'Spider' Llewellyn (Morton's 1889-1896) - 20 caps, 16 tries; E. 'Teddy' Morgan (Morton's 1892-1899) - 16 caps, 14 tries; H.T. Maddock (Hostel 1895-1898) - 6 caps, 6 tries; J.P. 'Jack' Jones (School House 1903-1904) - 14 caps, 6 tries and captain of the British team in the 1st Test v South Africa in 1910; J.F. 'Scethrog' Williams (Christ College 1896-1899) - 4 caps; A.F. 'Boxer' Harding (Morton's 1890-1897) - 20 caps. Arthur Harding also captained the Anglo-Welsh side that toured Australia and New Zealand in 1908, a side that included no fewer than six Old Breconians.

Willie Llewellyn was the first to be capped in 1899 but the news that he was to be joined by 'Teddy' Morgan and Arthur Harding to play for Wales against England in 1902 caused much excitement at his former school. The Easter term of 1902, due to begin on January 18th, was delayed by three days so that Christ College boys could watch them play the match at Blackheath. On February 1st the whole school went by train from Brecon to Cardiff to see them play for Wales in the team that beat Scotland 3-0.

In the famous 'match of the century' played at Cardiff Arms Park on 16th December 1905, four Old Breconians played in the Welsh side: A.F. Harding, W. Llewellyn, E. Morgan and J.F. Williams. It was 'Teddy' Morgan, though, who left the touring New Zealand team unable to claim they were undefeated and whose name will forever be associated with the game. Not only did he score the winning try in the Welsh 3 - 0 victory but before the match, in response to the New Zealanders' haka, he led the Welsh team and the 47,000 crowd in singing *Mae Hen Wlad Fy Nhadau* - the first time a national anthem had been sung before a sporting event. In a 'Letter from the War' published in *The Breconian* and written on 10th January 1915, the pride in victory felt by Old Breconians ten years later was still very evident:

> *Off Aden we were anchored beside troopships, which we were told contained 75,000 New Zealand troops bound for England. They shouted to us, "Where do you come from?" It would have made you smile if you could have heard our chaps reply, "South Wales, the place where the footballers come from. Ever heard of it?"*

The Calm Before the Storm

In the years immediately before the outbreak of war, Christ College was under the headmastership of Canon R.H. Chambers (Headmaster 1895-1921). He had previously been headmaster at Brighton College and, in his 25 years as headmaster, he saw Christ College through the Boer War and the First World War and into the second decade of the new century. His predecessor, the Reverend Bayfield had left, it was said, "a fragment of a school, since a large number of boys and several staff migrated to Eastbourne with him". Canon Chambers, highly respected by boys and staff, devoted his energies to the welfare of the school and its academic progress. Repairs were made to the Chapel and new Chemical Laboratories were planned to replace the wholly inadequate 'stinks lab' in the Big School building. Percy Morton's zealous persuasion brought generous donations from Old

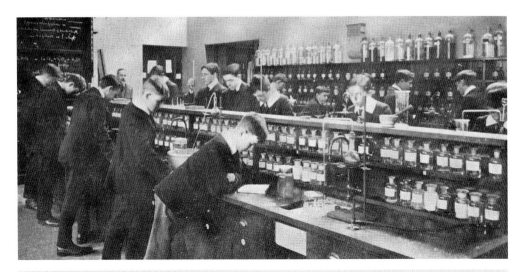

New Laboratory 1908

Breconians and benefactors and the first wing of the new laboratories was opened by the Lord Mayor of London, Sir Walter Vaughan Morgan, on 12th September 1906.

Under his guidance the school settled into a routine of preparations for examinations and sporting encounters on the pitches. In addition to the annual examiner's report at Prize Day, the more formal results of the Lower and Higher certificate examinations were listed in *The Breconian* - together with news of the 'schol. hunters' who had gone in search of scholarships to Oxford and Cambridge. The well-attended Prize Day was an opportunity for the school to reinforce its ethos and reveal its academic successes to an audience of parents and local dignitaries, many of whom were Old Breconians. The pages of *The Breconian* continue to be filled with match reports and player critiques as well as news of rugby football internationals and those who left school to play for senior clubs such as London Welsh. There were also reports of the hockey season each Easter term. Initially regarded as "contrary to the old traditions" and something of a poor substitute for rugby football by some of the diehard footballers, hockey had become a main team sport with detailed critiques of the players in *The Breconian* and news of Old Breconians in the Welsh hockey side, including W.E. Jones (School House 1895-1900) who won four caps between 1906 and 1913. In 1914 Lionel Baker-Jones (School House 1905-1914) set a record by being the Captain of Rugby Football (1913/14), Hockey (1914) and Cricket (1914), as well as being Captain of School.

There are also reports in *The Breconian* of the "doings" of current and former pupils: the election to Parliament of Henry Terrell (Christ College 1871-1872), a champion of the Unionist cause; the bravery of A.B.G. Biggerton-Evans (Hostel 1907-1912) who won an award in 1910 for rescuing a drowning swimmer off the coast of St David's; news of R.N.W. Leyson (School House 1900-1902) who was drowned in the sinking of the *Titanic*; the honours received by W.H.H. Vincent and J.R. Atkin in the New Years Honours of 1913; the death of Godfrey Charles Morgan, Viscount Tredegar, a governor whose martial fame stemmed from this being part of the ill-fated Light Brigade in the Crimea War; the work of Old Breconians such as J. Howell Evans (Simmons 1880-

1891) who, in 1912, was regarded as perhaps the greatest authority on the study of cancer, and Sir Evan Williams (School House 1886-1888), Chairman of the South Wales and Monmouthshire Coal Owners' Association who was one of the two Assessors assisting the Chief Inspector of Mines into the Senghenydd Mining Disaster of 1913.

On the lighter side, there was a great deal of humour recorded, not least in the suggestion that, given the severity of the Coal Strike of 1912, the Pavilion be used as fire wood because of its poor state. There was also news of E.F. Thomas (School House 1906-1912), an Exhibitioner at Emmanuel, riding at excessive speeds and dodging speed traps on his 'Douglas' around Cambridge in 1914, and of B.O. Davis (School House 1909-1912) who was receiving acclaim as a competition motorist with his driving of a 10 hp Mathias and 12 hp Talbot.

Noticeable is the prominent place given to correspondence regarding the need for Public School Boys to be involved in fostering the Empire by studying and working in countries such as Canada. Even more striking perhaps is the increasingly martial tone of some of the comments and letters in *The Breconian*. This is perhaps clearest in two letters, the first dated 8th July 1912 where the correspondent exhorts readers, especially those leaving school, to be trained in arms to defend "the Motherland". The second in early 1913 bemoans the lack of an OTC at school and blames lack of a Corps squarely with there being no officer on the staff, in the town or at the Depot willing to take it on. Signed 'Be Prepared', the letter is typical of its call to arms.

> … *"to preserve peace, prepare for war," is avowedly the best policy, yet - are we here doing our duty by slacking or playing games in our spare time? Games are all very well in their way, but perhaps a little too much is thought of them, and certainly a great deal too little is thought of the Empire.*

Town and School

B recon's inhabitants numbered over 6,000 just before the war and were involved in a wide variety of activities, not least in the very active lives of Church and Chapel. The town was well served by the railway which had replaced the canal in transport of goods. It had a fine reputation for banking and as a business centre. The barracks, home of the South Wales Borderers, had a strong relationship with the town. Agriculture came to Brecon with the weekly market and tourists came in increasing numbers to view the beauties of the Beacons.

The local news in early 1914 concerned hunt news and the vagaries of hunting foxes, badgers and otters; eisteddfods; land drainage improvement; Breconshire's Education Authority's problem of getting teachers and especially head teachers for "lonely county schools"; the latest cinema productions such as *The Battle of Waterloo* at The Palace Cinema in Brecon; Regimental Orders and news of the SWB and Territorials, including a recruiting tour by the Band of 1 Battalion, SWB. Other news concerned warnings on possible Foot and Mouth disease; news that on the morning of Monday 22nd June a fierce storm killed cattle and horses in several areas; news of ploughing and hedging competitions; as well as reports from the Council. Some national news crept in such as military unrest in the Army over the possible use of force in Ulster.

Thus in the long hot summer of 1914 the pattern of life, with steady change and improvements in the town,

1914 Cricket XI

was expected to continue within a country and Empire seemingly indestructible. At school there was a similar pattern of continuity: the early months of 1914 were filled with lectures and choir practices, Fives Competitions, Steeplechases and Athletic Sports, and hockey and cricket matches. The annual cricket match against Llandovery at Brecon was played to the largest known crowd of spectators and Big School was well-filled with visitors and parents on Prize Day. Held on the last day of term, the proceedings of the prize-giving ended with tea and music on Chapel Lawn.

However, at 6.30 pm on Tuesday 4th August 1914, the Chief Constable received a telegram ordering the general mobilisation of all forces of the Crown. Even this potentially alarming call to arms though was met with a desire to serve in a selfless way before 'the show' ended and recruits flocked to the colours, including reputedly one Old Breconian who was the first to volunteer in Cardiff. *The Breconian* of December 1914 remains an affecting record of the change that was wrought in the weeks that followed the last day of term: the Prize Day report from the end of the previous term, with its lists of examination results and scholarships, precedes the first Roll of Honour which lists the 137 Old Breconians "serving with the colours" and the first two Old Breconians to be killed in the conflict. The war of course did not end by Christmas 1914 and the bogged down armies were to slog it out for four bloody years. The Editorial in *The Breconian* of December 1914 noted that "everywhere we hear the bugle call to arms …" and continued

> *It is with a sorrowful but proud heart that we begin our first editorial by saying that some Old Breconians have laid down their lived for their King and Country, and that many others have responded to the call to arms in a manner worthy of the name and traditions of Christ College. They have died; but let us not forget those who have brought such honour and glory to the old School.*

As the months went on into years and the numbers of Old Breconians killed and wounded steadily mounted, *The Breconian* continued to bring news from the Front, mainly through printing letters from fighting old boys, publishing a roll of honour for those with the colours, poems and obituaries. There was also correspondence on school issues, such as matters of uniform, sporting colours and caps, as well as the usual detailed sport and other reports. The life of the school continued to flow in its ordered academic sequence. The Editorial at the start of *The Breconian* of July 1915, stated that "we cannot escape from the shadow of the War" and played much on the Cadet Corps as well as patriotism shown by two young members of the school who left school to join up at the very first opportunity: E.T. Akrill Jones (School House 1909-1915) and E.E. Arnott (School House 1913-1915) - both of whom were to perish.

1915 Hockey XI

Almost from the start of the war, away sports matches were curtailed but the sporting life of the school continued and even sports reports were imbued with the idea that "Our supreme task has been 'to keep the kettle boiling'". There are even occasional glimpses of defiance, such as the Hockey report for 1915 season written by the Reverend Donaldson who, with the departure of younger masters, had to return to coaching in December 1914 having 'retired' as a games coach in 1911:

> *In spite of all - Armageddon, The Deluge, and other minor catastrophes - we have enjoyed some pleasant games of Hockey. We have observed a growing development of skill throughout the School, and a creditable attempt to check excess of vigour in the form of "golf shots" and "shock tactics". The game has been keenly played as far as Fate has permitted it.*

THE TOLL OF WAR

The regular Letters from Cambridge and Oxford that were printed in *The Breconian* reported military activity. By the summer of 1915 "Games and athletics have almost disappeared from Cambridge, and the most active institutions are the OTC and the Military Schools". The Cambridge letter commented on Old Breconians arriving and then soon after "taking a commission". Light heartedly, it also mentioned an Old Breconian taking pictures, being keen on photography, and then being "mistaken by an overzealous constable, for a German spy"!

At school the lectures and entertainments included such martial themes as "the Whitehead Torpedo" as well as a popular sing-song evening. By the summer of 1916 the Cadet Corps numbered 70 boys, even if some were "younger and smaller than we should care to accept under ordinary conditions". Now affiliated to the Brecknockshire Territorials, the Corps even had uniforms, three bugles and a drum - although the band "require a considerable amount of practice in playing together on the march". Space was always found in *The Breconian* for 'Occasional Notes' which gave news of marriages, staff departures for the military, visits to the school and not infrequently, church appointments conferred on Old Breconians.

Further lectures such as a detailed report on the close-run Battle of the Marne, matches, amusing articles and sport continued to be reported alongside the growing list of those in uniform and dead, wounded or 'invalided out'. The April 1917 number of *The Breconian* offers a glimpse of the continuity of school routine that existed alongside the effects of war shortages:

> This term has been very like any pre-war Easter term in many ways. Hockey, fives, steeplechases and sports still flourish, though all are affected by war conditions. In place of a fixture card comes a curt notice on a classroom door, written on the back of a Greek exercise, and the array of cups usually distributed after the sports are to be replaced by very modest bronze medals.

The Editorial for the summer of 1917 ended by wishing readers "a happy, sunny, and patriotic summer holiday" but a slight element of war weariness was creeping in, as reflected in the whole country. The magazine had fewer jaunty militaristic poems and many references to those absent from the school. There was a report of an Old Boys' dinner held in Cairo, where at least eight Old Breconians were serving with the Egyptian Expeditionary Force in early 1917. The dinner ended with a promise to the Old School of "a love never swerving". Military awards continued to be noted in successive numbers of the magazine which also carried the continuous flow of obituaries.

The end of the war was greeted with "joy and thankfulness … (and a feeling of honour) … that "Alma Mater" has been granted the high privilege of helping to pay for that great Day with the lives of her sons". The Cadet Corps expressed the hope that they "be converted into a Junior contingent of the OTC". Military news of Old Breconians all but disappears although the War Memorial appeal, originally proposed at the end of 1917, remains to the fore. News of old boys is also to be found in the local newspapers such as the *South Wales Weekly Post* of January 1918 which reported that former Christ College Brecon boy (School House 1910-1914) Lieutenant William John Hamilton Morgan, RFC, son of the High Sheriff of Brecon, was the first airman to cross the Austro-German lines on the Italian Front.

Remembrance

Christ College Brecon
War Memorial & Chapel

Christ College remembers the sacrifice of those killed in the First World War and the Second World War in the ante-chapel. The names of those who fell are inscribed on white Sicilian marble tablets, surmounted by the school crest and bearing the words "To the glory of God and in proud memory of the old boys who gave their lives for their country". The memorial, placed just outside the Chapel, was created in the form of a crusader's cross on steps, mounted upon an octagonal base. On the memorial cross were inscribed the words "1914 - 1918 To the glorious memory of those Old Breconians whose names are recorded on the tablet in the Chapel".

Fittingly C.W.M. Best (Day Boy 1893-1900), the only one of four brothers not to die in action, oversaw the various stages of designing and building the memorial cross and tablet. It was unveiled by the Right Honourable Lord Glanusk in a very moving ceremony on Prize Day, 1922. Lord Glanusk, who had commanded many of the Old Breconians during the War, stated that public schools "had responded to the call of duty in the Great War with wonderful devotion. The record of Christ College, Brecon, was one that any school of its size might regard with pride and envy". He could personally "testify to their keenness, sense of duty, and loyalty". He continued that the memorial would "convey a message which they dared not forget: 'Play up, and play the game as we did'" and that it would be "an undying incentive to Duty and Valour". The School Choir sang from just within the Chapel, *The Supreme Sacrifice* and the Lord Bishop of St David's then dedicated the memorial. Prayers, Collects, *The Last Post, Reveille* and the laying of a wreath ended the Dedication.

Even before the First World War years but certainly throughout them, as well as in the subsequent running of the memorial appeal, the Reverend A.E. Donaldson stands out. To say that he was the stalwart of the school barely does him credit although the fact that he served as a Master at Christ College between 1902 until 1955 (including as Housemaster of the Hostel, Games master and Chaplain) gives an indication of the man. In the finest tradition of the Church, he clearly gave selflessly in caring for all those connected with Christ College and so it was not surprising that as well as being one of the chief donors for the War Memorial, he also aided the organisation and direction of the Fund. As it became clear that there would be a surplus after the erection of the Memorial in Chapel Yard, various suggestions were made as to its use. One was to subsume the money into much needed repairs but, given the sporting traditions of Christ College, by late 1921 the idea of a pavilion and possibly a gymnasium gained momentum. It was decided that with the additional money collected from a further appeal, there should be built "a Pavilion worthy of the School and of the dead O.B.'s, whose names will be associated with it". Thus it was that *The Breconian* of April 1924 was able to report that "The New Pavilion, which is the object to which the second part of the War Memorial has been devoted, is now finished, and it is proposed to open it formally on Saturday, May 10th". This happened but the rain meant the proposed Old Boys cricket match was cancelled as the ground was sodden.

In the summer of 1925 the War Memorial Committee was wound up. Reverend Donaldson reported that there was a surplus of £70 in the account and it was decided "to hand over the rest of the balance to the Games Committee to be expended on (1) Seating accommodation for visitors on the Cricket Field; (2) A flag and flagstaff; (3) Team boards and other furnishing for the new Pavilion. The Committee then adjourned sine die". This was all quickly accomplished so that "at the beginning of July the new flagstaff was also in position and a handsome green flag with the H in gold now floats from it on all important cricket occasions".

A total of 447 Old Breconians fought of whom over one third were killed or wounded, a not surprisingly high figure when it is clear that over 150 Old Boys were 'in at the start'. The final tally compiled soon after the end of the war showed 57 killed, 95 wounded, 68 decorated and 40 mentioned in despatches. Old Breconians who died in war service were represented with few exceptions from every joining class of the school year since 1881. Old Breconians served in all branches of the military as well as in civilian support roles such as the Mercantile Marine. Sixteen of those killed were sons of clergymen. In some cases, brothers served and four sets died together. Each death detailed in the coming chapters was a sacrifice, perhaps none so poignant as the three Best brothers, killed within a few weeks of each other in 1917.

F. H. BEST   A. S. M. BEST   S. W. BEST

The Best brothers, Bombay, December 1916

Chaplain the Reverend William David Abbott

Army Chaplains' Department

3RD DECEMBER 1918 ~ AGED 35

Hostel 1896-1898 and 1899-1901

William David Abbott was born to the Reverend David and Mrs Mary Abbott in the small village of Kirmington, Lincolnshire on 22nd July 1885. Three years later the family moved some 36 miles to the living of Cherry Wilmington where the Reverend Abbott was vicar from 1888 to 1891. Later that year he had again moved his wife Mary and young son, William David, this time to Knowbury, Ludlow. It was from there that William David joined the Hostel in January 1896.

Although short-sighted, William David was keen on cricket as well as amateur dramatics and music. He was also noted for his academic ability, and as well as studying, he threw himself into a mixture of activities. The first mention of him in school records is a plaudit for doing well in the Paperchase held on Saturday 30th January 1897. The next mention of him in the records is his success in the summer examinations of June 1897 when he achieved the Under 12 John Morgan Exhibition. Worth £10 a year, the academic award represented a significant contribution to school fees. William David's theatrical talents found an outlet in the Christmas Play of 1897, *The Sorcerer*, a two-act comic drama by Gilbert and Sullivan based on a Christmas story of love transcending all barriers. The 13 year old William David played the contralto part of Mrs Partlet, one of several boys in the cast who played female characters - including a chorus of 'village maidens'. The review of the production was not altogether complimentary but named him as one of the few actors who worked hard to make the complex plot "intelligible".

William David left Christ College in 1898 for uncertain reasons, but he re-entered the Hostel in September 1899. In 1900 he was playing for the 2nd Cricket XI and on 13th June of that year he had his best score of taking

8 wickets for 20 runs whilst playing for the 2nd XI against 'The Banks XI'. He rounded off the academic year by again winning a John Morgan Exhibition. His achievement was announced at Speech Day on 31st July 1900 when the newest member of the Governing Body, Frank Edwards MP, presented him with a Mathematical prize. He also gained First Class in the Oxford and Cambridge Board Lower Certificate Arithmetic examination. Reprising his dramatic success of a few years earlier, William David gave a stirring rendition of the then popular satirical song *The Vicar of Bray* at a musical evening held in the autumn term 1900. A suitable choice perhaps for a son of the Church given that it recounts the Vicar flexing his principles to retain his ecclesiastical post despite the vagaries of several English monarchs.

In early 1901 William David was playing half-back for the 1st Hockey XI and in the summer term he was selected for the 1st Cricket XI. His bowling was noted for its accuracy and the end of season critique for W.D. Abbott in *The Breconian* reads "On his day a very respectable bowler, with a tricky slow ball. Much improved as a bat, but a poor field owing to shortness of sight." Noted as a steady element in the team, it was no surprise that he finished the season by winning the 1st XI prizes for the 'Average Ball' (8.8) and 'Aggregate Wickets' (31), sharing the wicket honours with P. Spencer Smith (Hostel 1897-1901).

After leaving Christ College in July 1901, William David Abbott went on to University College, Nottingham where he played cricket for their 1st XI, and kettledrums for the orchestral society. After completing his degree he entered the teaching profession. In January 1907 William David moved to Bloxham School where he immediately joined the rugby football team. Although masters were not allowed to play against other school sides, he "excelled" as half-back in the XV matches against club sides. In the summer of 1907 he played his favourite game, cricket, again for the 1st XI. William David played rugby football and cricket again the following year, before leaving for Lichfield Theological College with another Bloxham Master. William David Abbott was made Deacon in 1909 and then ordained, by the Bishop of Worcester, in 1910. From 1909-1913 he was Curate of St John-in-Bedwardine Parish Church, Worcester. Whilst there, he married Miss Ruby Williamson on 7th October 1909; almost exactly a year later they had a son, Kenneth David George Abbott.

In 1914 William David moved the family to St Paul, Blackheath, from where he became organizing secretary for the Society for the Promotion of Christian Knowledge in the north west of England and Ireland. On 21st June 1916 a second son was born, John Williamson Abbott. The Reverend William David Abbott entered the Army on 7th June 1918 with the rank of Chaplain 4th Class, the rank always given to newly recruited Chaplains and equating to the army rank of Captain. He arrived in France on 7th August with the official designation of 'Clerk Chaplain' and immediately set to in one of a Chaplain's main tasks, the burial of soldiers. It was whilst undertaking this duty amongst the large number requiring burial that he caught a chill. Carrying on as best he could, his chill developed into influenza and then bronchopneumonia from which he died at No. 5 British Red Cross Stationary Hospital on 3rd December 1918. His Commanding Officer wrote:

> I have had an exceptional opportunity of learning what he was, what an inspiration he was to all around him; what a tower of strength he was on the side of everything manly and clean.

> He was one of the bravest men in moral courage I have ever met . . . he was loved by all

ranks, and his influence was unbounded; he was so human and so straight. His loss to us here is a calamity . . . the good he did and his inspiring personality will leave their mark till we all get home.

The Reverend William David Abbott is buried at the Janval Military Cemetery, Dieppe. He is remembered on the Memorial of The Royal Army Chaplains' Department in the Royal Garrison Church of All Saints, Aldershot, where his name is the first of 172 recorded, as well as on the War Memorial at Christ College.

Squadron Sergeant Major George Taylor Aitken MM

St. George's Cross
D Company, A Squadron, Canadian Light Horse

10TH OCTOBER 1918 ~ AGED 36

Hostel 1895-1898

George Taylor Aitken, born in Cork on 24th January 1882, was the oldest of three Irish brothers. He and his brother, Alexander, entered the Hostel in 1895 arriving from the family home in Kingstown, Dublin. George's younger brother, Gordon, followed the two older boys into the Hostel in 1897 and for a short time all three were together at Christ College.

George had an uneventful school life at Christ College. He left in 1898 and joined the Royal High School, Edinburgh. George then returned to Ireland to study Veterinary Science in 1899. His brother, Alexander, left Christ College in 1900 for Business; Gordon left in 1902 to become a rubber planter.

During his time back home in Ireland, George was a member of the South of Ireland Yeomanry. The Yeomanry were effectively a reserve force who, in the case of the South Ireland Yeomanry (SIY), met on a well-spaced although regular basis, and whose historian describes them "as a gentleman's club". After three years of studying, George decided to leave his home at 27 Clarinda Park East, Kingstown, Dublin and go to Canada, possibly with the intention of joining the Royal North West Mounted Police (RNWMP). Certainly very shortly after his arrival in Canada, 22 year old George did just that and enlisted for a five year term on 25th January 1904 at their Headquarters in Regina, Saskatchewan. To do this, he needed at least one recommendation and the people listed on the form were the Adjutant of the SIY, and his uncle John Aitkin MRCVS who was, at the time of George's attestation, living in White Hart Street, Dalkeith, Scotland. John Aitken was also a member of the Army Veterinary Department (AVD) as was George's father, also named George.

At the start of his first five years with the force, Constable 4174 Aitken was based initially at Fort Saskatchewan. In 1906 he applied for furlough to return home for "urgent family business". This was granted, with pay, and George left Fort Saskatchewan on 19th September and returned on 24th November. It may have been that his father, who at one time in his work with the AVD was attached to the 16th Lancers, had died. Certainly his mother remarried and became Mrs Shannon by late 1908. Shortly after his return, George was put on a charge that "on the morning of the 15th (December 1906) he was 35 minutes late returning off pass. Was intoxicated, however slight, at the same time and place". The evidence given shows there was clearly ill-feeling between George and the Sergeant-Major who had arranged for him to be put in a cell but there is no record of the judgment.

Two years later George was the constable in the rapidly growing hamlet of Hardisty, Alberta. The railroad had reached the once sleepy hamlet in 1906 and a huge number of people and businesses flooded in. In September 1908 there was a flurry of telegrams and letters between the first Attorney General of Alberta the Hon. C.W. Cross, the Assistant Commissioner, the Commanding Officer of Fort Saskatchewan, and the Commander of C Division concerning what was effectively a general dereliction of duty by Constable George Aitken. The Superintendent commanding the Division had requested Aitken be removed from Hardisty for delaying paperwork unnecessarily, not keeping up his record books and having an untidy office, despite several warnings. If Aitken remained, the Divisional Commander felt that his authority would be diminished. The Attorney General, however, wanted to look into the matter.

Private correspondence between senior RNWMP officers suggested that there was evidence George Aitken was "looking the other way" concerning illegal liquor whilst also imbibing. Also that he was in with the local politicians and this was perhaps standing in the way of efficient law enforcement. Phrases including "worse than useless" and "willful neglect or incapacity" go alongside reports of failing to provide information to superiors and lack of investigation of possible crimes. Pressure quickly mounted within the RNWMP to have him removed from Hardisty and this was done within days. George was kept in C Division for a short while before being transferred to G Division.

Despite all of this, George Aitken was allowed to re-engage in the RNWMP on 25th January 1909 for a further three years. However, his work did not go well and a little over a year later, George requested a transfer away from G Division. On 30th April 1910 he was reported as being "intoxicated however slightly at Edmonton while on pass for the purpose of going to Hardesty on business". At his hearing on 2nd May, he was found guilty, fined $10 and confined to Barracks for fourteen days. He was also made to swear the Oath of Allegiance and Oath of Office again later that month. At the end of his three years, George Aitken left the RNWMP in January 1912 having completed eight years' service.

In early May 1912 George attempted to re-enlist. A letter dated 12th May 1912 from the Divisional Commander of G Division to the Police Commissioner states that Aitken was "a heavy drinker" and "should ex-Constable Aitken be reengaged, I beg to request that he be not posted to this Division". Further enquiries within the force were made and the Commissioner decided not to accept him.

George Aitken remained in Canada and within weeks of the declaration of war he enlisted into the 19th Alberta Dragoons at Valcartier, Quebec on 23rd September 1914 at the age of 42. His choice may well have been influenced by the fact that, since their inception on 1st December 1905, C Squadron of the 19th Alberta Dragoons had been based at Fort Saskatchewan where George was initially based. His enlistment papers describe him as 6 feet tall, 38½ inch chest and single with his religion being 'Church of Ireland'. Under 'Trade or Calling' he wrote 'Mounted Police'. His rank on enlistment was Trooper, regimental number 1944. In October 1914 the Dragoons were sent to Britain eventually arriving at Bulford Camp where they were issued with better rifles and more modern weapons - the 1908 pattern cavalry sword replacing their 1890 pattern issue. The following month, George Aitken was one of ten men chosen from the Dragoons to ride in the Lord Mayor's Show.

After weeks of parades, lectures, sword exercises and drills, often in heavy rain, the Dragoons landed in France on 11th February 1915, the first Canadian Cavalry to arrive. The War Diaries record the sword and musketry practices, injuries to men and horses, the opportunities to have a bath, and various field punishments given to the men (usually for drunkenness), also a court-martial. On 23rd June 1915 George left for leave in England, returning on 2nd July. George was promoted to Lance Corporal on 7th August 1915. Later that month, on 29th August 1915, the General Officer Commanding awarded him the Russian Medal of St George, 4th Class, for his actions at the Battle of Ypres in the previous April and May. This was duly recorded in *The London Gazette*.

In early January 1916 George attended 'Grenade School' for instruction. At 2pm on 7th October, notification was received that Sergeant George Aitken had been awarded the Military Medal for bravery in the field. This was noted in *The London Gazette* of 9th December 1916.

Throughout 1917 George was involved in a variety of working parties and burial parties. His work included shooting wounded horses on the battlefield and collecting remounts from various depots to replace the ever increasing numbers of horses killed. He was also involved in attacks (which often seemed delayed for one reason or another) and training, as well as being part of the Canadian Corps inspected by Field Marshal Sir Douglas Haig on 14th February 1917.

A similar pattern of life continued in 1918 but increasingly fierce fighting took place as the troops advanced and, despite having fought throughout the war, George Aitken was killed shortly before the Armistice at the Battle of Iwuy on 10th October 1918. It was a particular bloody day with 5 men and 66 horses killed, and 17 men and 5 horses wounded. The official military report of his death reads:

> The Brigade to which Squadron Sergt. Major Aitken belonged was ordered to take the high ground to the East of Iwuy at one o'clock. The Canadian Light Horse were ordered to jump off after the infantry and make for the high ground in front of the Infantry, seize and hold it until they came up. (Squadron Sergeant) Major Aitken came over with the leading troop and was instantly killed by enemy machine gun fire.

Squadron Sergeant Major George Taylor Aitken was subsequently buried at Drummond Cemetery, Raillencourt.

Lieutenant Edward Trevor Akrill Jones
Royal Flying Corps
18TH MARCH 1918 ~ AGED 19
School House 1909-1915

Edward Trevor Akrill Jones and his brother, Robert Rowland Akrill Jones, were sons of the cloth, like so many others at Christ College. Their father, the Reverend David Akrill Jones, was not only a clergyman but also an Old Breconian. He was a member of School House from 1884 to 1886 before entering Merton College, Oxford. Thus it was no surprise when Trevor joined his older brother in School House in September 1909.

Trevor was born on 17th May 1898. On arrival at school he gained the sobriquet "The Babe" because of his small stature, big head and "large, wondering eyes". The name stuck throughout his school days. He evidently made a hit in various sports and acquitted himself reasonably in the academic sphere.

He was a keen and talented runner. On 16th March 1912 in the Junior Steeplechase he achieved the lead and "was never very seriously threatened". In the following year he similarly "secured a lead which he never lost". On a sodden course in heavy showers, he finished the race in 26 minutes 50 seconds, some 40 seconds behind his time in the previous year. At the Athletic Sports on Saturday 30th March 1912 he narrowly missed winning the Under 16 Half-Mile, coming a fraction behind the winner. The same result occurred in the same race on April 5th 1913 and again on April 6th 1914!

It was during 1913 that he also began to make his mark on the cricket pitch. He was selected for the 2nd XI and was regarded as a "solid player" in both batting and bowling, with six good innings to his credit. He was not in the rugby football 1st XV until the following year but in the autumn of 1913 he joined the Christ College XV that played a match on October 25th against Crickhowell to raise money for the families of the 439 miners who had been killed in the tragic Senghenydd Pit Disaster earlier in the month.

In the following spring he made his mark again in the Steeplechase. On Saturday 21st March 1914 Trevor gave a sterling performance in his first run in the Senior Steeplechase when he came second. *The Breconian* noted that he "ran splendidly and stuck to Baker-Jones (the leader) with great persistency; we shall expect to hear more of him in the years to come". The following month he came third in the Under 16 Quarter-Mile and a well-deserved first in the Under 16 Mile.

The summer term of 1914 saw Trevor playing for the 1st and 2nd cricket teams. On 17th June, in a match against Monmouth Grammar School, he was instrumental in the 1st XI's win by 49 runs. It was, claimed *The Breconian*, "…a most interesting game…The last wicket, Akrill Jones and G. Evans, gave great trouble and added 30 runs before the former was foolishly run out. He had played some good shots and looked like making a big score".

The match against Llandovery College on Saturday 27th June 1914 was played at home "in splendid weather". Christ College lost the match (120 runs to 224) but the game attracted more Old Breconians and visitors than could be remembered on any previous occasion. On that June day the clouds of war were already gathering and the contrast between the lives of the boys in that summer term and their lives just months later could not be more marked. The XI fought hard against their rivals and, in an unknowingly ironic statement in an account of the match, it was reported that "our tail (which included Trevor Akrill Jones) died fighting".

By the end of the summer term of 1914 Trevor had decided that an Oxbridge Scholarship to read Modern History would suit him but the onset of war aroused such patriotic feelings that he wanted to join up; his desperation to enlist is recalled in his obituary in *The Breconian*: "He was only sixteen but nothing would keep him quiet at School. He couldn't bear to think that he was out of it, while two of his dearest friends had just joined up". In all reports of him, it is clear that value of friendships was enduring, and that he wanted nothing more than to join his friends and "do his bit".

Unable to enlist until the age of 17, Trevor continued his sport in all three main games. During the autumn of 1914 when "a promising club fixture-list was cut to ribbons" due to the War, Trevor played Left Centre in the few matches remaining to the 1st XV rugby football team. One of these was the annual Llandovery match, played on 28th November. Trevor was noted as being "the soundest" of the three-quarters in an "interesting and well contested" Llandovery win. In the end of season report, *The Breconian* stated that Trevor was one of the "handiest men in the back division". His critique noted "Has genuine football in him; a good pair of hands and skill in running and kicking…A very reliable tackler".

In the spring of 1915 Trevor was playing left half-back as a member of the 1st XI Hockey XI. Thus on 3rd February 1915 he took part in the always popular hockey match against The Masters "Such did our opponents in our first match of the season call themselves". Another game he played was Fives and in the 1915 School Competition he reached but did not win the Final. On 20th March 1915 he did win the Senior Steeplechase and was appointed to the prestigious Sports Committee. Like his father before him, Trevor was also appointed School Prefect.

When Trevor's 17th birthday arrived, he left school to join up in the middle of what was for him a "promising cricket season", along with his School House friend, Euan Arnott. Well-liked and described as "singularly good looking, happy, sturdy, charming", Trevor was determined in character to do the right thing. *The Breconian* of July 1915 states "We congratulate T. Akrill Jones and E. Arnott on their patriotism, and we wish them and D.L. Jones, who is following them at the end of term, every success in their new sphere of duty".

Sixth Form in School House 1915. Standing: F. James and E.T. Akrill Jones. Seated: E.T. Sims, J.V. Evans, J.S. Eynon.

Trevor joined the Inns of Court Officers Training Corps, based at Berkhamsted, on 31st May 1915. From there he was commissioned on 10th September 1915 into the 4th (Reserve) Battalion, Sherwood Foresters (Nottinghamshire and Derbyshire Regiment). In September 1916 both he and Euan Arnott were wounded soon after arriving in France for the latter stages of the bloody carnage of the Somme. Euan never made it home but Trevor's injury, a shrapnel wound to the right calf sustained during an unsuccessful September attack on Thiepval on 3rd September, was a 'blighty'. He was sent to recover at Park Wern Red Cross Hospital, Swansea from where he wrote to Christ College on 15th September 1916:

> *I got a piece of shell in the top of my calf, which kindly came out 8 inches lower down, thus avoiding complications of any sort . . . The only officers left after our introduction to the Prussian Guard were the CO, Adjutant and Signalling Officer. We went over at a place that five Brigades had already failed to capture. Of course we were absolutely confident . . . Everything was beautifully synchronised, and we took the first two lines to time, with one rush-but then we found them untouched almost in a shallow trench, where they could just bomb into the second line . . . after 24 hours of practically hand-to-hand fighting, we had to retire. Another Brigade had failed! Personally I had rather an exciting time; I was buried once and then had a sheet of corrugated iron flung at me, temporarily 'doing me in' . . . I was just going back to the line to see what reserves I could scrape together, when I found myself sitting in a corner with the stretcher bearers bandaging up my leg. Quite the worst of all was getting back to the dressing station amidst a hail of shell.*

A letter calling him to his first Medical Board failed to find him at the Park Wern Hospital or at Swansea General. Official enquiries were made as to why he had not reported to the Medical Board and it was found that he had been allowed to recover at home at his father's living in Bolsover, Derbyshire. His next Medical Board, convened on 16th January 1917, found him still unfit for General Service but fit for light duties. Another, on 20th February 1917, found that, although he had improved, he still required "hardening". A third Medical Board, convened on 20th March 1917, finally found the 18 year old fit for general service.

Trevor was deemed too young to be sent back to the horrors of the Front but he successfully applied for training with the Royal Flying Corps. He gained his pilot's wings and was promoted to Flying Officer with 88th Squadron on 7th January 1918. However, on 18th March (just days before the Royal Flying Corps and the Royal Naval Service amalgamated on 1st April 1918 to form the Royal Air Force) 19 year old Lieutenant Edward Trevor Akrill Jones was killed in a flying accident at Harling Road Aerodrome, Thetford, Norfolk.

A Court of Inquiry was held with statements taken from four witnesses. The first witness - 2/Lt W.G. Westwood - reported as follows:

> I detailed Lieut. E.T. Akrill Jones, 4th Sherwood Foresters and RFC to fly SE5 B.604 during the morning of the 18th instant and at about 12.15pm he entered the machine and proceeded to run the engine up. At the first attempt at running the engine we found the carburettor required a little adjustment which was soon rectified. At the second attempt to run the engine everything proved satisfactory. About ten minutes later he proceeded to take the machine off the ground. I noticed as he was taking off, he allowed the machine to swing badly to the right and after leaving the ground and reaching a height of about 10 feet, the machine side-slipped into the ground and cartwheeled twice. The machine then smashed to pieces afterwards catching fire. I was with him at the time he ran the machine up and everything was satisfactory. The deceased had flown this machine several times previously making very successful flights. An instructor had flown this machine on its previous flight and everything was reported OK.

The fitter and the rigger of the aircraft, acting as witnesses two and three, confirmed the airworthy condition of the plane. The last witness was the RAMC doctor who confirmed that Trevor was dead "when extracted from the debris . . . (caused by) . . . shock due to extensive burns while in a state of unconsciousness".

The Court blamed "the pilot allowing the machine to swing badly on taking off. Seeing that he was approaching too near the sheds he took off too soon, stalled and slideslipped into the ground thus causing the machine to turn over and catch fire".

Whether Trevor's fault or not, his was one of the many deaths in training that caused questions to be asked in Parliament. So many young pilots were killed in or just after training, and such was the cost of the aircraft, that there were increasingly strident calls for lengthier and more comprehensive training.

Trevor's body was taken for burial to his father's living at Bolsover, and his kit was forwarded there to his father as well. The inventory of kit was extensive but perhaps reflected that Trevor's death took place whilst on service in the UK: inventories for officers abroad tended to be shorter. His kit included 15 ties, spools of film, a chain and cross, and a pencil.

The obituary for Trevor in *The Breconian* emphasised "The Babe's" talents and his popularity, reflecting on the youthful enthusiasm that would now remain unaltered: "So the war takes toll of our best and most beloved" … (He) remained a child at heart always. Death has but conferred on him an immortality of youth".

On Sunday 18th August 1918 Trevor's father officiated at what was a tradition in Bolsover on Feast Sunday, the "custom of memorialising the departed". The evensong service included a reading of the names of those buried in the churchyard that year. It must have been with heavy heart that David and his wife Ellen thought not only of their eldest son, who had been killed in action less than a year earlier, but also now the loss of their second son, Trevor, to the war.

Reverend David Akrill Jones was asked to be a Trustee of the Bolsover Branch of the Comrades of the Great War, one of four associations that amalgamated on Sunday 15th May 1921 to form the British Legion. The Bolsover Branch was given a small piece of land on which to build a clubhouse for serving and ex-servicemen and the Reverend Akrill Jones, as Trustee, proved to be assiduous in his duty.

The official records note that on 24th November 1920 the Reverend David Akrill Jones applied for the medals for both of his sons simultaneously.

Lieutenant Edward Trevor Akrill Jones is buried in St Mary's Church, Bolsover, Derbyshire. As well as on the Christ College War Memorial, he is remembered on War Memorial in the Market Place, Bolsover, Derbyshire with his brother, Rowland Akrill Jones.

Second Lieutenant Robert Rowland Akrill Jones
4th Battalion, King's Own Yorkshire Light Infantry
9TH APRIL 1917 ~ AGED 22
School House 1909-1910

Robert Rowland Akrill Jones, who was born on 30th June 1894, arrived in School House in January 1909 - two terms before his younger brother, Edward Trevor Akrill Jones. At the time, his parents were living in Prendergast Rectory, Haverfordwest. Later that year though, the Reverend David Akrill Jones was preferred to the living of Sketty, Swansea and then to Bolsover, Derbyshire in 1914. The Reverend Akrill Jones later moved to Llandaff where, amongst other posts, he was Treasurer and Canon at the Cathedral.

Rowland himself had little time to make his mark at Christ College before leaving in July 1910 to enter the engineering profession. The 1911 Census records the 16 year old Rowland as living at home and being a pupil in an engineering firm. However, this does not seem to have suited him and three years later, on 24th March 1914, he sailed for Canada with the intention of devoting himself to farming.

War was declared just a few months after his arrival. Though the Canadian War Records have no record of it, *The Breconian* records that "he came over with one of the earliest Canadian contingents". *The Breconian* continues "He suffered a good deal from ill-health during his course of training, but stuck pluckily to it, and after a short spell in the Flying Corps, secured a commission in the KOYLI (King's Own Yorkshire Light Infantry)." Rowland entered training with the Inns of Court on 16th September 1915, six days after his younger brother, Trevor, had left there to be commissioned. Possibly due to recurring health problems, Rowland was sent to 11th Officer Cadet Battalion on 7th May 1916 and on 4th September 1916 he was commissioned as a Second Lieutenant (on probation) into the King's Own Yorkshire Light Infantry.

On Easter Monday 9th April 1917 Robert was tasked with leading his men to attack the Hindenburg Line on the first day of the Battle of Arras. The battle commenced in a snowstorm but, nothing daunted, Robert "died gallantly going 'over the top' with his men".

The Battalion Diary for that day reads "TRENCHES 9/4/17 Battalion in action. Assault on HINDENBURG line unsuccessful owing to insufficient artillery preparation". The implication was that the wire in front of the enemy trenches had not been cut sufficiently and the result of the assault on the line was "Capt. A.G. Spark, 2 Lt. R.R. Akrill Jones and 2 Lt. S. Harvey killed. 8 officers and 176 other ranks killed, wounded or missing."

Second Lieutenant Robert Rowland Akrill Jones is buried in the Cojeul British Cemetery, St Martin-Sur-Cojeul, France. As well as on the Christ College War Memorial, he and his brother, Edward Trevor Akrill Jones, are remembered on the War Memorial in the Market Place, Bolsover.

Second Lieutenant Euan Edward Arnott
2nd Battalion, Welsh Regiment
23RD SEPTEMBER 1916 ~ AGED 19
School House 1913-1915

Euan Edward Arnott was born on 13 August 1897 in Aberdare and originally attended Monmouth Grammar School. Although Euan's family lived at The Garth, Monmouth, the 1911 Census records him being one of 30 boys living in The School House, Monmouth. In September 1913 Euan and his younger brother joined School House, Christ College.

Described as "physically strong and well grown", Euan soon plunged into the sporting life of the School. In the spring of 1914 he played in the Open Singles and Open Doubles of the Fives Competition and in the summer he was busily turning out for the 2nd Cricket XI and occasionally for the 3rd XI.

On 13th May 1914 Euan played for Mr. Munn's XI (captained by the Reverend A.E. Donaldson) in a match against other members of the School, and in which the notable all-rounder David Cuthbert Thomas bowled Euan out for 3. Euan also played an important part in the Christ College Cricket League, a league of teams (Tom-tits, Nibs, Leather-hunters, Wild Ducks and Fly-Catchers), which played fiercely contested matches. We don't know which of the five teams Euan played for but we do know that in 12 innings he scored 177 runs, including a half century.

The autumn of 1914 saw Euan playing rugby football for the 1st XV and, though noted as "a little spasmodic in his efforts", his end of term critique noted that he "Can at his best do much profitable work, and knows how to tackle". One rugby football match in particular typified both the time and spirit of wartime 1914 and may have played a part in further inspiring Euan, Trevor Akrill Jones and others to join up as soon as possible. On Wednesday 30th September an officer of the Barracks interrupted the 1st XV game being played on a half-holiday. The officer asked that they play a match against a team of those members of Newport Athletic Club who had joined the Colours at Brecon. Agreement being reached, the 'Usksiders' arrived together with comrades and a standard-bearer carrying the Newport colours. It was a formidable team which included two Internationals -

Wetter and Uzzell - and, unsurprisingly, the match was lost by the School 15-0. It was, says *The Breconian*, pleasant to play a game against those "who have so readily abandoned all to answer the call of their country".

In the spring of 1915 Euan turned to hockey and played left-back for the Hockey XI. He is described as "A determined and clean hitting back. He certainly improved, especially in the recognition of the superiority of skill over mere vigour". In the same term on 20th March he came fifth in the Senior Steeplechase, a race won by Trevor Akrill Jones. At the Athletic Sports of 1915 he won third prize in the Throwing the Cricket Ball Competition and, in his final term, he again turned out for the 2nd Cricket XI. He was also selected for the 1st Cricket XI, playing 5 innings and scoring 44 runs with 25 runs his highest score. Known for his physical strength, he is described as having "Much power in his hitting when he remembers to go down the pitch to the ball". Such was their keenness to join up, though, Euan and his School House friend, Trevor Akrill Jones, left school for officer training in the middle of the cricket season. Thus, although he gained the Mathematics prize on Speech Day in 1915, Euan was unable to receive it in person.

Euan entered the Inns of Court Officers Training Corps and was gazetted Second Lieutenant on 4th January 1916. He first joined the 3rd Battalion, Welsh Regiment and was later attached to the 2nd Battalion. He visited Christ College in the summer of 1916 before going over to France. Within a few weeks of his arrival, 19 year old Euan died of wounds sustained at the Somme on 23rd September 1916 - a few days short of the average life expectancy of six weeks for a young officer in a fighting battalion. Perhaps it was his youth or his "frank good natured comradeship" that inspired this poetical piece in *The Breconian* of December 1916.

To E.A.A. - A Tribute

War's awful toll has made us rue
The loss of sons, good, brave, and true;
But none more bitterly than you,
Our Arnott.

Still with us dwells your cheery face,
Although cold earth your form encase;
Still your keen ardour in life's race,
Our Arnott.

The School has oft with proud acclaim
Watch'd on the field, your sturdy game;
The 'greater game' you played the same -
God's Arnott.

Second Lieutenant Euan Edward Arnott is buried in the Worlencourt British Cemetery, France and is remembered on the Christ College War Memorial.

Lieutenant Sydney William Bell

8th Battalion, Canadian Infantry (Manitoba Regiment)

14TH JUNE 1916 ~ AGED 34

Hostel 1895-1899

Sydney William Bell was born on 25th February 1882 at Greasley, Nottinghamshire. Sydney and his slightly younger brother, Charles Courtenay Bell (Hostel 1895-1897), joined Christ College from Charlynch, Bridgewater, where their father was vicar. The Reverend William Atkinson Bell had been an engineer in India before entering Lichfield College to train for the Church in 1880. After a curacy in Derbyshire, he took the parish of Charlynch from 1884 until 1916.

Sydney was named after his uncle, a Lieutenant Colonel in the British Army (whose son, a career soldier, was killed in action in 1915). Sydney's six uncles and aunts were a mainly military family and were either in (or married to officers in) the Army, or more especially the Navy. Thus the family members could be found either in military service or business in many parts of the Empire. There does seem to be a particular family interest in South Africa where Sydney's grandfather, Sir Sydney Smith Bell, had been Chief Justice in the Cape and also where one of his uncles had gone to "grow oranges".

Given his namesake and his family's background, it is not surprising that Sydney had an interest in the military and soon after arriving at Christ College joined the Cadet Corps. Perhaps it was a little unfortunate that the Field Day on Tuesday 30th June 1897 was also the second day of examinations for Scholarships and Exhibitions. However, Sydney was able to take the papers early on the Tuesday morning and joined his fellow cadets later in the day. The report of the 1st Christ College 1st Volunteer Battalion South Wales Borderers (1CC 1VB SWB) Field Day, conducted with the cavalry and infantry of the Volunteers, records that arriving with A Company of the 1VB SWB was Private Bell "who had been left behind doing scholarship papers in the morning and had fallen in with the Volunteers on the march".

In the previous year Sydney's result in the scholarship examination was listed as *"Proxime accessit"* (the literal meaning of which is "he came next, or placed second"), still a prestigious placing. In the summer of 1897, he distinguished himself in the examinations by winning the Under 16 John Morgan Exhibition. In the same year, his brother, Charles, left school; after obtaining a Naval Cadetship, Charles joined the Royal Navy and later won the DSO.

In the autumn of 1898 school records show that Sydney became a House Prefect and in addition, a School Prefect after Christmas. He volunteered to set the spring Paperchase trail for the whole school and, by all accounts, did it extremely effectively. Remaining with the Cadet Corps, he was promoted to Lance Corporal in the summer of 1899. Clearly talented in many areas, at the Speech Day of 1899 Sydney was awarded his Lower Certificate of the Oxford and Cambridge Board together with the Drawing and the Geology prize, the latter newly offered by Mr. John Lloyd of Dinas.

After leaving Christ College in 1899, Sydney travelled to South Africa to study electrical engineering and mining. Once there, he soon joined up as an electrical engineer in the Royal Engineers, where he served for sixteen months during the South African Campaign (Boer War). In 1906 he enlisted as a trooper in the Transvaal Mounted Rifles who were taking part in the Natal Campaign of that year against the Zulus. Sydney was the recipient of medals for both campaigns but he also had other interests in the country. When not involved in military service he was mining on the Rand and in West Africa. His older brother, Edward Nevinson Bell was at that time looking into the iron and steel works in Burma and was noted for publishing a detailed and informative monograph on the subject in 1907.

At the outbreak of the First World War, Sydney was in Canada visiting his old school friend, George Aitken. Sydney and George had arrived at Christ College at the same time and both joined the same House, the Hostel. On 23rd September 1914 they enlisted together in the 19th Alberta Dragoons at Valcartier, Quebec. Sydney's records show him as being 5 feet 10 inches tall with a 38½ inch chest. His profession is given as 'electrical engineer'. Within days he was made up to Lance Corporal due to his previous military experience. He and George travelled to Britain and from there to France with the Dragoons. On 10th July 1915 Sydney was promoted to Temporary Second Lieutenant in the 8th Canadian Infantry (90th Rifles). This promotion reached the 19th Dragoons in orders on 17th July 1915 and appeared in *The London Gazette* on 27th July.

On 14th June 1916 the now Lieutenant Bell, whilst with his men at Zillebeke (Hill 60) near Ypres, was reported "Wounded believed Killed" and his death was confirmed when news arrived that his body had been "Buried behind the Support Trench". The official report reads "While on duty in the front line trench during a heavy enemy bombardment, this officer was hit in the head by a piece of shrapnel and almost instantly killed".

Lieutenant Sydney William Bell was described as "a gallant officer, much loved by his men". His body was never found. He is remembered at the Ypres (Menin Gate) Memorial as well as on the Christ College War Memorial.

Lieutenant Arthur Stephen Middleton Best
71st Field Company, Royal Engineers

23RD FEBRUARY 1917 ~ AGED 30
Day Boy 1897-1901

The Best family were local to Brecon and, through Mrs Julia Martha Diana Best (née Maybery), had inherited the family's large estate on the edge of the town. Through the maternal line the children of Julia and Charles Best had a strongly Welsh lineage. Julia's great-grandfather, John Maybery, had been an ironmaster in Dowlais and purchased a sizeable Brecon estate from the Marquis of Camden in the nineteenth century.

Julia Maybery married Charles W. Best, a civil engineer, in 1880 and for the early years of their married life they lived in Fulham. However, they decided to come to the family estate in Brecon and in 1887 a house was built for them, having been designed by John Morgan-Thomas JP. Charles W. Best took a detailed interest in the design and building, creating a water supply for the house and part of the town, and also installing a hydroelectricity plant for their home making it the first in Brecon to have electricity. Within a few years he had added central heating and an extension.

The 1901 Census lists Julia and Charles W. Best and their six children: Charles Walter Maybery (19), Arthur (15), Dorothy (14), Stephen (12), Frank (6) and Gwenllian (4) plus two servants. Walter, as he was always known, was the first of the four brothers to attend Christ College and joined as a Day Boy in 1893. In 1900 he won an £80 Scholarship to Jesus College, Oxford where he spent time playing "tennis for Jesus with success", boating, and occasionally playing cricket for the Old Boys XI. Obviously something of a character, he was elected to the University's 'Elizabethan Society' thus being allowed to wear "a tie of rainbow hue". He was also seen sporting a Panama hat around Oxford. After graduation, Walter entered business.

Mr. and Mrs Best senior were clearly also strong supporters of the school, giving a variety of prizes in successive annual Athletic Sports for over a decade and being noted for their regular attendance at the annual Speech Day. Following their example, in 1907 Walter gave a substantial donation of 100 guineas towards the new laboratories at Christ College. In 1922 Walter, the only one of the four brothers to survive the First World War, would design the Memorial Cross and Tablet at Christ College.

Arthur (born 25th May 1885) joined his older brother, Walter, at Christ College at the start of January 1897. He had previously been educated Le Brocq's, a small preparatory school in Brecon where pupils were taught by W.P. Le Brocq, a former Master at Christ College (1883-1886). The first record of Arthur at Christ College appears in a report on Speech Day 1899 when he received an honourable mention for his studies. At the following year's Speech Day in 1900 Arthur received a Mathematical prize (along with William David Abbott) whilst his brother, Walter, was mentioned for his Oxford Scholarship.

Described as quiet and serious, Arthur followed his father's interest in how things worked and spent a lot of time in the mechanics workshop his father had established, not least to tinker on his beloved cars. Arthur was good with his hands and was not without some academic ability. He left school at 16 and worked at engineering under his father before a course at the Central Technical College in London from where he gained a Diploma. He later went on to London University to study Engineering, gaining a BSc. He maintained his connections with Christ College, where his two younger brothers were still pupils, and visited the school on occasions, including for an Old Boys' match on 26th July 1909 when Arthur is recorded a being out for 0. He also regularly attended the Old Boys' Dinner held each December in Brecon.

In 1913 Arthur gained a post as an assistant engineer in the Public Works Department of the Federated Malay States, which he is said to have enjoyed very much. However, some months after war was declared, he "sacrificed his own preferences at the call of patriotic duty". He bought a passage home and on 1st April 1915 was commissioned into the Royal Engineers. Later that year on 10th November he was promoted to Lieutenant. For some time he was stationed as a company commander in North Wales but volunteered for duty in the East and arrived in Mesopotamia in October 1916. He was wounded in December 1916 and had the good fortune to be unexpectedly reunited in Bombay on Christmas Day with Frank and Stephen, who were serving in the same campaign.

In January 1917 Arthur was recovered enough to rejoin his unit, the 71st Field Company of the Royal Engineers. Within weeks, though, he was killed as the Company pushed on after fierce fighting towards Baghdad (which was not to fall until 11th March). Arthur's death on 23rd February 1917 took place ten days after Frank's, his youngest brother, and nine weeks before his younger brother, Stephen. Thus, in an eleven week period, the three brothers were killed in action. What indescribable grief must have affected the Best household in that time, compounded by the Administration of Effects for both Arthur and Frank on the same day at Hereford.

Lieutenant Arthur Stephen Middleton Best is remembered at the Amara War Cemetery, Iraq as well as on the Christ College War Memorial.

Lieutenant Frank Harrington Best

1/1st Brecknockshire Battalion, South Wales Borderers

13TH FEBRUARY 1917 ~ AGED 22

Day Boy 1904-1910

Frank Harrington Best, the youngest of the four 'Best brothers', was born on 27th June 1894. Frank became a pupil at Christ College in September 1904, joining his brother, Stephen, as a Day Boy. Their older brothers, Walter and Arthur, had left the school several years earlier.

Though he was "not by nature an athlete", Frank came third in the Under 16 Quarter-Mile at the Athletic Sports in April 1906 and was credited for showing "more activity in games than many Day Boys". He also seems to have had a flare for performing and was clearly well liked. He received a Mayor's Prize for Recitation in 1908 and was described in *The Breconian* as "a universal favourite; a wholly irresponsible but most charming boy with the gift of friendship".

Like the rest of his family, he showed an aptitude for engineering and, after leaving school in 1910, Frank followed Arthur and went to the Central Technical College for Engineering at the University of London. In July 1914 he passed his intermediate examinations, which would have eventually led to a BSc in engineering. However, on the declaration of war Frank volunteered for service with the Brecknockshire Territorial Force Battalion of the South Wales Borderers. Known as the 'The Brecknocks', this Battalion of the South Wales Borderers was uniquely known by its county name rather than a numerical designation (as was the case in other regiments). On 16th August 1914 Frank was gazetted Second Lieutenant and posted to the Cefn Coed Company with which he was to remain associated for most of his time.

Upon mobilization, the 1st Brecknockshire Battalion moved to its war station at Pembroke Docks. On 29th October the Battalion, which by then Stephen Best had also joined, sailed for India on board the 'Dilwara'. Once there, the Battalion Commander, Colonel the Lord Glanusk, received orders to garrison the important coaling station of Aden which was threatened by Turkish forces in the Yemen. They arrived on 16th December 1914. Both brothers saw action here, Stephen being more involved in it than his brother. A little after six months in

Aden, on 5th August 1915, the Battalion was ordered to India embarking on the transport ship 'Varsova'. Their task was to garrison Mhow, an important military centre in Central India where the Battalion was to spend the rest of the war. Whilst there, Frank was promoted to Temporary Lieutenant on 16th December 1915.

Meanwhile the 4th (Service) Battalion of the South Wales Borderers was fighting valiantly in Gallipoli where it suffered extremely heavy casualties. From there it was ordered to the Mesopotamian Campaign with the aim of securing Basra which, as it was at the heart of the Persian Gulf, would mean the safety of the nearby oilfields. With the Government in London keen to report victories at a time of a series of failures in Europe in 1915, the Mesopotamia Campaign eventually overextended itself in trying to reach Baghdad. As a result, Major General Townshend retreated to Kut where, on 29th April 1916, Townshend and over 12,000 British and Indian troops surrendered to the Turks. Nearly half of these would later die as Prisoners of War at Turkish hands.

British forces had tried to relieve Kut, amongst them the 4th (Service) Battalion, South Wales Borderers who had again taken heavy casualties in the action. Such were the losses that, for a short time, the 4th South Wales Borderers were combined in a composite Battalion with the equally decimated 5th Wiltshire. It was clear more men were needed to fill the ranks and the Brecknocks in India were asked to supply a draft of reinforcements with two subalterns. Frank and Stephen were chosen, possibly at their own request, to lead the draft of 140 Brecknock men. They arrived in Mesopotamia on 7th February 1917.

The Chief of the Imperial General Staff based at the heart of the Empire in London, Sir William Robertson, had been in favour of a defensive policy of oilfield protection but the Commander in Mesopotamia, General Maude, wanted an aggressive campaign and by delivering some military results had, over the winter of 1916/17, moved the forces on the ground into an offensive campaign. As part of this, the destruction of Turkish forces

Mhow, India late 1915. Old Boys of Christ College serving with the Brecknockshire Battalion.
(L to R standing) A.J. Hando, R.G. Heins, G.H. Fryer, M.V. Fryer, J.F. Phillips, G. Tudor, H St. J. Saunders Jones, A.G. Phillips, A.H. Coppage.
(L to R seated) S.W. Best, C.S. Butcher, M.F. Thomas, D.W.E. Thomas, G.D.E. Thomas, H.J.V. Rees, F.H. Best.

was imperative. On 9th February, two days after Frank and Stephen arrived, the British attacked a large Turkish force trapped in a bend on the River Tigris. 40 Brigade, of which the 4th Battalion of the South Wales Borderers was part, was in reserve.

Such was the ferocity of the fighting, though, that 40 Brigade was moved up to replace 39 Brigade on 13th February 1917. The 4th South Wales Borderers were on the Brigade's left flank in shallow and poorly sited trenches which were swept by enemy fire. The Battalion Diary notes "Trench very narrow and unsafe. At 2.00 p.m. bombing party sent forward … to try and bomb into enemy's line. Communication trench undug and party had to withdraw". During this day, the enemy fire took its toll with two officers killed and two wounded; six men were killed and sixteen wounded. Frank was one of the two officers killed, barely six days after his arrival.

The Battalion, though exposed, was kept waiting for the attack order throughout the next day and until 8.45am on the morning of 15th February. Stephen, who had lost his brother in action just a few days before, led his men 'over the top' that morning in what was to be a victory, although at some bloody cost.

Lieutenant Frank Harrington Best is commemorated at the Basra Memorial in Iraq. He is also remembered in the University of London OTC Roll of War Service as well as on the Christ College War Memorial.

Frank's obituary appeared in the same issue of *The Breconian* as that of his brother, Arthur Middleton Best. In addition to his detailed obituary, reference to the loss of the 'best young men' appeared in the following lines about Frank:

In Memoriam - F.H. Best

Optimus en iuvenum se quisque dederunt
Pro patria; gaudens, Optime, tuque cadis.

Behold all the best young men who have given their lives
for their country; you too, a very fine young man, are happy to fall.

Lieutenant Stephen Wriothesley Best
1/1st Brecknockshire Battalion, South Wales Borderers

30TH APRIL 1917 ~ AGED 28
Day Boy 1900-1906

Stephen Wriothesley Best was born on 16th January 1889 in the Parish of St John the Evangelist, Brecon. At the start of the summer term in 1900, he followed his older two brothers, Walter and Arthur, to Christ College as a Day Boy.

The first mention of him at school is in a report on Speech Day, Tuesday 29th July 1902, when Stephen was awarded the IVth Form and Greek prizes as well as receiving an honourable mention for his work in Mathematics and Arithmetic. At the following year's Speech Day, Stephen received the Greek Prize and also obtained his Lower Certificate with Distinctions in Arithmetic and Latin.

On 9th November 1903 the school was given a half-holiday at the request of the new Mayor of Brecon, Stephen's father, Charles W. Best. Charles Best had also given a prize for the High Jump and it must have been a proud moment when Stephen collected that prize at the Athletic Sports on April 1904. At Speech Day in July 1904 the Mayor took his place on the platform alongside local dignitaries from where he heard it announced that his eldest son, C. Walter Best, had taken his BA at Oxford.

The following year Stephen, described as a "quiet, steady boy (who) won general respect and not a little affection, among those who came into close contact with him", passed his Higher Certificate examination and in 1906 he received the Lower VIth Form Prize. He also completed further Higher Certificate subjects before leaving school in December 1906.

Stephen went on to gain a Civil Service appointment in Edinburgh where in 1908 he was listed as one of the "Second Class Clerks in the Estate Duty Office" (later known as the Capital Taxes Office). In 1912 he commenced studying Law at Edinburgh University and in January 1913 joined the Officers Training Corps (Infantry). On the outbreak of war Stephen returned home, becoming an 'Officer Cadet' in the Brecknockshire Battalion, South Wales Borderers and, following Frank's lead, was soon gazetted Second Lieutenant on 5th

October 1914. Arriving in Bombay on 3rd December 1914 and then trans-shipping to Aden, Stephen and the Battalion arrived on 16th December with the aim of defending this vital coaling station. In July 1915 the British forces faced an increasingly aggressive Turkish military and it was decided to send a 1,000 man moveable column to Lahej to support the local pro-British Sultan. More than 400 of these 1,000 men were from the Brecknocks and included Stephen.

During the 25 mile march in extreme heat over what was more of a track than a road, many men collapsed with heatstroke. The column was exhausted when they arrived and the Turks lost no time in attacking. Barely a quarter of the men from the Brecknocks could fight but the disciplined British column repulsed the Turks. However, the supply column of camels driven by local Arabs and bringing water, ammunition, machine guns and medical supplies had been lost when, hearing the battle, the Arabs fled. Without these supplies the column had little choice but to return to Aden. Although some water was sent to aid the troops over 30 men died from the heat, more than half that number from the Brecknocks.

Within a short time the Battalion was sent to India where it was to pass the war in relative peace, 'policing the Empire'. It was here that Stephen was promoted to Temporary Lieutenant on 9th August 1916. In early 1917 Stephen and his brother (almost certainly having volunteered) took 140 men from India to help rebuild the shattered 4th Battalion in Mesopotamia. Arriving on 7th February, the brothers were in the thick of action on 13th February 1917 and Frank was killed. Stephen, now the only one of the three fighting brothers left, led his men bravely forward the next morning.

The capture of Baghdad on 11th March 1917 was a huge morale boost to the Allied Forces and encouraged General Maude to destroy all Turkish Forces within his reach. Hard fighting ensued and the 4th Battalion with men of the Wiltshires and 8th Royal Welsh Fusiliers attacked Deltawa on 29th March 1913. The Battalion started its march towards battle at 1am and then advanced in "Artillery formation" just after 7.30am. Heavy shelling and opposition met the advance and Stephen was wounded, recovering enough to rejoin the Battalion on 21st April 1917.

At 5am on the morning of 30th April 1917 the 4th Battalion and men from the Cheshires attacked Adhaim Village where Turkish forces were entrenched. Brigade orders were to halt at the second enemy line but this was not discernible so the Cheshires pressed on. A and D Companies of the 4th Battalion, who were on the left of the Cheshires, followed but ended up a mile beyond their objective. Having lost touch with their support, their position was precarious. B and C Companies moved up in support but the Battalion Diary for that day states that the phone line had run out 1,000 yards before this position and runners were being shot by Turkish troops so any communication was difficult.

The 4th and Cheshires were suffering from shrapnel wounds but still hoped to advance; intense firing commenced before a Turkish counter attack took place. With the Turks barely 10 yards away, B and C companies retreated to the village but A and D companies were cut off. Two Turkish gun batteries were within 300 yards and Stephen appears to have led some of his men to attack them because, as the Battalion Diary records "there is no doubt a gallant attempt was made to capture one of these batteries, as soon afterwards the bodies of Lieutenant Best and several men were found close to the gunpits". As no officers witnessed this act of bravery, there could be no question of a gallantry award. The Battalion withdrew at about 10am to reform and the roll call showed 126 men surviving of the 340 going into battle five hours earlier. On 3rd May 1917 the brave and previously wounded Commander of the 4th Battalion, Lieutenant Colonel Kitchin, wrote to the family:

> *Dear Mr. Best,*
>
> *It is very difficult to express adequately the very deep sympathy which we all feel towards you and yours at the terrible loss you have suffered. I only rejoined the regiment yesterday to find that your son Stephen had on the 30th April given his life very gallantly for his Country as his brothers had previously given theirs. His death occurred during an overwhelming Turkish counter-attack and at the time he and his men had with the greatest gallantry attacked and captured 8 Turkish guns and apparently defended them with their lives for his body and those of 30 of his men were found lying around the gun positions when the Turks withdrew later in the day. From the wound found upon your son's body it appears that he must have been shot through the chest and would probably have died almost at once. He was buried the following day by the Chaplain near the spot where he fell which is about 36 miles up the Shatt El Adhain river, some 80 miles North of Baghdad.*
>
> *I had the pleasure of meeting all your gallant sons when I was in hospital last January, and it is with very great sorrow to me to feel that they have all passed away.*
>
> *Will you please accept our deepest sympathy.*
>
> *Your sons who were with us were extremely popular with all ranks and were both splendid officers and will be sadly missed by us all.*
>
> *Yours very sincerely,*
>
> *C.E. Kitchin*
>
> *(Lt. Col. Commanding 4th S.W.B.)*

Charles W. Best claimed the medals in memory of his three sons on 26th December 1920. Lieutenant Stephen Wriothesley Best is remembered at the Basra Memorial, Iraq. He is the third of the three Best brothers to be remembered on the Christ College War Memorial, a tablet designed by their elder brother, Walter Best.

Captain Arthur Basil George Biggerton-Evans

Chevalier of the Order of King George 1st (Greece)
3rd Battalion, South Wales Borderers

17TH DECEMBER 1919 ~ AGED 26
Hostel 1907-1912

Arthur Basil George Biggerton-Evans, known as Basil, was born on 10th April 1893. At nearly 14, he arrived as a Scholar at the Hostel from his St David's home in January 1907. He had previously attended St David's School, Pembrokeshire. His father, the Reverend A Biggerton-Evans, was a minor canon at St David's Cathedral.

While at school Basil wrote regularly to his parents. The letters they received from him are an evocative record of the life of a young boy at Christ College in the years before the First World War. Most of the letters are filled with pleas for more tuck because he is "simply famishing", or "oof", a bob or two that he could spend in the Dot café in town. He also sends news of school sporting successes, his musical performances and his academic progress (and sometimes lack of it, despite the encouragement of his Housemaster, "Donnie").

A more public record of his time at school exists in *The Breconian*. Basil came second in the 150 yards Under 14 race at the Athletic Sports on 4th April 1907 and ended the school year with the Form IV Prize awarded at the annual Speech Day on Tuesday 30th July 1907. At the Athletic Sports on 6th April in the following year Basil won the 100 yards Under 15 Consolation Race and once again, ended the school year with a prize at Speech Day - the Division III Mathematical Prize.

At Christmas 1908 Basil appeared, with some success, in the 'Christmas Theatricals' of 1908 - the comedy, *Heir-at-Law*, written by George Coleman exactly a century before. *The Breconian* records that the choice "required some courage on the part of Mr. Donaldson to stage the whole of a five-act play; and his courage, as courage usually does, paved the way to victory … Basil Evans as Dick Dowlas was a very popular figure. The part suited him to a button, and he revelled in it - his acting during his first meeting with Dr. Pangloss being especially good".

On 3rd April 1909, as in previous years, Basil gained a prize at the Athletic Sports and came third in the

Quarter-Mile Under 16 Handicap. He achieved further academic recognition on Speech Day when he received his Lower Certificate of the Oxford and Cambridge Board for Arithmetic.

Clearly a popular boy, he also displayed great bravery in the summer of 1910. Whilst bathing at Caerfai Bay, near St David's, he rescued a young boy who was in danger of drowning. In recounting this exploit, news of which was found in several newspapers, *The Breconian* of December 1910 gives "Congratulations to Evans on a timely act of gallantry, worthy of a Christ College boy". The following edition in April 1911 was able to record that the Royal Humane Society had awarded Basil a certificate "for his plucky action".

In the Athletic Sports of 8th April 1911, Basil won a pleasing first place in the 150 yards Open Consolation Race, which he completed in 19 seconds. In the summer term he played for the 3rd XI. In July, in a match against 'Mr. Large's Bible Class', the 3rd team won by 41 with a total of 73 runs. Basil scored 20 of these. He also took all 10 wickets in the first innings for 6 runs.

In the Certificate Examinations at the end of the summer term 1911 Basil gained his Higher Certificate (Latin, Greek, Elementary Mathematics, Scripture, English and Greek History). For the 1911/12 rugby football season, Basil was selected for the 1st XV, playing alongside fellow Hostelites David Cuthbert Thomas and Leonard Glynne Lewis ('Siwel'). His end of term critique is mixed but mostly positive: "A.B.G. BIGGERTON EVANS - Hard working and greatly improved. A good 'middleman' in the scrum, but inclined to be clumsy. A fair tackler".

In the spring of 1911 Basil played right-half for the 1st Hockey XI. His end of term critique was rather less flattering than the previous term's for his rugby football skills: "Very slow, but tries very hard, must learn to keep his place; is clumsy and inclined to 'give sticks'".

Finally for that busy term, he is recorded as being one of four editors of *The Breconian*, a role which Basil continued into the summer term, his last at Christ College. In that summer term of 1911, Basil was deputy organist to Mr. Large and also played cricket. He played three of the five official 2nd XI matches with varying success ranging from scoring 12 runs on 18th May in a match against the County School 1st XI to being bowled out for 0 on 8th June in a match against Brecon Sports Club 2nd XI.

He rounded off his school career by gaining his Oxford and Cambridge Higher Certificate (Latin, Greek, Scripture and Roman History). Basil did not obtain a scholarship place at either Queens' College Cambridge or to Jesus College in January 1912. Perhaps this is not surprising given that his school report for the previous term commented: "If he had given himself more time for scholarship work, he might have done quite well but he has run the margin very fine". He did however gain a place at Keble College, Oxford, matriculating in the Michaelmas Term 1913. This was in spite of his final school report for History commenting that he "Has done very sound work and has a pleasing if superficial style". The final report for Greek is rather more direct: "He has been inexcusably slack in getting up his set books by himself during the enforced absence of his master".

In September 1912 until going up to Oxford in 1913, Basil worked as an assistant master at Lucton School. Clearly life at Oxford suited Basil and reports back to his old school in the termly 'Oxford Letter' that appeared in *The Breconian* suggest he was making a name for himself. During his first term it was noted that one day after lectures "Biggerton-Evans came home with his face all black but I fancy he was the innocent victim of the wily scientist from BNC (Brasenose College). 'Biggers' Evans - as he is called in Keble - is quite a well-known character. Under the Presidential wing of H.B. Davies he is blossoming forth into a great orator in the Debating Society.

He also plays Rugger quite well, and worthily maintains the reputation of Brecon in this respect".

The Oxford Letter of the summer term 1914 concerns his romance and illness: "Biggerton-Evans wishes to deny the rumour of his engagement; nevertheless, he desires to thank all O.B.'s who wrote to congratulate him. He was quite a fine sight as an "Old Josser" (Walters' name for a "knight") at a Literature Pageant in the Town Hall. He fell a victim to infectious disease, viz., German measles, which prevented him from enjoying Eights Week. It is rumoured that he offered at least 4s to anybody to get rid of it".

After a successful first year at Oxford, Basil was set to continue his round of sport, entertainment and, of course, work towards honours in Theology. However, shortly after the 1914 autumn term began, Basil volunteered for service. After an intensive six weeks of training at the University, he was commissioned on 22nd December 1914, and his name was printed in *The London Gazette* on the list of 'Cadets and ex-Cadets of the Officers Training Corps to be Temporary Second Lieutenants'.

Second Lieutenant Biggerton-Evans joined the South Wales Borderers and was stationed at Rhyl with the 9th Battalion. He then went out to Gallipoli with the 4th Battalion and on arrival was transferred to the command of D Company, there being no other officers available. He was wounded in October 1915 during the fierce Gallipoli campaign which had only a few weeks earlier claimed the life of his school chum with whom he had shared classes, David Mansel Griffiths. Following a debilitating attack of dysentery, Basil was sent home in November to recover.

Four months later in March 1916, shortly after visiting Christ College, this already battle-hardened young officer was sent to the 10th Battalion in Ypres. He fought at Mametz Wood (Somme) in the bloody days of 10th, 11th and 12th July where nearly 250 of his Battalion were killed or wounded. Basil was part of the 38th Welsh Division, one of the New Army Divisions raised wholly in Wales. In this battle, the Division lost nearly 4,000 men in three days. Basil sustained another wound, this time to his hand.

He was able to send home some "Fritz souvenirs" and told his parents how he met a "Brother Breconian in the middle of the attack (at Mametz) a chap called Brooker who went to the Argentine and came over to fight in this war". Basil also wrote to Christ College from the Somme about meeting Jack Brooker, half way through operations, and how they "had a yarn together and shared rations. We even became reminiscent and talked of the time he bowled A.P. James the first ball after tea in 1907". Jack Brooker (School House 1905 to 1908) was in the 1st Rugby Football XV and the 1st Cricket XI as well as being a Prefect. Although having fought with the Canadians, by this time Jack was a Second Lieutenant in the Welch regiment. Jack was wounded soon after the encounter but returned to the Front and survived the war.

In the letter published in *The Breconian* Basil continues that

Captain Biggerton-Evans in uniform

the second in command is a Monmothian and one chap in his company is a Llandoverian "so we can go over some of the old squabbles again". He also reports on a few "Hun dug-outs" which he had toured in the woods and describes how well they are provided for: "They were 30 odd feet deep, with several entrances, match-boarded sides, easy chairs, comfortable well covered beds, stoves, plentiful crockery, and cigars and cigarettes which smoked very well indeed. Some comfort the old Hun seems to have enjoyed!"

In late November of 1916 Basil became ill with "gastric catarrh and rheumatism", the latter affecting a number of men. From his hospital bed Basil wrote to his parents "You will no doubt be pleased to know that the C.O. and the Brigadier are very pleased with a little job I did the other day and my promotion to full Loot has gone through . . . The old Hun is bucking up a little round here". From his "snug bed" at the 131 Field Ambulance Hospital, Basil was sent to the Corps Rest Station at Wormhoudt and then home to the 2nd Western General Hospital, Manchester where he remained until January 1917. In a letter from the hospital dated 5th January 1917 Basil writes "I want to get out of this place as soon as I can - I hate the town . . . I have gratuitously seen all the shows worth seeing . . . Sir Thomas Beeching is conducting some splendid Promenade Concerts here but as they run no matinees it is impossible to hear them . . . We had the usual ubiquitous Welsh choir here (singing) the usual stuff - Honour and Arms and things about the sea . . . It is raining here as usual".

After a spell at home, Basil was appointed Musketry Officer to the 3rd Battalion (part of what was known as the 'Mersey Garrison') at Sniggery Camp, Liverpool. In October 1918 he was sent to Salonika to a Battalion of his Regiment. Known as a good linguist (he could speak seven languages), Basil was selected to join the British Military Mission in Greece and Bulgaria where, amongst other things, he was responsible for the repatriation of Greek Prisoners of War. He arrived in Macedonia in October 1918 and was then sent to Sofia on a "special mission". From there he spent time with the Italian Garrison at Phillipopolis and finally with the French Garrison at Karagatch, Sofia. For his dedicated work, he was made a Chevalier of the Greek Order of George I by the King of the Hellenes in August 1919.

Basil was due to return home in December 1919 from the French Garrison at Karagatch. After a night out in Adrianople, he bought five bottles of stout from the Quarter Master Sergeant and boarded the train to come home. He had mentioned on the previous day to some French officers that he had a pain in his stomach and again he mentioned this to an Interpreter. The train was awaiting departure when some French officers visited him to say goodbye and between them, they drank two bottles of stout. They left at 4pm as the train had still not departed and he was briefly visited by an American Priest and his wife. A report reveals more of his unexpected death:

> (His) Russian batman, Nicolai Andreeff went to get some coal and on entering the (train's) saloon at about 4.30pm found Captain Evans lying on the seat, breathing heavily and his hands turning blue. The batman ran to the house of an Englishman, living near the station, for assistance. Mr. Deir, a Bulgarian Doctor, and Sapper Powell arrived within a few minutes but Capt. Evans was then dead . . . Colonel Harene, the A.C.O. arrived the same evening . . . and the British Medical Officer two days later and the body was taken to Adrianople in a motor car. In the afternoon the body was brought back and interred with military honours in the Protestant Cemetery. Those present included British Colonel

Harene . . . the French Commandant, Colonel Rondonnet and all the French officers of the Garrison. The French provided a troop of Moorish Cavalry, a guard of honour (about 2 Coys.) and a firing party . . . the Mayor of Karagatch and many of the inhabitants of the town.

The British Intelligence Officer at Karagatch collected Basil's personal effects and sent them home to his father at Gladestry Rectory, Kington. They included clothing, an automatic revolver, pipes and cigarette tubes, a pocket Kodak, a Sam Browne belt and two German war picture albums. Unfortunately though, these never reached his family. In St Mary's Church, Gladestry there is a bronze plaque mounted on a marble backboard. On the plaque is a head and shoulders within a laurel wreath. Underneath are the words:

To the dear memory of Captain Basil Biggerton-Evans, S Wales Borderes (24th Regt) aged 26 years, only and beloved son of the Rector of this parish. Educated at Christ College Brecon and Keble College Oxford. He served throughout the Great War 1914-1919 in Gallipoli (wounded), Flanders, France, Salonica and Bulgaria. For his distinguished service with the British Military Mission in the Balkans he was created a Chevalier of the Order of George I by the King of Greece. He died December 17th 1919 and was buried in Karagath Cemetery, Adrianople with full military honours by the French Garrison. A good soldier of Jesus Christ.

Captain Arthur Basil Biggerton-Evans is buried in Plodiv Central Cemetery. He is remembered on the Gladestry War Memorial and at the Llandrindod Wells County War Memorial Hospital. He is also remembered on the War Memorial at Keble College, Oxford as well as on the Christ College War Memorial.

Second Lieutenant Charles Geoffrey Boothby

177th Tunnelling Company, Royal Engineers

28TH APRIL 1916 ~ AGED 21

School House 1909-1913

Charles Geoffrey Boothby was born in Brixton on 13th December 1894 and was the only child of Charles and Alice Boothby. He was known as Geoffrey to distinguish him from his father. His father, a chemical engineer, seems to have moved around. In 1901 the family was living in Leyton but had moved to Putney by the time Charles joined Clayesmore School as a 9 year old boarder in the Trinity Term 1904. At some point Geoffrey's parents moved to Glenthorne, North Hermitage, Shrewsbury and it was from this address that Charles joined School House, Christ College at the start of the Easter Term 1909.

He immediately set about making his mark academically as well in sport. On the Speech Day of 27th July 1909, at the end of his second term at school, Geoffrey was awarded the Lower School Prize. At the Athletic Sports in April 1910 he came third in the Under 16 Mile and it was noted that he "ran well". In the following year, on Wednesday 11th March 1911, Geoffrey came eighth in the Senior Steeplechase and, in the Athletic Sports of 1911, he gained fourth place in the Open Half-Mile.

Clearly something of a runner, Geoffrey was expected to do well in the Senior Steeplechase in March 1912 but did not have a good day. In fact the record of the run states that "Boothby, a promising runner in the past, was a disappointing addition to the go as you please brigade". However, he was to make up for this two weeks later at the Athletic Sports when he took first prize in the 220 yards Open Handicap, winning by 13 yards.

1912 was academically successful for Geoffrey. At Prize Day on Tuesday 30th July he was awarded the Form V prize. He also gained his Lower Certificate in the summer examinations with passes in Latin, Greek, Arithmetic, Mathematics, Scripture, French, History, Physics and Chemistry. In the following autumn Geoffrey proudly achieved his place in the 1st Rugby Football XV playing alongside fellow forward David Cuthbert Thomas. Weighing in at 9st 7 lbs, the annual team critique records him as "A very moderate forward" who "works hard in the scrum".

The summer of 1913 saw Geoffrey as one of four boys sent to take the London Matriculation Examination. All four were successful and Geoffrey left Christ College after a happy stay of just over four years. He had made many friends "by his charming personality and cheery good fellowship" and was, noted *The Breconian*, "a boy of more than average literary taste and ability". By early 1914 the Boothby family was living at Charlemount, West Bromwich, where Charles Boothby was working for a firm of manufacturing chemists. Geoffrey was not enamoured with the Black Country but his close friend, Arthur Ainscow had a 16 year old sister, Edith, with whom he formed a close friendship.

In the autumn of 1914 Geoffrey entered the Medical School of Birmingham University. However, he stayed only a few weeks before enlisting and was sent to Camberley for officer training. He and Arthur Ainscow were gazetted Second Lieutenants on Christmas Eve 1914, shortly after Geoffrey's 20th birthday. Geoffrey was attached to the South Staffordshire Regiment and, by early February 1915, he was at Bovington Camp, Wool, Dorset for training and, in his letters to the now 17 year old Edith, he gives every indication that he was enjoying life.

The continuing correspondence between Geoffrey and Edith reveals a deepening attachment as the months pass. His letters to her are full of bravado and life is "topping" and "ripping". He records numerous instances of his new life such as in May 1915 when out riding his motorbike at 40mph "the bally thing seized up". He escapes serious injury to body but not to his wallet as the repair cost was estimated at about £6. He also reports on "bathing parades" in the hot weather they have been having. These are "very nice but for the fact that all the fair maidens of the village assembled on the cliffs, which was rather embarrassing, since both men & officers bathe - er, well, the government haven't issued costumes to us yet".

At the end of May the 8th Battalion of the South Staffordshire Regiment marched for four and a half days, sleeping in the open en route. At their destination, Flower Down Camp near Winchester, they trained in trench warfare and learned how to erect barbed wire. Geoffrey's letters continue to record accidents on his newly acquired motorbike (including one where he nearly killed a Corporal), getting a weekend's leave cancelled by telegram soon after arriving home (he was hoping to see Edith on the Sunday) and growing a moustache to match his red hair. Then, in early July 1915, the news is received that the Battalion are on two hours standby for France. In his letter of 11th July 1915, Geoffrey states that "Unlike many regts. we are going straight to the trenches, so says that unreliable dame, Mme Rumour, because the artillery are being given live shells, which would not happen if we were going to a base to finish training as usually happens". He also tells Edith that he has made Platoon Commander which is "jolly lucky" otherwise he would be transferred to the 11th Battalion and have to stay at home.

Within days he is writing from the British Expeditionary Force in France to thank her for cigarettes she had sent him. In August he notes that he is doing a short course in mining with the Royal Engineers and is hoping to be assigned a motor cycle which many mining officers have. Further letters detail his life in the Mining Section (51st Infantry Brigade), implore Edith not to study Science but Medicine at university (which she does), and record highlights such as seeing a "Bosche plane" come fluttering down to destruction.

In October 1915 he prevented the Germans blowing a mine under the British trenches. He was put up for a gallantry award but it was given to an officer just senior to him. On 7th October 1915 Geoffrey wrote to his friends at Christ College about the incident:

> I left the RE Company to which I was attached and proceeded with the Brigade mining section to a new lot of trenches. Though this was only a matter of a few yards from one of the hottest mining sectors in the whole line, the mines we took over were reported to be very quiet and peaceful. Quiet and peaceful! I should smile! I have been in the fighting line about 2 months now and only a couple of days ago did I have my first real adventure. The mines were handed over to two of us officers and one Brigade section. After we had been down there two days a RE officer came up to look around. He went down my two and found all correct; then he went down the other two. Out of curiosity he went along an old gallery half-full of water. Imagine their surprise when they suddenly came upon an instrument like an enlarged telephone receiver, stuck in the wall and connected up with wires, which ran along the gallery in front into the darkness. This thing had German writing on it; they disconnected it and brought it out. Of course it didn't require a Sherlock Holmes to deduce that the wily Bosch had broken into this old gallery further along. So we then decided to explore and find where the Huns had got in.

> We went along through the water until we came to the German gallery. This was properly joined up with ours and must have been done long before we took over the mines; which was scandalous, for the people before us should have heard the Germans working. There was a water pump for pumping water into our sap; there was also the rest of the telegraphic apparatus, a beautiful and complicated piece of workmanship in a mahogany box. This was a kind of wireless, by which they could tap the wires from our front trenches running back to headquarters, big guns etc. As we had only a rifle between us, we thought it dangerous to explore more than a few yards of the German gallery; so we cleared out and sent for explosives. Then we went down again, the RE officer, a corporal and little me! Two rifles this time. Our object was to get the rest of the instrument, which we had left in the first instance for fear the Huns should come and find it gone, and so give the alarm, before we were ready to blow them up. So we went along, I first with a rifle and a flash lamp. The water made a horrible noise round our legs as it was up to our knee. The gallery had a slight bend; when we were round this and in the straight into which the German gallery ran at right angles, suddenly as the novels and penny hair-raisers say "A shot rang out"!

> As a matter of fact it did not ring at all, but made a business-like "poop"! I had to drop the lamp to work my rifle and managed to get one shot off while the other two retreated. Of course it was useless to stay any longer, as the Bosch had us absolutely. You see he was in a dry gallery and right round the corner, his revolver poked into our gallery and firing at random without exposing himself at all. I dropped my rifle and after groping in the water for my torch while he got two more shots off, I beat an absolutely panic-stricken retreat, dashing through water bent double to avoid the roof. It was, you realise quite dark. I got to the others at the next corner round the bend about 15 yards from the German sap

and found the corporal had lost his rifle too. So the RE officer went up to the surface, while we stayed on guard in the dark. A rifle came down and my revolver. Then we made things hum. Men all along the galleries behind us dragging full sand bags up and leaving them for us to build a barricade. I boarded up the corner we were holding and piled sand-bags behind. Then the explosives were sent down and the corporal and I packed sandbags round them and filled our own gallery with sand bags 6 feet back from the charge. My word! How we worked! It took us four hours to get the whole thing done ready for firing. The sandbags had to be dragged through water; consequently we were absolutely wringing and then the heat and the bad air - phew!! The object of this haste was to get our charge off before the German got off his and buried us. About the toughest race I've run yet. Doubtless they were working as hard as we, but we won. Thank God! The explosion made a 12-yard crater on the surface. General staff seemed rather "bucked".

Two months later, on 18th December 1915, Geoffrey celebrated his 21st birthday in the trenches. In January 1916 he was transferred to the 177 Tunnelling Company and apologises to Edith for not seeing her. Instead it took two days of travel to visit his sick father, convalescing in Cornwall. Their correspondence, now becoming even more romantic, is tinged with sudden items of sadness such as in March 1916 when Geoffrey reveals that "Nearly all my friends in the Staffords have been killed in the fighting round Ypres a few weeks ago. It's a horribly sad thing … but it does make one proud to be an Englishman, when one knows how unselfishly one's friends go west". Over these months he has harsh words to say about those staying behind, and reveals that he is not sure that he will resume his medical studies as he will be so old by the time he qualifies.

Geoffrey hoped for leave but it was repeatedly cancelled. He wrote on the 27th April 1916 that he hopes to be "in Brum" near 9th May. Killed in action on the following day, he never received Edith's letter (also of 27th) in which she writes about her dream cottage of the future, nor did he receive the letter of 4th May in which she looks forward to them seeing each other again soon.

Geoffrey was killed about thirty feet underground at Railway Wood near Ypres. The Secret Weekly Mine Report of 177 Tunnelling Company, Royal Engineers 14th Corps, Guards Division gives the exact location as well as the information that the men were working in a shaft 4 feet 6 inches wide and 2 feet 3 inches high. It goes on to report that at 7.45am the enemy blew a camouflet, an underground explosion that did not break the surface. Geoffrey and two other men were killed.

According to his friend and fellow officer, Second Lieutenant Alex Wilson, in a letter to Geoffrey's parents, it had been reported by men working at the face of their tunnel that German miners could be heard talking through the earth. He investigated and agreed, so ordered that work be stopped. Second Lieutenant Wilson then reported to the Commanding Officer, as it was "the custom in tunnelling for the less experienced to report to the officer in charge if time permits, to get the benefit of his experience and help". Geoffrey was just getting up and decided to go with him, apparently saying that they had to make really sure before alarming the men and stopping work. "It was just that self-reliance and careful weighing of facts and absence of flurry that made him so valuable to his junior officers and men," wrote Second Lieutenant Wilson. He went on to say that the gallery space was small so Geoffrey, followed by the Corporal, went forward with Second Lieutenant Wilson at the gallery entrance. Thirty seconds later the Germans blew the mine, instantly killing Geoffrey, the Corporal and another man, and severely injuring Second Lieutenant Wilson and four men.

When the telegram announcing his death reached his parents at their home Park View, Astwood Bank, Redditch, his father telegraphed the War Office with a plaintive request: "I cannot think it true please confirm". Confirmation was explicit and letters from Geoffrey's fellow officers soon arrived at the family home. All write of his bravery and popularity. Describing the circumstances of Geoffrey's death, a senior officer wrote "The only consolation is that they must have been killed absolutely instantly and painlessly. He was a most likeable man and a very keen and efficient officer, and both I and all my officers feel his loss very deeply, both on social and military counts." Another senior officer from the South Staffordshire Regiment wrote that "He was very popular in this Battalion … We were all disappointed that he did not get decorated for a very plucky bit of work which he did last October, when he was acting as mining officer in out trenches. An officer just senior to him got the decoration, but I have also understood that he was responsible for the work done … We shall always remember him as a very gallant officer and a very upright, clean-minded English gentleman." A third officer wrote that "… everybody misses his cheery smile … (and that he was) fearless."

Like many soldiers at war, Geoffrey turned to poetry in his idle hours. Two of his works survive in manuscript form; the second of the poems, *Hope the Siren*, is a mournful reflection on the uncertainty of the future.

Hope the Siren

Hope the Queen of Sirens sits on the Rock of Future besides
The sweet waters of Oblivion, and ceaselessly sings a song
That lures us cheerfully onwards into the doubt and darkness
Of the Unknown.

Hope sits in a beautiful garden besides the Lethian stream,
And at her feet the poppies creep round many a troubled dream,
She gazes across the waters and turns with a smiling face
To where the shadows of sadness lie dark o'er the human race.
And to her toiled-stained children, wrapped in a mist of tears,
She sings her gladsome song of mirth of sunny coming years.

Hope is the merriest jester, with her treasures seeming fair,
The mirage gleams of empty dreams, and "castle in the air",
But when the Heart is aching and thorns the vain toil's prize;
When the cold, cold world grows colder, and sorrows dim the eyes,
Hope pities her stricken children, the suffering souls opprest,
And sings her songs of brighter days, with the poppies at her breast.

Hope's but a delusive Siren yet grief is the world below,
When athwart her face the storm clouds brace and doubting night winds blow.
Slowly the heavy links of years grow on the chain of time,
When hushed the song of the Siren and silent her searching rhyme.
So though fond hands are parted and joyless hang the hours
Hope sings her song of brighter days among Eternal flowers.

Edith wrote a farewell poem and then locked away her letters from Geoffrey, together with those she had written to him and which the family gave her when Geoffrey's belongings were returned.

Will you come back when the Tide Turns?
After many days? My heart yearns to know!
And I seem
To have you still the same
In one world with me
As if it were part and parcel,
One shadow, and we need not dissemble
Our destinies: do you understand?
For I have told you plain how it is.

The poem and the letters were discovered by her son in 1990 and later published in a small volume that told the story of their "affair of letters", *Thirty-Odd Feet Under Belgium*.

The body of Second Lieutenant Charles Geoffrey Boothby was never recovered. He is remembered at Railway Wood near Hooge in Belgium as well as on the Christ College War Memorial.

Second Lieutenant Cecil Hoyle Broadbent
4th Battalion, King's Own Yorkshire Light Infantry
1st March 1916 ~ Aged 34
Classical VIth Form Master 1903-1906

Cecil Hoyle Broadbent was born at Cannock, Staffordshire on 25th October 1881 to Eliza and James. James Broadbent was a bank manager for the Manchester and Liverpool District Bank. By 1891 he and Eliza had moved to Rochdale where they lived in relative comfort with their seven children, Eliza's sister and three staff.

Cecil Broadbent was educated at Oundle School and then matriculated at Trinity College, Cambridge in the Michaelmas Term 1900. Trinity College records show his family as living at Ravenswood, Wood Road, Whalley Range, Manchester. Three years later, in 1903, Cecil Broadbent gained a 1st Class Classical Tripos. In the September of that year he started his teaching career at Christ College. His role is described somewhat formally in school records as 'Classical VIth Form Master'. There is little doubt, though, that he soon became a popular master and actively involved in many areas of the school.

With other staff he attended the Old Boys' Dinner of 20th December 1904 and again in 1905. He gave the second prize for the Mile Open race at the Athletic Sports of 1905 and 1906. Clearly a man of wide interests, he performed in the end of term production of *HMS Pinafore* on Tuesday December 19th 1905. He took the part of Captain Corcoran and received a glowing review in *The Breconian*: "Captain Corcoran had a bass voice of nice quality and considerable compass. He had a trying part to sustain, but came through the ordeal, for a first appearance, very creditably". In an ironic twist, the star of the show, Josephine (Captain Corcoran's daughter) who was played by Martin Spencer Smith, would be killed in action a few months after his fellow actor.

One of Cecil's final extra-curricular acts at Christ College was to be a judge in the Athletic Sports of 1906, and it was a mark of the man that *The Breconian* singled him out as being a familiar face missed on their return to school for the new term in September 1906. He was clearly much loved and his work with the VIth Form in particular was described as being very successful. Though he was keen to make the Classics more accessible by editing and explaining Classical works, his main passion was English Literature and he would frequently regale his classes with the connections between the Classics and English. Apparently of weak health, he nevertheless also enjoyed billiards and golf. In fact, he had been a prominent member of Brecon Golf Club.

C.H. Broadbent as Captain Corcoran (to the right of Dick Deadeye) with the cast of H.M.S. Pinafore

After only three years at Christ College, in the summer of 1906 he moved to be second Classical master at Bradford Grammar School, a school of similar age to Christ College. Whilst there he achieved his long held ambition of editing not just one but two books: *Camillus* in 1910 and *Selections from Ovid's Heroides* in 1911, both of which have been republished in recent years - a century after their first publication. In 1912, Cecil Broadbent received his MA from Cambridge.

On 20th November 1914 Cecil Broadbent was gazetted Second Lieutenant, Bradford Grammar School Contingent, Junior Division, Officers Training Corps. From his house at 4 Apsley Crescent, Bradford, in August 1915 Second Lieutenant Broadbent joined the 1/4th Battalion King's Own Yorkshire Light Infantry (TF) - a territorial battalion based at Wakefield. After brief training at Beverley and Leeds, he entered the French theatre of war on 20th September 1915.

After some months in the trenches at Ypres, he was appointed Officer Commanding of the Brigade Bombing School near Albert. He died of wounds on 1st March 1916 following a premature explosion of a bomb whilst he was acting as instructor. His Commanding Officer wrote "He was an excellent officer and very popular alike with officers and men; his death is a great loss to the Battalion". His Colonel wrote "We all regret the death of such an able officer and one of the best of comrades".

Second Lieutenant Cecil Hoyle Broadbent is buried in the small 46 grave Warloy-Baillon Communal Cemetery on the Somme. As well as on the Christ College War Memorial, he is also remembered on the War Memorial in the Chapel at Trinity College, Cambridge and on the Colwyn Bay War Memorial.

Lieutenant James Cassels Cobb
5th Battalion, Queen's Own (Royal West Kent Regiment)
23RD AUGUST 1918 ~ AGED 33
School House 1900

James Cobb was born on 26th September 1884 at Pontypridd, Glamorgan. He was the third of six children. His father was a bank manager and their address at the time was given as Bank House. James attended the then famous Blackheath Proprietary School in Lewisham, a school known for its sport and for being a founder member of the Football Association. James was only at Christ College for two terms, between Easter and Christmas 1900, living in School House. There is no indication why he left at Christmas 1900 although it may well be that he wanted to return to the family home. He was known to have a great interest in English language and literature so it was not surprising that his ambition was to be an author. In 1915 his first novel *Struggles* was published by the recently established general publisher Mills and Boon. *The Breconian* noted in his obituary that "It seemed that he might have had a successful future before him as an author. His life has gone to pay part of the price of recent victory."

James evidently joined up as soon as war was declared. On 6th November 1914 he was promoted with great rapidity from Private to Second Lieutenant. In 1915 he found himself attached to what has been described as the "most unusual of Kent units", the Kent Composite Battalion. The 53rd (Welsh) Division was based at Cambridge but, such was the ferocity of the fighting over the Ypres Salient in April 1915, one Brigade of the Division, the Monmouthshire Brigade, was sent to the Front at short notice. In order to bring the Division back to full strength, a composite Brigade from various troops in the Home Counties was formed and became known as the 160th Brigade. This Brigade was made up of 3,000 men and the Kent Composite Battalion comprised 1,000.

The Kent Composite Battalion consisted of a Headquarters Company plus four other companies and James was attached to D Company. Reporting to Cambridge on 14th June 1915, a few weeks of Battalion and Brigade training ensued before they sailed on 20th July from Southampton to Alexandria in Egypt on board the SS

'Norland'. From there, the Battalion sailed, still on the SS 'Norland', to the important allied port of Mudros on the Mediterranean island of Lemnos. This was a key staging post in the Gallipoli Campaign. Indeed, a crucial and ultimately final attempt at breaking the Gallipoli deadlock started on 6th August 1915 with an amphibious landing at Suvla Bay. The landings were to commence at 10pm with two diversionary attacks starting a little earlier from the ANZAC lines. One of these diversionary attacks was aiming at Lone Pine and became known as the Battle of Lone Pine. One of those taking part in this particularly bloody battle was another Old Breconian, Trooper David Mansel Griffiths of the Australian Light Horse, who was killed in action on 7th August 1915 in what was ultimately a Pyrrhic victory.

James and the Battalion landed at Suvla Bay on 10th August 1915, three days after the death of David Mansel Griffiths. Unfortunately those in high command at Suvla Bay were amongst the most incompetent of the war and an easy victory was turned into a prolonged and bloody battle. James was in the thick of the fighting during the second part of August. He and his men were fighting alongside the 2nd Battalion of the South Wales Borderers until 13th December, when the Battalion was evacuated along with the rest of the Allied forces.

During his four months at Suvla Bay James was under frequent shelling and rifle fire, even in the reserve area. When not defending the front line, he and his men were loading or unloading supplies. Although few men were killed, many succumbed to illness. They also suffered from a terrible blizzard in November and torrential rain which resulted in trenches flooding to three or four feet deep, creating almost impossible fighting conditions. Upon withdrawal, the Battalion was sent to Egypt and re-designated the 2/4th Queen's Own (Royal West Kent Regiment). Thus the Kent Composite Battalion was short lived but also known as a dependable and determined body of men and officers.

On 8th May 1917 James was promoted to Lieutenant (backdated to 1st June 1916). A few months later, on 25th September, he was further promoted to Acting Captain, commanding a company in the Royal West Kent Regiment. James, by now an experienced soldier, was a valuable addition to the 7th Battalion fighting in France. This Battalion was involved in fierce fighting during the brief but successful Third Battle of Albert (21st - 23rd August 1918) which itself marked the start of the Second Battle of the Somme (21st August - 3rd September 1918).

The Germans were quickly ousted from Albert but held Tara and Usna Hills, east of the town. The 7th Battalion plus two Brigades attacked at 'zero hour', 4.45am on the morning of 23rd August 1918. To the minute, the Battalion "pushed forward behind the barrage along the light railway which runs up the Tara Valley. The attack was an immediate success". Large numbers of prisoners were taken and the Battle of the Somme was able to move forward. James was seen to fall during the advance, bravely leading his men. The attack on 23rd August and further fighting on the 24th August cost the 7th Battalion three officers killed, five officers wounded and 142 other casualties but, unlike in so many previous battles, its gains were noted as significant.

Lieutenant James Cassels Cobb is buried at the Dernancourt Communal Cemetery Extension in the Somme area of France and is remembered on the Christ College War Memorial.

Private Cecil Arthur Collins

78th Battalion, Canadian Expeditionary Force

SURVIVED THE WAR

Hostel 1906-1907

Cecil Arthur Collins was born in Lucknow, India on 9th November 1891 and entered the Hostel on 19th February 1906. He was the oldest of three brothers and named after his father. Along with both his brothers, Percy Leonard Collins (Hostel 1906-1907) and Malcolm Reginald Collins (Hostel 1906-1907), Cecil Arthur arrived in Christ College on 19th February 1906. The boys' home at the time of entry is listed as Chakrata, India.

All three boys left school at Easter 1907, having stayed for three and a half terms. During his time at school, Cecil made an impression and was noted as "a dark, keen, active lad . . . a determined protector of his younger brothers; a vigorous promising boy in many ways". He seems to have been keen on cricket and is recorded as playing well for the 3rd Cricket XI, including in an "easy victory" on 14th July 1906 when the 3rd XI played the Drummers of the South Wales Borderers Depot.

In 1912 Cecil moved to Canada, eventually joining the Royal North West Mounted Police. He served with them for a year and two months before enlisting at Calgary on 24th August 1915 to fight in the First World War. Strangely he seems to have enlisted a second time (on 20th October 1915) as there are two different copies of his attestation papers. These papers describe him as being 5 feet 10½ inches tall with a dark complexion, brown eyes and black hair. His religion is shown as 'Church of England'.

Cecil Arthur arrived with his fellow Canadians in England on 29th May 1916 and exactly a month later was made up to Acting Sergeant. The following year he reverted to the rank of Corporal and was then further reduced to Lance Corporal and then Private. Having been transferred between Reserve Battalions, he reached France on 11th November 1917. In and out of the front line as a result of gassing, influenza and trench fever, he eventually returned to England on 14th April 1918. He was reported as fit for duty on 30th May 1918 and then attended a number of courses before returning to Canada and his eventual demobilisation on 4th February 1919.

During the war all three brothers joined up, Cecil Arthur and his brother, Leonard (as Percy preferred to be called), both in 1915 with the Canadians. By that time their father had moved to Silakoth, Punjab, India. In 1918 the youngest brother, Malcolm, was in training for a commission. Leonard is reported as having "copped a blighty one" when his elbow was shot off and a message reached Christ College saying that Cecil had been killed. *The Breconian*, however, notes that "We know at present no details of his rank or regiment or of the circumstances of his death."

Such is the confusion and rumour in wartime. Though his death is recorded on the Christ College War Memorial, he actually returned to Canada where he married Margaret Bowles and settled in Victoria, British Columbia. His brother, Leonard, also returned to Canada and, until his death in 1949, lived a happily married life in nearby Saanichton, British Columbia.

Cecil Arthur Collins died in Vancouver of tuberculosis in 1930, probably unaware that his old school had already been mourning him for many years.

Second Lieutenant David Harold Davies
1st Battalion, Wiltshire Regiment

18TH NOVEMBER 1918 ~ AGED 21
School House 1912-1914

David Harold Davies was born on 29th September 1897 and entered Christ College in January 1912 at the same time as his older brother, Thomas Henry Ronald Davies (School House 1912-1913), from their family home at Gowerton, Glamorganshire. Both boys had previously attended Gowerton County School. Their father, Dr. Abel Christmas Davies, was the local GP in Gowerton; he had played rugby football for London Welsh and was also a former Welsh international who had gained his cap in 1889.

David Harold seems to have enjoyed the various sports on offer at Christ College. At the Athletic Sports of 13th March 1912 he came second in the 220 yards Under 15 Handicap. In the summer he played for the 2nd Cricket XI and, although stronger as a bowler than a batsman, on 1st June 1912 he scored a useful 13 in a match against Sketty 2nd XI. On Wednesday 12th June he played in a 2nd XI match against Brecon Sports Club 2nd XI. Short of numbers on the day, Brecon Sports Club had borrowed a couple of Christ College boys. Thus one poignant entry in the score book reads "T. Akrill Jones, c Yendoll, b D.H. Davies 4". All three - Trevor Akrill Jones, Gordon Yendoll and David Harold Davies - were killed in the war as was a fellow bowler in the game, Basil Biggerton-Evans.

During the autumn of 1912, and aged barely fifteen, David Harold played the occasional game for the 1st Rugby Football XV alongside Geoffrey Boothby and David Cuthbert Thomas, two other boys who were also to die in the war. Thus six of Christ College's best sportsmen of 1912 were to be killed, four of them 21 years old or younger.

In the spring of 1913 David Harold is reported as playing Fives and, at the Athletic Sports in April 1913, he received a string of prizes. The Junior Cup had "produced some very exciting races". Of these he won first prize for the Long Jump, the 100 yards - in a dead heat with E. W. Corbett (Day Boy 1910-1914). He also won the 220 yards and the Quarter-Mile, in which he "broke away at once and won comfortably, but in moderate time" beating Corbett and Trevor Akrill Jones. When the results of the Junior Challenge Cup were announced, it was no surprise that David Harold was the clear winner by 37½ marks.

He played cricket again in the summer term of 1913, this time for the 1st XI. Still only fifteen, he took a good number of catches but the record shows he was a decent all-rounder. The critique of his performance reads "A most promising cricketer, but at present is too subject to 'nerves' to produce his true form. Has very nice style and a strong defence. A fair change bowler and a smart field; should be very useful another season".

His brother, Thomas, had left Christ College at the end of that summer term to go to university to follow his father into a medical career. Thomas had played for the 1st Cricket XI and 1st XV and, in the autumn of 1913, David followed his brother into the Rugby Football XV. His position was at three-quarters and the match reports praise him for his conversions. However, the usual critique of the team at the end of term cannot have pleased him: "D.H. DAVIES (right centre) - A failure as a centre, has no resolution and confidence. Can kick well and run straight at times, but his tackling and defence are deplorably weak. A good place kick". Similarly, the 1st Hockey XI the critique in the spring of 1914 was no better: "D.H. DAVIES (outside right) - A very weak forward; rarely beats his half, and practically never centres. Very inclined to give 'sticks'".

The cricket season of 1914, though, saw David having some good matches. The two day match in which the 1st XI played the Masters resulted in a draw, and David Harold was responsible for the fall of seven wickets. On 23rd May he scored a quick 40 runs in a match against Brecon Sports Club at their ground. The School lost the match but not before David Harold had taken 4 wickets in 11 overs. The following week he went on to take 5

1914 Hockey XI including D.H. Davies (standing far right back) and D.C. Thomas (standing far left back)

wickets in just over 6 overs at home in a match against Swansea Wednesday in which the opposition scored 27 (all out within the hour) to the School's 198.

On 10th June, despite heavy morning showers, the School won against Hereford Cathedral School, thanks to some hard hitting by David Harold with a top score of 35. On Wednesday 17th June 1914, the School won against Monmouth Grammar School on a warm, sunny day with "the wicket in perfect condition for run getting". David Harold was quickly dismissed for 3 runs but had a better day with the ball by taking 6 wickets for just 33 runs.

David Harold missed the match against Builth Wells on Saturday June 19th as his father had died unexpectedly at the age of 53 the previous day. However, he reappeared for the all-important match against Llandovery on Saturday 27th June 1914, which was played at home "in splendid weather" to a large crowd. Christ College lost 120 to 224 and, despite bowling 20 overs, David Harold failed to take a single wicket. However, he made up for it in the return match against Swansea Wednesdays, played at Swansea on 1st July, when he bowled 16 overs and gave away only 28 runs. Unfortunately, despite the hard work of David Cuthbert Thomas and the support of Trevor Akrill Jones, the match was lost by 19 runs. At the end of the 1914 season, David Harold was placed amongst the top bowlers in the 1st XI alongside Trevor Akrill Jones and David Cuthbert Thomas. David also made occasional appearances for the 2nd XI and, of course, in the House matches.

Not just able on the cricket field, he gained passes in Latin, Greek, French, Dictation, Arithmetic, Geometry, Algebra, Scripture Knowledge and Chemistry in the 1914 summer examinations. His ten passes in the Cambridge Junior Examinations were the most in the year. Poignantly, the name on the list that follows D.H. Davies is that of N.V. Evans, Neville Vernon Evans, who was also to die in the War.

David Harold and Thomas, his brother, both joined the Army. Thomas joined the Royal Field Artillery and David Harold the 28th (County of London) Battalion (Artists' Rifles). David Harold was later recorded in *The London Gazette* of 29th April 1918 as being commissioned into the 1st Battalion, Wiltshire Regiment. The Regiment was involved in heavy fighting throughout much of 1918 and in late summer David was reported as wounded and missing in action. It transpired that he was a Prisoner of War at the extensive Prisoner of War Niederzwehren Camp in Germany. It was here that he died on 18th November 1918 and was subsequently buried in the camp cemetery.

Second Lieutenant David Harold Davies is remembered on the Christ College War Memorial and is buried in the Niederzwehren Cemetery in Germany.

Second Lieutenant Harold Blakeney Davies

1st Battalion, West Yorkshire Regiment

23RD APRIL 1916 ~ AGED 25
School House 1909-1911

Harold Blakeney Davies was the younger brother of Walter Bomford Davies (School House 1901-1908). A third brother, Ronald Brynmore Davies (School House 1908-1910), was also at Christ College. Harold was born on 17th February 1891 at Blakeney, Gloucestershire (and named after the village). His father, the Reverend Walter Pandy Davies, was a Baptist Minister living with his family at 3 Victoria Avenue, Penarth. He entered Mill Hill School in 1904, joining School House. Mill Hill School had been established by Nonconformists a century earlier and many sons of ministers attended.

Leaving Mill Hill at Christmas 1908, Harold joined School House at Christ College, five months after his brother had left and shortly before his 18th birthday, and around the time his father had become a Minister in the Church of England. In his first term Harold represented the School in a hockey match against Abergavenny. Several other matches followed where he played alongside Martin Spencer Smith, who would become another casualty of the war. The following term started with a hot May and then a rainy June before improving again. The 1st Cricket XI's success seemed to fluctuate with the weather - good, poor, good. Harold was a prominent member of the team with some decent early efforts such as in the match against Sketty on Saturday 15th May 1909 where he bowled 16 overs and took 6 wickets. His performance in later matches was not as successful, although he redeemed himself in the Llandovery Match of 3rd July 1909 when, through "playing quietly and correctly", he helped to carry the score to well over 100 before falling to a catch.

He finished the season with a prize for his bowling. At the end of his first summer term Harold was described in the cricket summary in *The Breconian* as "unexpectedly useful, till he overbowled himself". The critique of his performance, published at the end of the term, reads "Did excellent service with the ball in the first half of the season, but lost his sting latterly … Good field, and bats solemnly and very straight."

In the rugby football season of 1909/10, Harold turned out regularly for the 1st XV. Later described as one

1909 Rugby Football XV. HB Davies is third from the left in the back row

of the "almost invincible" teams of Christ College, the side was captained by H.J.V. ("Jack") Rees (Day Boy and School House 1902-1910) who would go on to achieve a rugby football Blue while at Oxford. In the Llandovery Match of Saturday 27th November, Harold is described as being "splendid, as long as he lasted". In a match where several key players were down with flu, Christ College "won at Llandovery, by 2 goals (10 points) to 3 tries (9 points) for the first time in the history of these long established matches". His critique in *The Breconian* reads "H.B. DAVIES - A converted back, and has certainly found his right place in the scrum. His line-out work has been invaluable, and while not neglecting to push, he is to the fore in every rush. Tackles low and effectively."

Harold was made a School Prefect during the autumn term and the spring of 1910 found him hard at work in his study and on the games field. As well as working in the January on entry papers to Oxford University, he was the Captain of the 1st Hockey XI. He played right-half and was described as "A player of considerable ability, using his stick cleverly and breaking up opposing combination well."

In the cricket season of 1910 Harold again played for the 1st XI. In the opening match on 4th and 5th May against the Masters, Harold caught out two of the Masters, although was himself later bowled and caught by Mr. R.T. Rees (Master 1908-1909) for 0. A few days later, playing against Mr. Donaldson's XI, he had the misfortune of being run out, again for 0. However, his bowling was clearly far superior both for the 1st XI and the House, and by the end of the season, Harold had bowled 183.5 overs for 512 runs, taking 39 wickets.

The end of season report stated "H.B. DAVIES - A bowler of much merit. On his day swerves in very deadly fashion and has not always had the best of luck. A good field, but has been singularly unsuccessful with the bat".

For this he was awarded the cricket prize for the 'Aggregate Ball'. In fact his team mate, W.A.G. Howell (Hostel 1907-1911 and Master 1920-1959), had actually won all the cricket prizes that year - not least for his stunning bowling resulting in 65 wickets taken (a School record) - so it was decided to award some of the cricketing prizes to the next in line.

In addition to his cricketing prowess, Harold was a member of the Games Committee, an Editor of *The Breconian* and a School Prefect. On Prize Day 1910, held in the Big School Room, Harold was awarded the VIth Form Mathematics Prize. He was clearly something of an all-rounder.

The rugby football season of 1910/11 saw Harold again to the fore. Although in a match against Brecon Town, played on 9th November 1910, the forwards were described as "lacking cohesion ... individually (they) played well". On Saturday 26th November the 1st XV played Llandovery in the annual match and, although eventually losing 11 points to 3, Harold got involved in the game from the start. He very nearly scored in the opening moments when, after "J.V. Rees kicked off, (Harold) followed up so well that he charged down the return. The ball rolled into touch right on the Llandovery line, but we could not force our way across". The end of season report stated that Harold was "A first-rate forward, particularly valuable in the line-out and in loose rushes. One of the soundest tacklers on the side, and can kick or take a pass when necessary."

Harold captained the 1st Hockey XI during the spring of 1911. The side had mixed fortunes and Harold's end of season report stated that he was "A little uncertain at the start but has gradually found his best form. Has the true half-back genius for interception of passes, uses his stick neatly and feeds his forwards with judgement". In the House Fives Competition, he and J. Cooper (School House 1907-1912) were beaten in the first round of the Doubles but Harold went through the rounds in the Singles competition, unfortunately being knocked out in the semi-finals - by J. Cooper! At the Athletic Sports on Saturday 8th April, Harold won a closely contested Senior Cup by winning the 220 yards Open Handicap, the Quarter-Mile, the Mile and the Steeplechase, where he broke the School record by coming in at 35 minutes 24½ seconds.

In his final summer at the school, Harold again proved himself an excellent bowler and in one match, on 7th June against Swansea Wednesday, he took 5 wickets for 29 runs. On 24th June in a memorable match against Reverend Donaldson's XI, Harold scored a magnificent 65 which was described as "a fine effort and easily the best innings he has played so far". He also bowled out David Cuthbert Thomas whose death in 1916 was just a few weeks before Harold's. In a repeat of the previous cricket season, W.A.G. Howell took all the prizes (and smashed his own record to take 78 wickets) but "handed down two to the next in order of merit". Thus Harold again received the prize for the 'Aggregate Ball' once more. In the end of year examinations, Harold gained his Higher Certificate, with a Distinction in Additional Mathematics.

At the time of his leaving school, Harold's successes were legion: a "distinguished member of the Mathematical VIth ... one of the best bowlers of the Cricket XI of 1909-10-11; he played with great success in the XVs of 1909 and 1910; he was a long distance runner of more than average merit, winning the Senior Steeplechase in record time in 1911 and carrying off the senior Challenge Cup in the same year. He was also a member of the Hockey XI 1910-11 and captain in his last year. In every branch of our life his force of character brought him to the Front." As well as being a Prefect, Captain of the School and an Editor of *The Breconian*, he was also known as a "witty and eloquent speaker" and on occasion, turned his hand to poetry (see epigraph at front of book). Going up to Keble College, Oxford in the autumn of 1911, Harold "won distinction and popularity". He played cricket, tennis, and rugby football for his college and the London Welsh. As well as enjoying romantic encounters and continuing his not inconsiderable debating skills, he also led the very strong Oxford Old Breconian Society. Harold took a brief spell as Lower School master back at Christ College in September 1913 during the sudden incapacitating illness of Mr. Lance. Harold was welcomed back in this unexpected capacity and it clearly had no effect on his studies. In the summer of 1914 Harold took "Honours in the Final School of Modern History", later deciding to prepare to read for Holy Orders.

Though he was known to have felt a strong dislike for war and militarism, he "at once obeyed the call of duty and joined the Officers' Training Corps". *The London Gazette* of 25th June 1915 records that Harold was commissioned into the 3rd (Reserve) Battalion, West Yorkshire Regiment. This was a training unit based at Whitley Bay as well as being part of the

Second Lieutenant H.B. Davies in uniform

Tyne Garrision. That summer Harold became engaged to be married. However, time was limited and demands on the young officers continuous. In the spring of 1916 Harold was attached to the 1st Battalion, West Yorkshire Regiment, which had seen heavy action since landing in France in September 1914 and was now based on the Ypres Salient.

On 23rd April 1916 he moved up to the front line for the first time in order to take part in a small scale attack on a German trench. He died at the start of the attack, less than an hour after arriving at the Front. *The Breconian* recorded "With his death Christ College loses one of the most striking personalities of recent generations".

Second Lieutenant Harold Blakeney Davies is buried at Essex Farm Cemetery. He is remembered on the War Memorial at Keble College, Oxford as well as on the Christ College War Memorial.

Second Lieutenant Walter Bomford Davies

1st (Garrison) Battalion, Somerset Light Infantry

3RD NOVEMBER 1918 ~ AGED 29

School House 1901-1908

Walter Bomford Davies, the older brother of Harold Blakeney Davies, was born on 20th August 1889. He arrived in School House, Christ College in 1901. The first mention of Walter in *The Breconian* is in the report on the Speech Day of 29th July 1902 when he received the Form V prize for Greek, with Stephen Wriothesley Best the next in line to receive the same prize for Form IV. Walter was also given his Lower Certificate which included four first class passes and an honourable mention in Lower French.

In the following year at Speech Day on Monday 27th July 1903, Walter received the French Prize as well as the Upper V Greek Prize. Again Stephen Best followed him on to the platform, this time to receive the Lower V Greek Prize. Walter was also awarded a Mathematical Prize. His prowess in Classics and Mathematics had, by this time, earned him the sobriquet of 'Genii'.

He received his Oxford and Cambridge Higher Certificate and the second place Upper VIth Classical prize in 1905. In the following year he received the VIth Form Latin prose Competition Prize, and further Oxford and Cambridge Higher certificates were presented to Walter, along with Stephen Best and Charles Piper Hazard. He was made House Prefect in September 1906 as well as becoming an Editor of *The Breconian*.

Given this academic prowess, it was not surprising to hear in the Speech Day of 1907 that Stephen Best and Walter Bomford Davies had passed the London University Matriculation, First Division. Walter was also awarded the overall VIth Form prize, the Higher Certificate for Divinity, as well as the VIth Form Classical Composition prize. Second place for the Composition prize went to Charles Piper Hazard. The three boys who had so often shared the academic limelight on Speech Day would all die in the conflict yet to come.

Throughout 1907 Walter remained an Editor of *The Breconian* and in the autumn he was made a School Prefect. With a long-standing academic record, it was no surprise that he gained the Senior Open Scholarship at Trinity College, Oxford in 1908. The Scholarship was worth £80 and the school was awarded a half-day holiday on 5th March in honour of the award; Walter must have been an especially popular fellow on that day. For the rest of the year he continued as School Prefect and was, by now, an experienced editor of *The Breconian*. He was also a member of the Games Committee and on a cloudy but dry April day Walter took an active part in the smooth running and organisation of the Athletic Sports of 1908.

That summer his school career ended in a blaze of academic glory. He received the VIth Form Classics, History and Composition Prizes, and had the academic success of gaining three Distinctions in his Higher Certificate Examinations in Latin, Greek and History. In addition, he was awarded the prestigious Senior Anthony Death Exhibition in Classics worth £90 for four years.

Going up to Trinity College, Oxford University in 1908, Walter immediately got to grips with rowing as well as his academic studies. He remained interested in this sport and reports of his "stentorian" voice that would reach the rowing eight are found in the Oxford Letters in *The Breconian*. However, academic studies can never have been far from his mind and in the summer of 1910 Walter took a First in Classical Moderations. He was also becoming a noted speaker and was reported as "blossoming forth into a great orator, and holds the members of the Cambrian Society spellbound by his flowery rhetoric. Rumour says that he is in the habit of practising "animation" before his looking-glass every morning and night". No doubt pleased when his younger brother Harold also went up to Oxford to join him in the autumn of 1911, Walter continued to study hard and, according to his contemporaries, was cultivating "a look of studious innocence". With commitments to the river and oratory, as well as his studies, Walter was unfortunately not well during his Finals. Nevertheless he achieved a Third Class Honours degree in 1912.

Having decided to learn German, Walter was in Germany when war broke out. Like so many of his countrymen, he was interned, eventually obtaining release in late 1916. Shortly after arrival home, he joined the Army and after a period of training, on 15th December 1916 Walter was appointed Second Lieutenant in the Royal Welsh Fusiliers. Trinity College, Oxford records that, at the time of his death, he was a Second Lieutenant in the 1st (Garrison) Battalion, Somerset Light Infantry. The Commonwealth War Graves Commission does not have a record of him but it is confirmed that he died of influenza on the way back from India. Thus, *The Breconian* notes "a career of great possibilities has been cut short". The same obituary notes that one brother, Harold Blakeney Davies, had already died in the War and the third brother, Ronald Brynmore Davies, had been "severely wounded".

Second Lieutenant Walter Bomford Davies is remembered on the War Memorial at Trinity College, Oxford as well as on the Christ College War Memorial.

Lance Corporal Harry Skeel Duncan Dempster
7th Battalion, King's Royal Rifles
3RD AUGUST 1915 ~ AGED 27

Harry Dempster was born in early 1888 in Bromyard, Herefordshire, one of ten children (five boys and five girls). His father, Robert Duward Dempster, was a huntsman and shortly after Harry's birth, Robert, his wife Margaret and the family moved to Kennel Cottage, Canal Bank, Brecon. Robert then spent many years working for the Breconshire Hunt Club.

There is no record of Harry entering Christ College nor conclusive mention of him in the extant school records. He is included here solely on account of the mention of his having been killed in action (although without the usual obituary) in *The Breconian*. He is also in the later list of pupils, dates and occasional additional information conscientiously compiled by the Reverend Donaldson. Harry's attestation papers record him as being a member of the Cadet Force, adding weight to the initial research that he had been a Christ College pupil. However, these papers also state that Harry's school was Brecon County School and recent research has shown that this school had its own Cadet Force. On balance of probabilities, therefore, it seems unlikely that Harry was ever a pupil at Christ College.

After leaving the County School for Boys in Brecon, Harry became a clerk and the 1911 Census shows him as a printing canvasser in Llanelly, Carmarthenshire. He enlisted on 2nd November 1914, at the age of 26 and a half, into the 7th Battalion, King's Royal Rifle Corps at Haverfordwest.

Harry spent the next six months training as a rifleman, gaining promotion to Lance Corporal on 28th April 1915. He entered France on 19th May 1915 but died of wounds on 3rd August 1915, less than three months after his arrival. A telegram forty eight hours earlier, from the Officer Commanding 24 General Hospital, Etaples reported Harry dangerously ill with a gunshot wound to the head. Tragically, three years later, on 10th October 1918, Harry's older brother was killed in action in France.

Lance Corporal Harry Skeel Duncan Dempster is buried at the Etaples Military Cemetery.

Second Lieutenant Frederick William Evans
13th Battalion, Welsh Regiment
28TH OCTOBER 1916 ~ AGED 21
School House 1908-1910

Frederick William Evans was born in Swansea on 17th January 1895, the third of four children. His father, also called Frederick, was a Millinery Traveller. Frederick's mother, Mary, was a local Brecon girl and this may explain the choice of school.

Frederick entered Christ College in September 1908 and remained in School House until December 1910. During this time he was known for his "engaging simplicity and natural happiness of character". He was something of a sportsman and won places in the events of the Athletic Sports. On Saturday 3rd April 1909 Frederick came second in the Under 15 100 yards and first in the Half-Mile Open Handicap, a race he "won easily". In the afternoon, he went on to come second in the 220 yards Under 15 Handicap. During the summer term Frederick also turned out for the 2nd Cricket XI occasionally.

In the spring of 1910 Frederick and D.E.K. Llewelyn (School House 1907-1910) beat Hostel and then the Day Boys to become Fives Doubles champions and take the House Cup for School House. In the Fives Singles competition he was knocked out in the fourth round semi-final. However, on Monday 4th April, Frederick again shone in the Athletic Sports when he came second in the Quarter-Mile Under 16 Handicap. He was in scratch position and "ran in splendid style, and the long start men were out classed". In the Half-Mile "he was too fast for the other competitors" even though he made his "final burst much too soon" and must have been delighted with the first prize (awarded by the famous jewellers Mappin and Webb).

Frederick clearly had some talent in rugby football, playing for the 2nd XV in both 1909 and 1910, and was noted "as 'the most impudent seller of dummies' that ever graced the 2nd game three-quarter line". In the following summer, he again turned out occasionally for the 1st XI and it was recorded in the 1910 cricket report for the 2nd XI that he was "likely to make (his) mark in the future". A noted athlete, principally in middle distance running, Frederick had little time to develop his talents before leaving school at fifteen.

Frederick returned to live at the family home at 20 Bryn-y-mor Crescent, Swansea and followed his older brother, Walter, into the electricity industry by becoming an electrical apprentice. He still kept up his love of sport and on Tuesday 17th December 1912 returned to play for the Old Breconians alongside Harold Davies and Mr. J.S. Robinson against a 1st XV which included Geoffrey Boothby, Frank Best and David Cuthbert Thomas - all six of whom were to die in the ensuing war. Frederick returned on a number of other occasions, maintaining his connections with his former school.

Frederick entered France as a Second Lieutenant with the 13th Battalion, Welsh Regiment on 23rd August 1916. He died not far from Poperinge just over two months later, having been shot through the right lung and surviving a mere 24 hours.

The Breconian noted that "everything he did was done cheerily and gaily; no doubt he went into battle with such a gallant joyousness. The world is the less bright for his untimely death". The Editors also accorded him a poetical tribute with the poem 'F.W.E.'

F.W.E.

Turn the list o'er, and see . . .
What was the name you read?
Evans, F. W. . . . 'tis he
Our little Fred!

Of the 5th Welch, 'tis writ,
Second Lieutenant . . . dead! . . .
Twenty-one years . . The Pity of it!
Poor little Fred!

O Death, O Glutton Death,
Hadst not enough instead,
That thou must stop such joyous breath?
. . . Our little Fred!

Second Lieutenant Frederick William Evans is buried in the Lijssenthoek Military Cemetery and is remembered on the Christ College War Memorial.

Second Lieutenant Neville Vernon Evans
2nd Battalion, South Wales Borderers

16TH AUGUST 1917 ~ AGED 19
School House 1913-1916

Neville Vernon Evans was born on 19th December 1897 and was the eldest son of the Reverend J.D. Evans, Vicar of Treherbert. Neville joined School House from Leatherhead at Easter 1913 and "soon won a genuine popularity for his sterling qualities and cheery good nature". Keen at games and known as "Neddy", "he was everyone's friend and nobody's enemy". At the Prize Day of 1914 it was recorded that in the summer examinations Neville had passed the Cambridge Local Examinations in Latin, Greek, French, Dictation, Arithmetic and Algebra.

In the spring term of 1915 Neville took part in the Open Single Fives Competition and in the summer did remarkably well in the cricket league. Playing 16 innings for the 'Fly Catchers', he scored a total of 335 runs with a highest score of 62 runs. At Prize Day on Tuesday 27th July 1915 it was announced that Neville's academic work had won him "Exemption from Certain Professional Qualifications".

In the autumn of 1915 Neville played for Christ College 'A' team at rugby football and, although not in the 1st Hockey XI, Neville "did good service in League and House games" in the spring of 1916. That summer he played some cricket, including turning out on 20th May to play for Reverend Donaldson's XI in a match against the School and the occasional match for the 2nd XI. Indeed his playing was improving to the extent that he was "not far from winning his place both in the XV and Hockey XI". The summer term of 1916 also saw Neville promoted to Lance Corporal within the now "Fully-fledged and recognised Cadet Corps . . . now affiliated to the Brecknockshire Territorials". Within months he would be fighting for real as a commissioned officer.

Having "worked his way steadily up the school", he was in Va "when the time came for him to serve his country". Thus, 18 year old Neville - a School House Prefect, member of the 2nd XI, recipient of the Lower V Prize (presented at a privately held Speech Day that year), and keen member of the Cadet Corps - left Christ College in late July 1916 and enlisted in the Army on 28th August.

After being a private for some months, the 19 year old Neville was transferred to the 12th Officer Cadet Battalion and subsequently commissioned Second Lieutenant in the 3rd Battalion South Wales Borderers on 28th March 1917. He was almost immediately sent as one of three new Second Lieutenants to join the 2nd Battalion South Wales Borderers in the Autheux (Picardy) training area on 11th June 1917. The days that followed were initially taken up with the Divisional Horse Show, Church Parade and training. The Battalion Diary notes that, after moving up to the Front, at 1.05am on the morning of 5th July an "enemy patrol met our patrol just after it left our trench" resulting in several men wounded, one missing and the officer in charge dying of wounds. There were further periods of training and reinforcements arriving, and then further front line activity around Woesten. On 14th/15th August came the preparations for a major attack.

After reconnaissance parties reported back, "The Battalion formed up very satisfactorily without hitch or noise on the tape previously laid". Neville was attached to C Company. A barrage opened up at 4.45am on the morning of the 16th August. All objectives were reached, with 53 prisoners captured and several enemy guns damaged. However, 163 officers and men were killed, wounded or missing. Second Lieutenant Vernon Neville Evans was one of the officers killed in the bloody slaughter around Woestan, having been with the Battalion for a little over two months. His body was "buried in a shell-hole near Forick Farm, west of Langemarck, by the Steenbeck River". His Colonel wrote that Neville "was a most promising officer; he was leading his men most gallantly when he was killed".

In his obituary, *The Breconian* recorded that Neville "had not been more than a few weeks abroad before the last call came" and that he would be remembered as "dear old Neddy, who was everyone's friend and nobody's enemy". Also quoted in *The Breconian* was a letter from the Chaplain who similarly reflected on his friendliness: "We all loved him; many will remember his cheery manner and encouraging smile. The men appreciated his sympathy with their difficulties and hardships. In order to bring in his body they worked continuously for nearly nine hours - a significant tribute to their affection".

Second Lieutenant Neville Vernon Evans is buried in Artilliery Wood Cemetery in France and is remembered on the Christ College War Memorial.

Major John Kenrick Lloyd Fitzwilliams MC

25th Army Brigade, Royal Field Artillery

30TH AUGUST 1918 ~ AGED 33

Christ College 1896-1898

The Fitzwilliams were a family imbued with a sense of social justice and duty. John's grandfather, known as the 'Emlyn Lawyer', is regarded as the brains behind the Rebecca Riots which swept West Wales in the 1840s. John's father, Charles Home Lloyd Fitzwilliams, was a Justice of the Peace.

John Kenrick Lloyd Fitzwilliams was born at the family home at Cilgwyn, Newcastle Emlyn, Cardiganshire on 13th December 1884. He was the youngest of ten children (eight boys, two girls). John and four of his brothers were at Christ College in the 1890s. Cuthbert Collingwood Lloyd Fitzwilliams (School House 1890-1893), William Logie Lloyd Fitzwilliams (1892-?) and Duncan Campbell Lloyd Fitzwilliams (Horsburgh's 1891-1894), were followed by John Kenrick Lloyd Fitzwilliams and Gerard Hall Lloyd Fitzwilliams (Horsburgh's and School House 1896-1899).

All eight of the Fitzwilliams boys entered military service and four were to die while serving their country prior to the end of the First World War. William Logie Lloyd Fitzwilliams, one of two Old Breconians who died in the Boer War, is memorialized in the Christ College Chapel.

John and Gerard Fitzwilliams arrived at Christ College in September 1896. Their brother Duncan, who had left the school two years earlier, had been a School Prefect and member of the 1st Rugby Football XV. He was also one of the first four corporals of the newly formed Cadet Corps in 1894. After leaving school he went to study Medicine and served in the Boer War as well as in Romania and Russia in the First World War. Gerard also went on to study Medicine and later served in the First World War. Duncan and Gerard were both Army surgeons spending much of their time on the Eastern Front tending to wounded Russians and Romanians. At one time, they were in Romania together, attached to the British Red Cross setting up and working in Queen Maria of Romania's military hospital. Following the war, Gerard was in Vienna during the disintegration of the Empire, working as both doctor to the Emperor and Passport Control Officer (1919), then Hong Kong as a doctor and

JP, and then in 1921 back to Russia as part of a Trade Mission before 'chucking it all up' and going to Africa to shoot elephants and then come home and carve ivory. Evidence from declassified secret service files notes that Passport Control Officers were posts created by MI6 to install their agents in various embassies!

John and Gerard had previously been educated at The Philberds School, Maidenhead, an historic house with close links to Charles II and Nell Gwyn. Entered for the Christ College scholarship examinations of Tuesday 30th June and Wednesday 1st July 1896, they took papers in Latin Translation, Grammar and Composition, Greek Translation and Grammar, Arithmetic, Euclid and Algebra, and General Knowledge. Both boys achieved a House scholarship and the award to each of them of £20-30 per annum would have been a significant contribution to the school fees. They joined Christ College in September 1896 and the following year, 1897, John received an honourable mention in the Under 13 John Morgan Exhibition, losing out to William David Abbott. By a sad coincidence the Under 15 John Morgan Exhibition went to another boy who was also to lose his life in the First World War, Titho Glynne Jones.

In 1899 John Kenrick Fitzwilliams gained a scholarship to Dover College, and then went on to the Royal Military Academy, Woolwich in September 1902. Passing out two years later, he joined the 139th Battery Royal Horse Artillery based at Kildare. The following year he was ordered to the 43rd Battery, stationed at Woolwich. Between 1907 and 1908 John was sent to Moscow for a year to learn Russian and in 1909 he went to Germany to learn the language. The Army needed interpreters, and John was a fine linguist.

On 7th June 1910 John married Margery Laura Hyde and, over the next four years, served in India and England. In late October 1914 Temporary Captain John Fitzwilliams and his Battery (G Battery, Royal Horse Artillery) sailed on the SS 'Minneapolis' for France, disembarking on 6th November. He wrote every few days to his wife and the letters reveal a sharp mind and honesty not quashed by censorship. John comments in a letter of 13th November 1914 that "We know nothing here of the war … stalemate … trenches are only 100 yards apart … discipline is not altogether satisfactory and a certain number of men have had to be shot as examples. I punish mine by making them sleep out with the horses in the rain."

John's many letters reveal a great deal about his life in the trenches. In one incident the German anti-aircraft guns cunningly opened up on a plane, leading the British to think it was one of theirs. They only realized the error when the pilot came close and dropped bombs on them. John also had to go round killing pigeons in peoples' houses in case they were used for messages, although in one case he could not do it as the young boy owner cried so much. Instead, John ordered that the pigeons be put into a cage every morning and brought out for inspection. John was also clearly frustrated by the lack of trust between the Allies as well as in the "tactless and bad delivery" of a supposedly inspiring speech by the British Commander-in-Chief, General French.

In March 1915 he writes of the bloody Neuve Chapelle when 481 British guns fired on the German trenches and "the air was mixed with loose legs, arms, heads and bits of bodies". After an urgent order to fire on Germans filling sandbags behind the enemy trenches, he writes "I popped in forty-three shells … I hope I may have bagged a brace or two". Significantly he mentions the smell of gas in one of his letters, dated three weeks before the first official notification of its use, and says of the enemy "They are pigs, aren't they?"

On Easter Sunday some the Bavarians opposite John were "fraternizing with our men, just as they did at Christmas. There will be fearful trouble about it, I expect". Next day we writes that there has hardly been a shot fired in forty hours except for a sleepy sentry who accidently let off a round and someone at work with a revolver trying to bag the only remaining rabbit on the hill.

By the end of October he had been given command of a battery, as its previous Commanding Officer's nerves had broken down - and that this is happening to his men as well. He writes that rats and mice are a plague (although he has a mouse that is quite tame but doesn't like tobacco smoke) and that rest billets for six weeks are good. Best of all, he reports, his Battery Sergeant Major was awarded the Victoria Cross, and John and his men had a roast beef dinner on December 25th. A couple of days later John headed home on leave.

After his leave, John returned in January 1916, knowing full well by now "the rules of the games". In his letters he shows annoyance at the effort the German troops put into guns and shell fire on the Kaiser's birthday as he cannot get much sleep. Also going to see a "Frammenwerfer" (flame thrower) demonstration with a lot of other fellows (except due to a military blunder there was no demonstration arranged so the day was wasted, which John found amusing).

Further letters refer to inoculations, having to dig men out after a mine explosion near a gun-pit, and receiving a four page official letter complaining against his Battery for returning 124 pairs of dirty socks instead of 125 to the laundry. This "shows you how serious this war is and how busy everyone is". He also writes of having to be nice to the Ordinance and Supplies Officers (whom he privately calls the "Mammons of Unrighteousness"), the rate of using artillery shells, and of a young enthusiastic officer who during the evening of 24th/25th June crawled out under the wire during a large raid only to get lost and end up raiding his own trench further down the line.

He refers to the exhaustion and how some officers look twenty years older, especially with 18 days in the line and seven out, month on month. He is obviously proud of his men and what they can achieve with their guns. On the morning of 3rd August 1916, they take up a position on the Somme. There is a constant bombardment as the Somme battles play themselves out and even tanks make an appearance.

In early November 1916 John was awarded the Military Cross. The citation reads:

> For conspicuous gallantry in action. During the attack and capture of an enemy position he observed the fire of his battery from the infantry front line, often under heavy shell fire. Throughout the day he sent back most accurate and valuable information. He has proved himself a gallant and capable battery commander.

It was not surprising that on 25th November John was promoted to Major. The following month he writes about the new officers "none of them over twenty years of age ... not much officer, and less gentleman". In January 1917 he fell ill and in the following month was sent home. His previous letters refer to the "large amounts of rheumatism and pneumonia that abound". Soon after his return to the Front, he sends news home of the extreme cold where one chap's false teeth froze together. In April 1917 he was wounded and sent home once more.

In early July 1917 he returned to the war, this time on the Eastern Front where his job as Propaganda Officer was specifically to rally the Russian Troops to the Allied cause. He toured the Front speaking to officers and men alike and on one occasion he heroically saved the life of a Cossack officer, for which action he was awarded the Order of St Stanislas. During this time, it is clear that he is not surprised by the increasing unrest and describes the violence between opposing Russian factions and the desperation of the people.

Following the Treaty of Brest-Litovsk, John's position became untenable and he left Moscow heading for

Vladivostok on the Trans-Siberian Railway. Having taken it on himself to ensure the safety of the British Red Cross Mission, he and twenty others, including his brother Gerard (and John Smith, real name Thomas Masaryk, soon to become President of the new Czechoslovakia), had some difficult moments on the month long rail journey. His brother Duncan had stayed at Archangel, the only British officer to do so, until he was joined by the North Russian Expeditionary Force whose aim was to support the White Russians.

John reports on the disturbances he finds created by the Bolsheviks at Vladivostok and after travelling to China, on 19th April 1918, a meeting with Admiral Kolchak in Peking (Kolchak later led an Army against the Bolsheviks before being executed by them in February 1920). With relief, John sails for Japan, America and then on to England.

John had requested that he be sent back to his unit in France and was allowed to return on 16th August 1918. In his letters he notes changes after being away for a year, not least that prices have doubled, the presence of Americans and having to attend "Gas School to be fitted with our gas masks". On August 18th 1918 he took command of the Artillery Company of the 126th Army Brigade. On 30th August, just two weeks after arriving back in France, this "very gallant soldier and gentleman" was killed by a German shell in the little wood known as "Bois du Sart", not far from Vimy Ridge and the towns of Arras and Douai, whilst the Allies were pushing on in the Great Advance to Cambrai.

Major John Kenrick Lloyd Fitzwilliams MC is buried at the Vis-en-Artois Cemetery, Haucourt and is remembered on the Christ College War Memorial.

Lieutenant Wilfred St Martin Gibbon
2nd Battalion, 89th Punjabis
24TH APRIL 1918 ~ AGED 29
School House 1899-1906

Wilfred St Martin Gibbon was born on 4th July 1889 in Glasbury where his father, the Reverend Hugh Harries Gibbon, was Vicar. Wilfred was the second of five sons to join School House, Christ College. Reginald Hugh Gibbon (School House 1896-1899) was the oldest and joined Christ College a few years ahead of Wilfred. At school he obtained his Higher Certificate and left to go up to Keble College, Oxford having been Prefect, musician, soloist, Lance Corporal in the Cadet Force and a member of the 1st XV. He took holy orders and served as an Army Chaplain in the First World War. Wilfred joined Christ College in the term after his eldest brother left and was soon followed by their younger brothers, Geoffrey Vincent (School House 1905-1908), Stuart Ralph (School House 1905-1910) and Eric Montague (School House 1909-1910).

Although Wilfred "took no very conspicuous part" in school life, he was one of the first boys to take part in the "new feature in the School sports", the Steeplechase. In the first junior race on 26th March 1904 he came last but one; later, at the Athletic Sports held on Easter Monday 1904, he came first in the Quarter-Mile Under 16 Handicap. The following year Wilfred and a friend, A.S. Pleace (Morton's 1903-1905), won the three-legged race. In 1906, his final year at school, he played for both the 2nd and 3rd Cricket XI. His most notable score was 15 when he opened the batting for the 3rd XI in a home match on 14th July against the Drummers of the South Wales Borderers Depot and in the same match he showed his forte as bowler by taking 6 wickets.

After leaving school Wilfred was "appointed by examination" into the National Provincial Bank - at the time one of the country's leading banks. In the 1911 Census, he was recorded as being a bank clerk with them. Later he joined the United Counties Bank.

Soon after the outbreak of war, Wilfred volunteered for the Army and was commissioned into the 12th Battalion, Welsh Regiment which was formed in Cardiff on 23rd October 1914. The following year, on 1st May, 25 year old Wilfred married 21 year old Majorie Isobel Forester at Holy Trinity Church, Formby, Liverpool.

They subsequently had one daughter, Honor Amelia Gibbon.

Wilfred saw a great deal of service in Salonika, although he suffered three serious bouts of malaria. He transferred to the Indian Army and was promoted to Lieutenant. On 24th April 1918 Lieutenant Wilfred St Martin Gibbon died in India. His father received a telegram on Friday 26th April informing him of Wilfred's death from enteric fever. The local newspapers reported that "A short memorial service was conducted at St Peter's (Glasbury) on Sunday morning…and muffled bells pealed in the evening." *The Breconian* memorialized his death in the context of so many that had already been reported in its pages during the previous four years and paid "a last tribute to one more promising and useful life freely given in the service of his Country".

His daughter, Amelia, later married Major-General Sir Robert Anthony Pigot, 7th Baronet Pigot on 7th October 1941 and had two children, a girl and a boy. The latter, George, became the 8th Baron Pigot upon the death of his father in 1986.

Lieutenant Wilfred St Martin Gibbon is buried in the Nowshera Military Cemetery and is remembered on the War Memorial at Christ College.

Second Lieutenant Henry Norman Grant

A Company 1st Battalion, Lancashire Fusiliers

1ST JULY 1916 ~ AGED 23
Hostel 1907-1909

Henry Norman Grant was born on 5th December 1892 at Hay. He was the second of four children and joined Christ College in January 1907 at the same time as Basil Biggerton-Evans. His family lived at 6 Castle Street, Hay and his father was listed as a paper stationer (Shopkeeper) in the 1901 Census, and as a bookseller some years later.

Within a very short time of joining Christ College, Norman (as he was usually called) came second in the Junior Steeplechase on Saturday 23rd March 1907, winning a silver medal. He also won the Handicap prize for Golf, a game which he seems to have much enjoyed. The following year, Norman again played golf both in the annual Golf Competition of Saturday 28th March 1908 and for the School against the Depot of the South Wales Borderers on 2nd April. Four days later, at the Athletic Sports held on Monday 6th April, Norman won the Under 16 Long Jump. In the autumn he made the occasional appearance on the rugby football pitches for 'A' team and once for the 1st XV on the rugby football field playing alongside Benjamin Leeder and Martin Spencer Smith.

In the spring term of 1909 Norman took a full part in the increasingly popular golf matches, including one against the Choir. He continued his sporting interests and played in the Fives Competition, losing to Martin Spencer Smith (15-8, 15-4). In the Athletic Sports of 1909 Norman won the Open Consolation Race and was awarded the Junior Games Rugby Football Challenge Cup for his work as a forward.

After leaving school Norman moved to Hereford to work for the United Counties Bank as a bank clerk. Like so many young men from Christ College, he joined up shortly after the war broke out. In fact Norman joined the Public Schools Battalion of the London Royal Fusiliers and was one of 25 successful candidates for a commission in the Regular Army.

After Sandhurst training, Norman joined the 1st Battalion, Lancashire Fusiliers as a machine gun section officer in February 1915. He entered France on Friday 5th May 1916 and almost immediately took part in a number of raids on enemy trenches. Of his arrival and early days, he wrote home on 16th May 1916:

1st Battalion, Lancashire Fusiliers,
86th Brigade, 9th Division

Dear Father and Mother,

I received your letter yesterday. Thanks for sending on my letters. I started my trench life with very wet weather and all the trenches about 8 inches deep in very muddy water. I am covered from head to foot with mud and it is all stuck to my clothes. I have not had my clothes off since I came. I have done nothing but dig since I came the first night. I was on top of the trench and in front, doing repairs about twenty yards from the Boshes, but as it was not more light, it was comparatively safe. At any rate I don't think they discovered us.

The Bosh smashed up our water pipes the other day and caused us much bother, not being able to get any water. I have a little dug-out which I crawl into. It is about two and a half feet high. Last night I have just finished digging and was en-route for my dug-out when the Bosh started to shell us properly coming over thirty at a time for about two hours. I should think they put in twenty to thirty thousand shells - quite the largest bombardment the 1st Battalion have had yet. Anyhow they did not attack us, otherwise I might have been mincemeat.

We have continual artillery fire going on all day and night - sort of playing tennis - and we are the net. Yesterday when repairing a bit of trench I had some come within fifteen yards of me. The Sergeant got one of part of the shells. I have never done so much work in the army before, if I can snatch about four hours sleep now and again, I am very lucky. We shall be going back to rest camp when I hope to get a bath. But of course, when we are in rest, we come up to the trenches for digging during the day. The only aircraft about here are our own which fly over the lines all day and the Bosh generally waste about a 1000 shells daily on them, none of which ever touch of course.

It has been a beautiful day today, the first fine one we have had, and I have quite enjoyed it. It makes an awful difference out here if we get fine weather.

Food is difficult to get here. Only rations and it is not very good, so I will get you to send me some cakes now and again. At any rate I shall see what I can get when we get back to the village on rest.

Would you please send me the paper called "Truth" every week. Well goodbye for the present,

Love to all,
Norman

On 1st July 1916, eight weeks and one day after arriving in France, Norman was killed in action - another of the young officers whose average life expectancy on the front line was six weeks. He was at first posted as missing, as were over 2,000 men in the aftermath of the 'Big Push' of the first day of the Battle of the Somme on 1st July 1916. This first day saw 19,240 British dead, 35,463 wounded, 2,152 missing and 585 taken prisoner. Sixty percent of all officers involved on the first day were killed. The Battle of the Somme was to last for some five months and the combined casualty figure for all sides was well over 1.1 million men. It also caused the destruction of so many of the 'Pals' battalions which formed an integral part of the new Kitchener's Volunteer Army.

A few days before Norman's death, the Divisional Commander, Major General H.B. de Lisle addressed the men of the 1st Battalion with the words "To you has been set the most difficult task, that of breaking the hardest part of the enemy's shell". The Battalion, already bloodied in Gallipoli, was part of the force tasked with capturing the heavily defended Grandcourt-Serre Ridge which lay to the north of the River Ancre. One of the most heavily defended parts was the village of Beaumont-Hamel. This was the specific objective of Norman and the 1st Battalion, Lancashire Fusiliers.

The Battalion was to attack from the sunken road, following a huge artillery barrage and the detonation of the mine at the Hawthorn redoubt. Hawthorn, with its 18 tons of explosives, was one of three mines to be blown - the others being Locknagar and La Boisselle. The mine was blown at 7.20am, ten minutes before the attack was due to begin, and it gave the Germans ample warning as well as time to send men to defend the lip of the crater. Thus the Battalion started the attack in the face of withering machine gun fire to the front and sides. Of the Battalion officers, 7 officers were killed and 14 wounded; 156 other ranks were killed, 298 wounded; 11 were missing presumed dead. For a large number of acts of bravery on the day, members of the Battalion were awarded four Military Medals and eight Military Crosses.

The last positive sighting of Norman was just after 7.30am, when the attack on German lines started from the sunken road outside Beaumont Hamel. Norman was in command of the Lewis Gun Section. The witness report taken on 18th July stated:

> The attack was made from a sunken road about 50 yards in advance of our front line trench and 130 yards from the German lines. During the advance, when about 40 yards from the enemy lines, witness saw Mr. Grant fall about 10 yards to his right. We failed to reach the enemy front line but witness did not regain our lines before about 10.30 pm. He did not see anything of Mr. Grant on the retirement.

Further enquiries at the end of the month stated that according to the Lewis Gun Section Sergeant, Norman had been wounded and his leg broken. Yet another witness stated that, soon after 7 o'clock in the morning, he saw Second Lieutenant Grant "on reaching top of the parapet fall, wounded by a shell".

Second Lieutenant Henry Norman Grant is buried at Redan Ridge Cemetery No. 2 at Beaumont-Hamel. He is remembered on the Hay-on-Wye War Memorial as well on the Christ College War Memorial.

Driver Cyril Norman Green
55th Division Ammunition Column, Royal Field Artillery

11TH MARCH 1917 ~ AGED 21
School House 1911-1912

Cyril Norman Green was born on 20th December 1895 at Pembroke Dock. He was educated at Greenhill Grammar School, Tenby and lived at Mount Pleasant. In September 1911 he arrived at School House, Christ College and left just over a year later in December 1912. "Best described as one of 'the rank and file' of the School, he took no very prominent part in its life or games, but was a solid, steady working, much respected lad". After leaving school Cyril went into business. He clearly had a deep love for the school and in *The Breconian* it was recalled that he "often came up to see it again, or wrote for news of the old place".

On joining up he became a member of the 55th Divisional Ammunition Column whose job it was to supply the many elements of the Divisional Artillery for the 55th (West Lancashire) Division. Having fought through 1916 at the Battles of Guillemont, Ginchy, Flers-Courcelette and Morval, the Division found itself on the Ypres Salient in October 1916, not far from Railway Wood, with enemy on three sides and under frequent shelling. In March 1917 it was reported that Cyril received a face wound and was moved to the rear for medical care. However, his wound, "which unhappily turned out more serious than was expected", caused his death on 11th March 1917.

Driver Cyril Norman Green was buried at the Boulogne Eastern Cemetery. He was a Methodist and is commemorated in Tenby on a plaque at St John's Methodist Church, as well as on the Tenby Town War Memorial at Trafalgar Gardens. He is also remembered at Greenhill Secondary School as well as on the Christ College War Memorial.

Trooper David Mansel Griffiths
8th Australian Light Horse

7TH AUGUST 1915 ~ AGED 22
Christ College 1907-1909

David Mansel Griffiths was born on 1st August 1893. His father was Robert Christopher Griffiths, a Bridgend Solicitor, Conservative Agent for South Glamorgan and Election Agent for Colonel W.H. Wyndham-Quin, 5th Earl of Dunraven and Mount Earl, who was elected to Parliament in 1895 and 1900. The family lived at the Cottage, Laleston, Bridgend. David went to school at Llandaff Cathedral School and then entered Christ College at Easter 1907, staying until October 1909.

The first mention of David in school records comes in the Athletic Sports on Monday 6th April 1908 when he won both the Under 15 100 yards and the 150 yards Under 15 Handicap. During the summer term he played for the 2nd XI, alongside Benjamin Leeder and Martin Spencer Smith. David also had a talent for the theatricals and in the Christmas Theatricals of 1908 he took the part of 'Kenrick' in Coleman's three act comedy Heir-at-Law, reviewed in *The Breconian* as an "excellent show". On stage with him were Martin Spencer Smith and Basil Biggerton-Evans, who played Henry Morland and Dick Dowlas respectively. The cast also included the 'refined and womanly' Caroline Dormer, played by Charles Hunter.

In 1909 David continued his sporting interests when he was selected to play right-half for the 1st Hockey XI, in which position he was described as "a painstaking and persistent tackler, with a sound idea of feeding his forwards". He also played in the Fives Competition but was knocked out by Martin Spencer Smith in the second round. At the Athletic Sports on 3rd April 1909, he won the Under 16 Long Jump with a distance of 15 feet 3 inches. He also came second in the Quarter-Mile Under 16 Handicap. In the summer he again played cricket for both the 1st and 2nd XI as well as scoring a very creditable 71 for School House A-M against the Day Boys in the House Matches.

Though enjoying his sport and making the most of the opportunities offered, David left in the autumn to take up a "business appointment". This was a blow to the Rugby Football XV as he "and Howell had already established a good understanding together, and looked like making a capital pair of half-backs". There was, *The Breconian* lamented, "no one available to fill the serious vacancy thus caused".

Whatever the business opportunity was, in September 1911 David sailed to Australia and settled at Wilcannia, New South Wales as a rancher. As soon as war was declared, he settled his affairs and volunteered for Imperial Service, joining the Australian Light Horse. In December 1914 his Battalion landed in Egypt and from there, on 25 April 1915, he landed in Gallipoli as part of the Mediterranean Expeditionary Force.

Just over three months later, and just six days after his 22nd birthday, he was killed in action on 7th August 1915 at Lone Pine whilst taking part in what became known as 'the charge of the 8th Light Horse'. His Squadron Commander, Captain H. Beath, wrote to his parents:

> *Your son was in my squadron and I was near him when he was killed. I thought a lot of him, and am proud to say he was a pal of mine. Poor old Griff (that is what we used to call him) was killed on the morning of 7th August in a bayonet charge on the Turkish trenches. Our regiment was badly cut up; very few of Griff's troop got back. Only 120 of over 500 men are left to tell the tale. We were in such a very bad place; our regiment made a grand name for themselves. You can always feel proud he belonged to the 8th L.H. We were set a very bad task that morning, but console yourself he died nobly doing his bit like the fearless boy he was.*

Trooper David Mansel Griffiths is remembered at the Lone Pine Memorial, Gallipoli and on the Christ College War Memorial.

Second Lieutenant Howard Locke Harries
18th Battalion attached 10th Battalion, Royal Welsh Fusiliers

13TH NOVEMBER 1916 ~ AGED 28
School House 1901-1905

Howard Locke Harries, the middle of three sons, was born on 19th May 1888 in Cardiff, to David and Frances Harries. David was a Chemist/Pharmacist and lived at 108 Queen Street (1891), 102 Queen Street (1901) and later, 181 Newport Road (1911). His mother, Frances died soon after the birth of her youngest son in 1890 and David remarried 18 years later.

Howard entered School House in September 1901, at the same time as Walter Bomford Davies. At Speech Day on Tuesday 29th July 1902, Howard received an honorary mention for his work in Mathematics and Arithmetic (as did Stephen Best). He left school in the same year as his elder brother, Frank Shearme Harries (School House 1898-1905). Frank had won his colours for rugby football, cricket and hockey and was sergeant in the Cadet Corps while at Christ College. Being rather younger than his brother when leaving school, there are no extant records of Howard's other activities while at Christ College.

After school Howard became a clerk in a coal shipping company and developed quite a talent for business and, it seems, for mastering modern languages. He soon prospered and gave every indication that he was to become a successful businessman.

When war broke out he joined the Glamorgan Yeomanry and then, after officer training, took a commission on 10th September 1915 into the 18th (Reserve) Battalion, 2nd London Welsh, Royal Welsh Fusiliers who were based in the United Kingdom. The following year he was attached to the 10th Battalion which had been sent to France on 17th September 1915.

Howard himself entered France on Saturday 7th October 1916. He was killed by an exploding shell five weeks and two days later, becoming yet another young officer who fell short of the six week average life expectancy of an officer in a fighting battalion. In *The Breconian* he was remembered as "a boy of many solid and manly qualities, for whom respect and affection grew as acquaintance developed".

Howard's brother, Frank, also saw active service in the First World War and was Mentioned in Despatches. A solicitor by profession, he was a Governor of Christ College from 1944 to 1965 and a generous benefactor to the school until his death in 1976.

Second Lieutenant Howard Locke Harries is buried at the Euston Road Cemetery, Colincamps. He is remembered in the War Memorial at Cardiff (Cathays) Cemetery as well as on the Christ College War Memorial.

Second Lieutenant Charles Piper Hazard
1st Battalion, King's Shropshire Light Infantry
21ST APRIL 1916 ~ AGED 28
School House 1904-1907

Charles Piper Hazard was born on 20th April 1888 at Bournemouth. His father was a retired Chemist (although only in his early 40s) who later went on to open a boarding house with his much younger wife. Charles joined School House in January 1904.

Although ostensibly interested in sport and acting, at Speech Day on Tuesday 17th October 1905 Charles was nevertheless awarded the VIth Form Prize for Divinity. However, rugby football was his sport and he worked hard at securing and keeping his place in the 1st XV. In the autumn of 1905, weighing in at 9st 8lbs, he is recorded as "A steadily improving forward" and "a conscientious worker all the time." Charles played for the 1st XV again in the following season; the end of season critique of him reads "A useful forward of the persevering sort. Uses his feet well in the open, and has improved in skill in the tight scrums. Always in the thick of it".

Indeed, the autumn term of 1906 was an important and busy term for Charles. He was made House Prefect, School Prefect, sub-Librarian, and appointed to the prestigious Games Committee. This was in addition to his beloved rugby football and the Cadet Force. To crown it all, on 18th December, Charles performed in the end of term production of Sheridan's *A Trip To Scarborough*. With a cast selected, coached and "licked into shape" by the Reverend Donaldson, Charles played 'the jeweller'. For several years prior, the school play had been of a musical variety and it had been decided to revert to "legitimate drama". Once *A Trip To Scarborough* had been selected, it was discovered that it had been performed "upon the College 'boards' most successfully in 1889"; it was revived with enthusiasm and its two performances were judged to be of a high standard.

Clearly talented in many areas, Charles, described as of "studious habits (and having) made a mark in the Classical VIth", went on to reap further rewards. In January 1907 it was announced that he had been awarded an £80 Classical Scholarship at Jesus College and would go up to Oxford that October. The School was given a half-day holiday on 4th February 1907 in honour of this award. In his final terms he proved his all-round talents: he was awarded a Silver medal for shooting in the School Cadet Corps; he came second in the Senior Steeplechase; remained a member of the Games Committee; he was awarded the VIth Form Prize in Classical Composition as well as Higher Certificate History and French on Speech Day 1907.

He went up to Oxford in the autumn of 1907 and, once there, Charles seems to have enjoyed his sport. He played regularly for the Jesus College XV and occasionally for the hockey team. During that first term, he also played for the London Welsh in their match against the Varsity. In July 1908 he was elected Secretary of Rugger at Jesus College whilst apparently being "an exponent in the gentle art of doing nothing". However, he was spotted wearing "the rainbow hues that illuminate his collar (and which) show that he has been elected to the 'Elizabethane Societie'". Rugby football and work continued to occupy his life, along with occasional tennis.

Graduating from Oxford with Honours in 1911, Charles joined the Colonial Civil Service and obtained a posting to Agbor, Southern Nigeria. He sailed on board SS 'Elmina' in March 1912. In the autumn of 1913 he was appointed Assistant Commissioner, South Nigeria. However, once war was declared, like so many of his contemporaries, Charles decided to resign his post and return home to fight. Charles joined up on March 13th 1915. He was commissioned and entered France on 10th July 1915.

Shortly after arriving in France he was wounded in action but later returned to the Front. On the night of 21st April 1916 he and his men of 1st Battalion, King's Shropshire Light Infantry were ordered to counter attack to resist an earlier successful German attack on Morteldje Estaminet, Ypres Salient. This part of the line had been fought over many times, and during the winter it had been impossible to keep a continuous front line; those trenches that did exist had low parapets and were not that bullet-proof, with little wire in front. At this time there were few dug-outs or communication trenches. The bombardment for the counter-attack due at 10pm started that morning at 8am. The ground, already well fought over, was thick mud. Later battle reports confirmed that several men suffocated in the cloying mud during the attack. Indeed, the only way for the troops to move forward in places was to crawl on hands and knees, throwing their rifles in front of them. Such Germans who were found were bayoneted or shot.

The counter attack was successful but only at severe cost to the King's Shropshire Light Infantry. The Battalion Commanding Officer, Lieutenant Colonel E.B. Luard DSO, was killed as were three other officers (and five wounded). 22 other ranks were killed, 135 men were wounded and six were reported missing. Charles was at first reported as missing in action but news soon came in that "he had been seen to fall shot through the head while trying to assist a wounded fellow officer under very heavy fire".

Praise was heaped upon the Battalion for their action. Lord Haig singled them out for their actions as did the Corps Commander, Lord Craven, who wrote to Colonel Luard's widow:

> *I do not think any battalion was ever set a much more difficult and necessary task, yet in inky darkness, over shell-destroyed ground, in pouring rain, the KSLI went straight to their work, and under your husband's splendid and gallant direction once more secured the safety of the left of the British line.*

The Brigade General wrote to the new Commanding Officer:

> *The Brigadier also wishes you to say to the Battalion, that in his opinion the action of the night 21/22nd April will rank very high among the many glorious exploits of the Battalion in the past, that its success is due to the careful arrangements made by Lieutenant Colonel Luard, to the gallant leading of the officers of the Battalion, and to the high standard of discipline, soldier-like conduct and personal gallantry which prevails throughout all ranks of the Battalion.*

The Breconian, in recording the circumstances of Charles' heroic death, stated that "His death seems to have been worthy of the high character and name he won for himself at Christ College and elsewhere".

Charles had two brothers, Cecil and Douglas. Cecil was a Major in the Hampshire Regiment and survived the war. Douglas was also a Second Lieutenant in the King's Own Shropshire Light Infantry and was killed in action on 23rd May 1915 on the Ypres Salient. Douglas and Charles would be buried within a few kilometres of each other outside the town of Ypres, although eleven months apart, Douglas at Sanctuary Wood and Charles at Essex Farm Cemetery.

Second Lieutenant Charles Piper Hazard is remembered on the Christ College War Memorial. The wooden cross originally placed on his grave in France was given to his former school by his relatives and dedicated on Easter Sunday in 1932. It still hangs in the ante-chapel today.

Second Lieutenant Bertram Hincks
5th Battalion attached 10th Battalion, King's Royal Rifle Corps

18TH DECEMBER 1916 ~ AGED 26
School House 1904-1908

Bertram Hincks was the sixth and youngest son of Hay doctor Thomas Samuel Hawkesford Hincks and Emily Fairbanks. He was the third of three boys to attend Christ College. His older brothers, Harold Austin (1896-1898) and Arthur Cecil (School House 1896-1900), joined Christ College at the same time, several years before Bertram. Harold later emigrated to Canada but Arthur remained a staunch supporter of the Old Breconians, returning to play in Old Boys' cricket matches and attending Old Boys' Dinners. On one occasion he played for Hay in a hockey match against the School when it was noted that the Christ College side were "too fond of fouling their opponents".

Bertram was born at 13 Broad Street, Hay on 1st May 1890. He entered School House, Christ College in 1904 from his home at 27 Broad Street, Hay. He left at the end of the Christmas Term 1907. This was almost exactly the same time period as another School House boy Charles Piper Hazard, though the latter was two years Bertram's senior.

Described as "a quiet, reserved boy with considerable force of character", he had "a good name for steadiness and industry". He also enjoyed sports and at the Athletic Sports in 1905 took first prize in the 220 yards Under 15 Handicap as well as third in the Half-Mile Open Handicap. At the Athletic Sports of 1906 Bertram was presented with a Rugby Football Cup for his work in the junior side as a forward. Through the summer term of 1906 he played cricket for the 2nd and 3rd XI and was noted as a good fieldsman. This sporting promise was carried into the 2nd Rugby Football XV in the autumn of 1906, when Bertram was described as "a promising forward".

This was the pattern of Bertram's life at Christ College - cricket, football, hockey and some athletics. During the spring of 1907, Bertram was a reserve for the Hockey XI and played as a half-back in four matches (including against his home town of Hay during which the umpire, the Reverend Donaldson, received a nasty facial injury in a game which displayed "unnecessary vigour"). Overall the team record was described as "a record of quite average skill and success. 13 matches were played, 6 won, 5 lost, and two drawn. 38 goals were scored for and 42 against".

In the summer term Bertram was selected to play for the 1st XI. *The Breconian* noted that he "promises to be useful another year". In total he played 9 innings for the 1st XI, scoring 52 runs; he also played occasionally for the 2nd XI. At Speech Day on Tuesday 30th July 1907 Bertram received his only recorded academic success with an honourable mention in Mathematics. In the autumn Bertram again played rugby football, occasionally turning out for the 1st XV.

After leaving school Bertram went into banking and spent four years in a London bank whilst lodging at 10 Bramerton Street, Chelsea. In 1912 he emigrated to Canada where he settled into the life of a Land Agent and farmer at Victoria, Vancouver Island. His older brother Harold had gone out earlier and had already established himself as a fruit farmer in Vancouver Island. Harold had been invalided home from the Boer War whilst seeing service with the Pembrokeshire Imperial Yeomanry. Arthur followed his father's footsteps and went on to study Medicine. He became a doctor and early in the war joined the 26th Field Ambulance, 8th Division, BEF. He wrote many detailed and interesting letters home, clearly showing the rapid movements in the early stages of the war and the large amount of work in dealing with the casualties. In one letter he noted that on Christmas Day 1914 "The Germans in the trenches opposite us had their Christmas tree, and put rows of candles in front of the trenches; our men met them half way and exchanged cigarettes, chocolates, etc".

On 12th August 1914 Bertram joined the 50th Regiment of Canada (Gordon Highlanders). Two days earlier the Regiment had been placed on active service for local protective duty. Many of the Highlanders, including Bertram, then volunteered for Imperial Service. On 23rd September 1914 he joined the Canadian Expeditionary Force and came over to England. He entered France on 14th February 1915 serving in France and Flanders, taking part in the fighting at the Second Battle of Ypres (April 1915) as well as the Battles of Festubert (May 1915) and Loos (September 1915). He was later promoted to Lance Corporal, serving with No. 1 Company, 16th Battalion (Scottish), 1st Canadian Contingent British Expeditionary Force.

In September 1915 Bertram applied for officer training with the desire to be attached to the 3rd Battalion, South Wales Borderers. His application form, complete with copy of birth certificate, shows that Lieutenant Colonel John James, a JP for Herefordshire, certified him to have been of good moral character for the last ten years. Also that he was recommended for training and commissioning into the South Wales Borderers. The Brigadier General Commanding 3rd Canadian Infantry Brigade signed the form recommending officer training on 5th February 1916.

Bertram was ordered to join officer training at Pembroke College, Cambridge, on 25th February 1916. He visited Christ College in the spring of 1916 and later that year, on 7th July 1916, he was gazetted Second Lieutenant, King's Royal Rifle Corps. On 18th December 1916 he was killed "by a stray shot" just south of Morval and buried there although the exact location of the grave was not recorded.

His Major wrote "He created a most excellent impression by his soldierly qualities, and the way in which he did his duty at all times." His Captain added "I had the greatest of respect for the way in which he handled his men and knew his job. In him we lose a fine officer and a brave man."

At the time of his death, three of Bertram's brothers were serving with the Colours, namely Thomas Ernest (Captain, Royal Army Medical Corps, Mesopotamia), William Harvey (Sergeant, South African Mounted Regiment), and Arthur Cecil (Captain, Royal Army Medical Corps, France). Harold Austin was still farming on Vancouver Island and his only sister, Emily Dorothy, had married a Mr. Todd and was living in Broad Street, Hay.

Papers in Bertram's War Office file show that he served as a Commissioned Officer at the rate of 7/6 per day. There is also a copy of an inter-war letter to Dr. Hincks of Cartrefle, Church Street, Hay. It refers to Bertram's exhumation and reburial, a pattern with many of the fallen that continued into the 1930s.

> *Sir,*
>
> *I beg to inform you that in the process of exhumation for the purpose of the concentration of isolated graves into cemeteries, the grave of 2nd Lieutenant Bertram Hincks, 5th attached 10th Battalion, King's Royal Rifle Corps, was located at a point just south of Morval.*
>
> *I am to inform you that in accordance with the agreement with the French and Belgium Governments to remove all scattered graves, also certain other cemeteries which were situated in places unsuitable for permanent retention, it has been found necessary to exhume the bodies buried in certain areas. The body of 2nd Lieutenant Bertram Hincks has therefore been removed and re-buried in Delville Wood Cemetery, Longueval, North East of Albert.*
>
> *I am to add that the necessity for the removal is much regretted, but was unavoidable for the reasons given above. You may rest assured that the work of re-burial has been carried out carefully and reverently, special arrangements having been made for the appropriate religious service to be held.*
>
> *I am Sir,*
> *Your obedient Servant*
> *(Sgd). Stopford*
> *Major, D.A.A.G.*
> *for Major-General.*
> *D.G.G.R. & E.*

Second Lieutenant Bertram Hincks is therefore buried at Delville Wood Cemetery, Longueval. He is remembered on the Hay-on-Wye War Memorial as well as on the Christ College War Memorial.

Private Lewis Hughes
31st Battalion, Canadian Infantry (Alberta Regiment)

6TH NOVEMBER 1917 ~ AGE 32
Hostel 1900-1902

L ewis Hughes was born on 29th October 1885 in the Parish of St Peter, Carmarthen. His father was a local doctor and the family lived at 10 Spilman Street, Carmarthen. Lewis entered the Hostel in September 1900 and was a contemporary of his cousins, J.V.R. (Jack) Rees (Day Boy and School House 1902-1910), W.E. Coldicutt (Hostel 1900-1904) and V. Coldicutt (Hostel 1900-1906). The Census, which took place in April 1901, shows that he was also contemporary with several boys living at Christ College who were later to fall in the First World War: William David Abbott, Wilfred St Martin Gibbon, David Roy Jenkins and Titho Glynne Jones.

Known as 'Lewie', he was "one of the brightest and more cheerful of mischievous spirits, ever happy and ever ready for a jest". He clearly had an excellent voice and "led the trebles in the choir for some time". He also had an interest in drama and, just before Christmas 1900 Lewis found himself first treading the boards as one of the bridesmaids in *Trial by Jury*. Christmas 1901 again saw Lewis in dramatic mode, this time taking the part of Little Buttercup in the end of term production of *HMS Pinafore*. He was described as "one of the most emphatic successes of the play. His voice and enunciation were both good, and he deservedly earned more than one encore 'on the night' though the omission of this delicate attention at the dress rehearsal nearly upset us but was adroitly put right by a timely piece of gag by Deadeye".

Lewis left Christ College at Christmas 1902, having been a member of the Cadet Corps. In summer 1902 he received a prize for Science and the Form prize for Greek, following Walter Bomford Davies and Stephen Best up to collect his prize on Speech Day. The following year he started training at an Agricultural College. His family had moved to Enmore, Cirencester after the death of his father. Lewis then spent some time working at the Capital and Counties Bank. Like so many of his contemporaries, he decided to emigrate to Canada to commence farming; this he did in 1911, living at Dog Pond, Cochrane, Alberta.

On 18th February 1916 he enlisted at Calgary with his attestation papers recording him as 5 feet 9½ inches tall, of fair complexion with brown hair and eyes. His religion was given as 'Church of England'. Having joined the 31st Battalion, Canadian Infantry (Alberta Regiment), Lewis arrived in France on 21st January 1917. He took part in the vicious but victorious Battle of Vimy Ridge (9th-12th April 1917) in which four Canadian Divisions, made up of men from right across Canada, fought together for the first time. Lewis was one of the 7,000 Canadians injured, receiving a serious wound which hospitalized him for several months. A further 3,598 Canadians died in the battle which was to symbolize Canadian sacrifice for the British Empire but also for many, to mark the birth of Canada as a nation.

Lewis arrived back to his Battalion in time for the Second Battle of Passchendaele (26th October-10th November 1917). As his Battalion successfully took the village of Passchendaele on 6th November 1917, Lewis was killed. *The Breconian* records that having fallen in the "hour of victory last November on the slopes of Passchendaele, 'Lewie' lies in a soldier's grave, but will not readily be forgotten by his old comrades and friends of 15 years ago". The Wiltshire and Gloucestershire Standard stated that "Lewis Hughes was a good son, a fine straightforward, honourable, manly, steady young fellow, whose death at the early age of 32, is, as well as being a severe blow to his relatives and friends, a very great loss to the country of his adoption, where he was just beginning to make his mark. He was not only the right type for a colonist, but also just the type of man so badly needed in his native land".

Private Lewis Hughes is buried at the Passchendaele New British Cemetery and is remembered on the Christ College War Memorial.

Lieutenant Charles Gawain Raleigh Hunter
2nd Battalion, King's Own Yorkshire Light Infantry
24TH APRIL 1915 ~ AGED 21
School House 1907-1910

Charles Gawain Raleigh Hunter was born on 10 September 1893 at the family home in Hunningham, Warwickshire, the eighth of ten children. His father William was the 11th Laird of Burnside (Forfarshire) and, until he retired in 1879, had been an Army Officer. His mother Isabella was the daughter of an officer in the Indian Army and had been born in Kashmir, India. After selling his estate in Scotland, William Hunter purchased The Elms, Hunningham from where he controlled his land holdings and dispensed justice as a JP. Charles was baptised in the local Parish Church on 5th November 1893.

Charles joined School House from St. Chads, Prestatyn in October 1907 and left in December 1910, having "won the affection and respect of all who knew him". He was a member of the school's Cadet Force. His one memorable contribution to school life though came in 1908 when he took the part of Caroline Dormer in the well received Christmas Theatrical *Heir-at-Law*. He played his part so well that his character was described as "refined and womanly. A boy knowingly remarked, 'you wouldn't have known if you hadn't known'; and in its way the criticism was correct".

In the New Year of 1911, having just left school, Charles became a clerk to the manager at the Triumph Motor Cycle Works in Coventry. However, he appears to have decided to follow his father into the Army, the sixth generation of his family to enter British military service. In August 1911, 17 year old Charles was gazetted Second Lieutenant in the Reserve Battalion, King's Own Yorkshire Light Infantry. He immediately transferred to the full time 2nd Battalion and completed six months duty in Ireland.

Returning to the reserves, Charles sought experiences abroad, particularly in the Argentine, although he completed his annual training in 1912, 1913 and 1914. Ten days after Britain declared war on Germany, he was posted back to the 2nd Battalion and landed with them at Le Havre on 16th August 1914 as part of the British Expeditionary Force. On 23rd August Charles and his Battalion were in action in the Battle of Mons and the subsequent retreat, Battle of Le Cateau (26th August), Battle of Marne (6th-12th September) which successfully stopped the Germans taking Paris, Battle of Aisne (13th-28th September), Battles of La Bassée and Messines (10th October-2nd November), and then on to take part in the First Battle of Ypres (19th October-22nd November).

During September 1914 Charles was promoted to Lieutenant and may have sustained a wound at some point. The Battalion Diary notes that Charles and 60 men rejoined the 2nd Battalion at Wulverghem, between Ypres and Armèntieres on 6th December 1914. Mud, rain and general filth seemed everywhere and made living difficult, let alone fighting.

On 18th April 1915 the Battalion was ordered to take Hill 60, three miles south-east of Ypres, "at any cost" in order to frustrate increasing German activity in the area. The Hill was in fact a 45 foot high and 250 yard long heavily fortified spoil heap from the nearby railway cutting. It had been fought over during previous days but was taken and then held in a tremendous defensive action by Charles and the remnants of his Battalion who stayed with red hot guns until relieved. On 21st April 1915 the Second Battle of Ypres started and Canadian soldiers fought their first major battle of the war. On 22nd April they were faced with a new German weapon, Chlorine Gas. Despite being slowly forced back, the Canadians were tenacious. Charles and his men were ordered to reinforce the Canadian line and if possible, advance with them.

Charles' Battalion Diary for 24th April states "At midday, the 13th Brigade was called upon to assist the 10th Canadian Brigade in retaking the lost line north-east of Wieltje. The Canadian line was at the time being subjected to a heavy bombardment and the trenches preparatory to an advance were crowded with Canadian Highlanders. So the newcomers had to lie out in the open under the shell-fire, where they suffered. Lt. C.G.R. Hunter was killed…"

Suffice to say that large number of men died whilst lying out in the open and the body of Lieutenant Charles Gawain Raleigh Hunter was never found. He is remembered at the Ypres (Menin Gate) Memorial and on the Christ College War Memorial.

Lieutenant Frank James
1st Battalion, South Wales Borderers

1st November 1918 ~ Aged 22
School House 1913-1915

Frank was born on 31st July 1896 in Maesyrhyddid near Pontypridd where his father, also a local man, was the colliery manager of the Maesyrhyddid Mine, which had opened in 1814 and continued to develop, as did many others in the area, to feed the increasing demand for house coal.

Frank, one of seven children, joined School House from Pontypridd Boys Grammar School in January 1913. At Prize Day of 1913 on Thursday 25th September, he was awarded *proxx. acc.* (second place) in Mathematics as well as his Oxford Local (Junior Examination) Certificate in Dictation, Arithmetic, Scripture, English, History, Latin, French, and Mathematics.

On Prize Day on Monday 27th July 1914 it was announced that Frank, along with several others had, through their academic prowess, won an "exemption from Entrance Examination of the Law Society and of Certain other Professional Bodies". He also received prizes in History, Scripture and French with a *proxx. acc.* in Mathematics. Finally he was presented with his Oxford and Cambridge Board Lower Certificate in Latin, French, Arithmetic, Additional Mathematics, Scripture, and English History (the last four with Distinction).

Though not a natural athlete, he was said to have "played all games keenly". In the Senior Steeplechase in March 1914 Frank had a creditable run, although he lost to Trevor Akrill Jones. In the autumn of 1914 he took part in the Fives Competition and was 16th man in the 1st Rugby Football XV. He played in a number of matches alongside Trevor Akrill Jones, David John Thomas and Euan Edward Arnott, including the annual match against Llandovery held at Brecon on 28th November. *The Breconian* recorded that Frank "filled a gap in the middle row of the scrum with much perseverance and courage" and commented that he "should be useful all round next year".

Frank took part in the Senior Steeplechase in March 1915, a good few places behind the outright winner, Trevor Akrill Jones. For his last two terms he was a School Prefect along with Trevor Akrill Jones. Upon leaving

Christ College in July 1915, he followed his father into the mining industry. This was a reserved occupation and Frank was exempt from military service. However, despite being described as "Studious and gentle by nature, he seemed to have little of the soldier within him; . . . he gladly volunteered for service . . . and did his part steadily and well".

Frank joined the Inns of Court Officers Training Corps and received his commission in early 1916, joining the 1st Battalion, South Wales Borderers in time to see action at a number of significant Battle of the Somme actions, all between 1st July 1916 and 28th September 1916: Battle of Albert, Battle of Bazentin, Battle of Pozières, Battle of Flers-Courcelette, and Battle of Morval.

In 1917 Frank was again involved in action during the German retreat to the Hindenburg Line of March and April of that year. On 4th July 1917 Frank was promoted to Lieutenant and saw action during the ultimately successful but very bloody Second Battle of Passchendaele. Throughout 1918 Frank again saw action at the Battles of Estaires, Hazebrouck, Bethune, Drocourt-Queant, Epehy, St Quentin Canal, Beaurevoir, and the Battle of Selle.

Due to commence on 4th November, the Second Battle of Sambre (in which Wilfred Owen was killed) was to be the final British offensive of the First World War. In late October a large number of prisoners had been taken in the Battle of Selle and the German resistance in some units was fading fast. However, the German artillery kept pounding away and was, in fact, to cause extensive casualties on the 4th November. A few days before the commencement of the Second Battle of Sambre on 1st November, Frank was bringing up rations to his men on the front line when an artillery shell exploded nearby, a piece of the shell killing him.

Frank's Commanding Officer wrote "Everyone loved little Jimmy, everyone from myself to the humblest private. Grief at his loss is universal". *The Breconian* stated that "It was Frank James' ill-luck to fall just in the hour of victory, and all who knew him will be deeply grieved at the news of his death. No Brecon boy of recent years bore a higher character and left a more honourable name behind him . . . We mourn in him one of our best and most honoured sons".

His obituary in *The Breconian* also refers to spirituality: "His influence was all for duty and right. He took delight in the Chapel services and in every higher department of our life". Buried on 5th November, six days before the Armistice, the last line of his obituary in *The Breconian* is especially fitting: "So he rests till the day of final victory".

Lieutenant Frank James is buried at Vaux-Andigny British Cemetery in France. He is remembered on the War Memorial of Pontypridd Boys Grammar School (now at Coedylan Comprehensive School) as well as on the War Memorial at Christ College.

Captain David Roy Jenkins
Royal Flying Corps

21ST JANUARY 1917 ~ AGED 28
School House 1901-1903

David Roy Jenkins was born at Bridgend on 24th September 1888. He was the youngest son of Jacob and Margaret Jenkins of Aberthaw House, Bridgend. His father, Jacob Jenkins, was a timber merchant. He joined School House in January 1901.

Known as Roy, he was a popular boy at school and "won many friends". He was remembered as a "bright, happy boy, with considerable gifts in mind and body". He seems also to have had promise as an athlete and in his obituary the writer recalls how "as a mere youngster, he won a House match for School House A-M by brilliantly hitting against 1st XI bowlers". The writer goes on to say that "His cheery smile is also not easily forgotten on this and similar occasions".

He also had something of a talent for amateur dramatics. In the Christmas 1902 production of Gilbert and Sullivan's opera *The Sorcerer*, Roy was noted for "a successful impersonation" of a young maiden. The opera was much enjoyed and clearly great fun was had by all, despite the fact that "the curtain refused to fall at the end of the first act" and that "the gasman nearly asphyxiated us all by putting out the footlights and then turning on the tap".

Roy left Christ College in July 1903 at the age of 14. He followed the footsteps of an older brother, Charles Fraser Jenkins, to Clifton College. Whilst there, he resided in Wiseman's House where, after an initial spell in the Sanatorium with typhoid, his subsequent termly reports showed Roy 'S' for satisfactory, "very dull - tries", "improving" and then, shortly before he left at Easter 1906, "doing well".

Clearly the Jenkins family had a flair for business. Roy's older brother Charles Fraser Jenkins had already established himself as a lime merchant. Roy, after some time helping to manage his father's business, based at Fforestfach, set up as a Brick merchant. When not working, he was achieving considerable success as a "Brilliant Hockey player" and was Captain of the Bridgend Hockey Club for two seasons. He also played for Swansea 1st

Hockey XI for one season and was a County Player.

He was also a keen Territorial Officer and obtained a commission in 1904 as a Second Lieutenant in the 2nd Welsh Brigade, Royal Field Artillery. He rose to Lieutenant on 20th January 1911. At the outbreak of war, his unit was mobilized and Roy and his unit spent some time in further training in England before heading for France. With his experience, he was soon promoted to Captain in the Royal Field Artillery (TF), on 13th November 1915. The local newspaper carried the news and stated that Roy "was very well known and exceedingly popular amongst all classes".

After seeing service in France and Flanders for two months, he was sent to Egypt with his Battery for another nine months. At the end of that time he successfully applied to join the Royal Flying Corps, joining the 7th Reserve Squadron as a pilot and training for France from October 1916. During his RFC training at Oxford, he captained the RFC hockey team. He was flying alone on Sunday January 21st 1917 over Salisbury plain when the aircraft crashed some three miles from the aerodrome and he was killed.

Such was the high esteem in which Roy and his family were held that there was "An Impressive Military Funeral At Bridgend". A firing party from the Bridgend platoon of the Glamorgan Volunteers headed the cortege and there were "widespread manifestations of sorrow and sympathy . . . At the church it seemed as if nearly all who stood for the corporate life of the place had assembled to pay their last tribute to their gallant young townsman". The service was described as "unusually touching and impressive" with large numbers of military and civilian mourners, letters of sympathy and wreaths. One veteran Volunteer, Colour Sergeant John Lane, attended in the scarlet uniform of the old 2nd Volunteer Battalion, Welsh Regiment. It was a notable funeral and a few days later, at a meeting of Bridgend District Council, the councillors had a minute's silence in memory of "a young man full of promise in business and in the Army".

Captain David Roy Jenkins is buried at Nolton (St Mary's) Churchyard, Bridgend and is remembered on the War Memorial at Christ College.

Captain Percy Barrett Jones
3rd Battalion, Middlesex Regiment
28TH SEPTEMBER 1915 ~ AGED 34
School House 1896-1898

Percy Jones was born on 2nd February 1881 in York where his father was a solicitor. The family lived at 26 St Mary's, Marygate, York. He was educated at St Peter's School, York and the family moved during this time to 109 Clifton Terrace, Bootham, York.

Percy entered Christ College at Easter 1896, one of several brothers to do so. His brother, Edmund Stanley Jones (School House 1891-1895), had left Christ College the previous year. He had been a noted games player and left school to enter the Law. Edmund became a Captain in the Yeomanry and fought in the Boer War as well as the First World War.

In the autumn of 1896 Percy played several rugby football matches as a member of the 1st XV, 2nd XV and the 'A' XV. In the 1st XV's first match of the season, against Brecon Town held on Saturday 26th September 1896, the match report stated that "it was considered advisable to give a trial in the middle to P.B. Jones, whose ignorance of the passing game lost us several chances; he ought to do fairly well on the wing however". In several matches he played alongside Edward Leyshon who was also to die in the War.

After Christmas the term began on 19th January 1897 following weeks of hard frost. The ground was too hard for rugby football and so, to keep the boys fit, ice skating was allowed and proved popular. Snowfall was also welcomed for tobogganing. With ground still hard to play on, a Paperchase, also known as 'hare and hounds', was arranged Saturday 30th January. The two hares gave the hounds a good run and after a couple of hours the leading hounds arrived back at school having caught one hare but missing the other. Among the leading hounds were three boys who would lose their lives a few years later: Percy Jones, George Aitken and David William Abbott.

Percy really came into his own with the cricket season. The first match of the season was on Saturday 8th May 1897 against Mr. Morton's XI. Percy got off to a great start taking five wickets for 38 runs. He continued to play well and on Wednesday 26th May, in a match against W.L. Harris' XI, he amassed 51 runs before stumps were drawn, having already taken four wickets for 21 runs in the same match.

Success followed success and at the start of an away match against Hereford County College on 2nd June 1897, Percy "immediately caught Davies (Hereford) in the slips, and followed it up by taking three more wickets in his first two overs". He took nine wickets for 16 runs in total. The season's play culminated in the annual cricket match against Llandovery College held on 3rd July. To the disappointment of Christ College, Llandovery won by 68 runs. Percy took two wickets for 32 but the side was marred by poor bowling. The match report considered this was the reason for the defeat, although it was also reported that the nerves of the batsmen did little to help.

During the cricket season he had "played some vigorous innings" and the end of season 1st XI report described him as "A steady bowler but lacks experience, keeps a good length and comes fast off the pitch". At Speech Day on Monday 26th July 1897 he received the prize for the best bowling average. Three days earlier, in a match against the Old Boys, he did better at batting and scored a creditable 22 (second best score) against a stiff opposition.

Percy was selected for the 1st XV in the autumn of 1897 and his end of season rugby football report described him as "A useful forward, but blundering; keeps well on the ball and plays well from start to finish; should improve a lot next season".

Throughout the summer term of 1898, Percy played for the 1st Cricket XI again. On Wednesday 6th July he led Christ College in a match against Monmouth Grammar School. The match was lost by Christ College. Percy, the acting captain, scored 14 runs before he was caught out. His end of season report was rather mixed: "Disappointing after last year's promise: can hit with effect, but is weak on the 'off': bowls well at times. A painstaking field, usually safe, but somewhat clumsy".

The summer term of 1898 also saw Percy successful in a number of areas of school life. In the Athletics Sports he won three prizes, including a first at Putting the Weight; both he and Charles Spencer Smith were made School Prefects; and at the Speech Day held on Tuesday 26th July in the Big Schoolroom, Percy Jones, Charles Spencer Smith and George Aitken all received Science Prizes.

The autumn term of 1898 was to be Percy's last at Christ College before entering the banking profession. He was again a School Prefect and on 15th October he was promoted from Private to Corporal in the Cadet Corps, just in time for two important inspections. The first, on 18th October by Captain Going of the 1st Volunteer Battalion South Wales Borderers, was moved to Big School as the weather was so bad. The second, three days later, was by Colonel Browne VC (commanding 24th Regimental District). Unfortunately there was a mix up over timing and the Colonel arrived before the Corps was ready. The Colonel thought that "the turnout of the Corps was very much improved . . . (but that) . . . the marching was not good" and it would have helped "if the commanding officer had known the right words of command." Despite this, Percy was promoted to Sergeant.

On the rugby football field in that term, Percy had a number of good games for the 1st XV in a forward position where he could dribble well and "was always there when wanted". Overall he was described as "An honest though never brilliant man. Always did his fair share of pack work, and now and then dangerous in the loose". At the end of the term, Percy left Christ College in December 1898 having "played a prominent part in the school life of his generation".

In 1901 Percy was living at 26 Upper Northgate, Chester and working as a bank clerk but later that year he went out to India and it was there that on 9th November 1901 he married Mabel Maddison at St Peter's Church, Fort William, Calcutta. Percy then joined the Army and took a commission as a Second Lieutenant in the 3rd Battalion, East Yorkshire Regiment on 21st February 1902. He transferred to the Prince of Wales' Own (West Yorkshire Regiment) on 28th January 1903. A further move saw him as a British officer in the Indian Army serving in the 77th Moplah Rifles. He was promoted to Lieutenant on 18th December 1906. He became Captain P.B. Jones after another promotion on 23rd October 1911.

The following year he 'exchanged' with a fellow officer and joined The Duke of Cambridge's Own, The Middlesex Regiment on 6th December 1912. The Regiment was, at that time, at Lebong (Darjeeling). Percy was later posted back home to the Regimental Depot at Mill Hill where he was at the outbreak of the First World War. At that point he was sent to Chatham and later joined his Battalion in France in April 1915, taking part in a number of engagements, including the Second Battle of Ypres.

He was killed in action near the coal mining town of Hulluch during the Battle of Loos on 28th September 1915. A fellow officer wrote "Percy was killed in Big Willie Trench. We lost so many good fellows in the 'hell'; it was much the hottest fighting I have ever been in, and I cannot put into words how sorry I am and how much we all miss him."

By the end of the war, Percy's three brothers were all in the Forces and his father was a member of the Volunteers. At the time of his death, Percy's daughter, Margaret Mabel Jones, was not quite two years old.

Captain Percy Barrett Jones was buried on the battlefield. He is remembered on the Loos Memorial and on the Christ College War Memorial.

Lieutenant Titho Glynne Jones
1st/7th Battalion, Royal Welsh Fusiliers

20TH APRIL 1917 ~ AGED 30
School House 1897-1905

Titho Glynne Jones was born in Soham, Cambridgeshire on 30th March 1887. His father, Edmund Osborne Jones, was a Church of England clergyman who had taken 1st Class Honours in both Mods and Greats at Merton College, Oxford. A former pupil of the Reverend Daniel Lewis Lloyd (Headmaster of Christ College 1879-1890) at Friars' School Bangor, the Reverend Jones was a notable scholar in the Classics and in Welsh. In the summer of 1889 he took a teaching position at Christ College and moved with his family to Brecon, thus Titho had a connection with the School from an early age.

The Reverend Jones (known as 'Titho' to his contemporaries) stayed at Christ College for two years and in June 1891 it was announced that he had been "presented with the living of Llanidloes, Montgomeryshire, by the Lord Bishop of Bangor, his old schoolmaster". The notice in *The Breconian* added its congratulations to Mr. Jones "on his well-deserved appointment, which has given universal satisfaction". The four year old Titho and his family moved to the Vicarage, Llanidloes after the end of the summer term.

Titho Glynne Jones entered School House at Easter 1897, thus renewing the family's connection with Christ College. At Speech Day in 1899 he received an honourable mention for his performance in the Scholarship examination as well as the Remove Form Prize. At the end of the year his father, who was an active member of the Old Breconian Association, was elected chairman of the committee which was planning to erect memorial brasses in the school chapel and elsewhere to the Right Reverend Daniel Lewis Lloyd, Bishop of Bangor, late Headmaster of Christ College and former Headmaster of Friars' School Bangor.

At Speech Day in 1901 Titho received an Arithmetic prize and in the following year he gained several passes in the Oxford and Cambridge Lower Certificate summer examinations, including one First Class. In January 1904 he was made a House Prefect. In the autumn of 1904 Titho was selected for the 1st Rugby Football XV as he had "come on very rapidly and just secured the last place". Thus he was part of the line up that won against the

Llandovery team (9-3), and was described as "a trier all the way". The end of season report described him as "Light at present but can dash and tackle".

At Speech Day 1905 it was announced that Titho, Stephen Best and Walter Davies had all passed their Higher Certificates. It had been Titho's last term but during his time at school he had clearly distinguished himself, particularly in the VIth Form where he had "revealed some gifts in Classical Scholarship not unworthy of his father's example".

After leaving school, Titho decided on a career in the law. He served his articles with an Aberystwyth solicitor, W.P. Owen (Christ College 1879-1880), who was one of 'the Reverend Lewis Lloyd's boys' who had joined Christ College from Friars' School, Bangor. (He was also a former Association Football International who had gained 12 Welsh caps between 1880 and 1884.)

Titho later emigrated to British Columbia, Canada to establish his own practice but was visiting England when war was declared. He immediately enlisted as a Private in the 9th (County of London) Battalion, The London Regiment (Queen Victoria's Rifles). Titho arrived in France in early November 1914 and fought for just over four months during which time another Old Boy saw him looking "quite thin ... We had a 'banquet' of boiled eggs and coffee ... and I was able to show him the list of O.B.'s which I had". On 12th March 1915 Titho was commissioned into the 1/7th (Merioneth and Montgomery), Royal Welsh Fusiliers. The 1/7th had been raised in Newtown in August 1914.

Titho reported to his new Battalion, who were training at Cambridge. In May 1915 the Battalion moved to Bedford and on 19th July they sailed from Devonport for Suvla Bay. The aim of the landings at Suvla Bay was to break the stalemate that the Gallipoli Campaign had become. Titho and his Battalion landed on 9th August 1915. The following day his younger brother, 21 year old Second Lieutenant Russell Hafrenydd Jones of the Royal Welsh Fusiliers, was killed in the Bay area.

All troops were evacuated from the failed Gallipoli Campaign in December 1915 and the 1/7th were sent to Egypt. Apart from defending the Suez Canal and Egypt, the troops became part of the Egyptian Expeditionary Force whose aim became pushing into the Ottoman Empire (today part of Egypt, Israel, Jordan, Saudi-Arabia and Syria).

On 22nd July 1916 Titho was promoted to Lieutenant. On 26th/27th March 1917, the First Battle of Gaza was repulsed by the Turks. The following month, on 17th-19th April, a Second Battle of Gaza took place and was again bloodily repulsed. Titho died on 20th April from wounds.

Lieutenant Titho Glynne Jones is buried in the Gaza War Cemetery. He is remembered on the Christ College War Memorial and the Llanidloes War Memorial. He is also commemorated, with his father, Reverend E.O. Jones, and brother, R.H. Jones, in a memorial window in Llanidloes Church.

Master Mariner Herbert James Graham Kell
Merchant Service

26TH JUNE 1918 ~ AGED 44
School House 1888-1890

Herbert James Graham Kell was born in Edinburgh on 23rd September 1874. His father, James, was a Civil Engineer who, soon after Herbert's birth, moved the family to Wales. By the time of the 1881 Census, the family were living at Gwernant, Newcastle Emlyn and the household contained eight staff two governesses, a lady's maid, dressmaker, parlour maid, domestic cook, dairy maid, and house maid. The family still lived at Gwernant a decade later, though with much reduced staff..

Herbert, with older brother Fergus Aenas and younger brother Philip Arthur Graham, entered Christ College in 1888 and left in 1890. All three were involved in athletics with Fergus taking first place in the 150 yards Under 15 Consolation race at the annual Athletic Sports held on Saturday 7th April 1888. In the following year, Herbert received his only mention is *The Breconian* by gaining second place in the Under 15 High Jump. At the end of the year though, it was Fergus who took to the stage when Sheridan's *Trip to Scarborough* was presented in the Big Schoolroom. He played the "youthful and beautiful widow "Berinthia".

After leaving school both Herbert and his brother Philip decided on sea-going lives and both boys became apprentices in the Merchant Navy in 1892. On 13th October of that year, eighteen year old Herbert signed on for a two year apprenticeship to the shipping firm of Wright, Graham and Company of Glasgow which he successfully completed in 1894. On 4th July 1895, shortly before his twenty-first birthday, Herbert passed his examination enabling him to be employed as a Second Mate .

On 3rd November 1899 he passed his examinations as First Mate and on 12th April 1901, he received his Master's certificate and was duly entered into The Captains Registers of Lloyds of London, a year after Philip. Herbert then emigrated to Australia and on 4th March 1909 married Christina Mary Wallas at St. Augustine's Church, Neutral Bay, Sydney. He joined the shipping firm of Huddart Parker & Co of Melbourne, Australia and by early 1915 was the Captain of the SS 'Wimmera', a passenger ship of 3022 tons. In April of that year Herbert was fined £2 for excessive speeding of his ship on the River Yarra.

The SS 'Wimmera' had been ordered by Huddart Parker & Co and was built by Caird & Co. of Greenock, Scotland in 1904. Named after the Autralian region of Wimmera, the ship was mainly used on the trans-Tasman Sea run between Australia and New Zealand. She left Auckland bound for Sydney at 10 a.m. on the morning of 25th June 1918. On board were 76 passengers and 75 crew. At 5.15 the following morning, she hit a mine laid by the German commerce raider SMS Wolf, eighteen miles North of Cape Maria Van Dieman. Although the Wimmera's stern was shattered the ship remained on an ever keel for some thirty minutes before her bow shot into the air and she plunged stern first to the bottom.

Herbert Kell remained on the vessel throughout, ensuring that the lifeboats were launched and those who could be evacuated from the ship were safe. Six of the eight lifeboats survived their launching and eventually landed at various locations over the next 48 hours. Herbert along with the Chief Officer, the Chief Steward and twenty three others died in the sinking. He is remembered on the Tower Hill Memorial, London. This Memorial commemorates those of the Merchant Navy and Fishing Fleets who died during war time and have no known grave.

Subsequent to the sinking of the SS 'Wimmera', a Court of Enquiry found that Captain Kell had ignored confidential Admiralty instructions to steer much further to the north of Cape Maria van Diemen. Herbert had signed to acknowledge these orders on 17th June, eight days before his ship was sunk. However, the discovery of the wreck of the SS 'Wimmera' in 2010, North of Cape Reinga and near the Three Kings Islands, suggests that Captain Kell had indeed followed orders correctly.

Herbert Kell died at sea in 1918 as his brother Philip had done in 1914. The third remaining brother, Fergus Aenas Graham Kell was a tea inspector for Boyd & Co. This Company, originally founded in Amoy on the south-east coast of China in 1862, traded in opium and sugar. In 1899 they opened offices in Tamsui (Formosa) to concentrate on the booming tea trade. It was in that year that Fergus joined them and often travelled between Formosa and the Chinese mainland. After a very successful sixteen years though, Fergus unexpectedly died at Amoy on 18th October 1915 and was buried in Tamsui Cemetery.

Lieutenant Philip Arthur Graham Kell

Royal Naval Reserve, HMS 'Cressy'

22ND SEPTEMBER 1914 ~ AGED 38

School House 1888-1890

Philip Arthur Graham Kell was born in Cardigan on 2nd May 1876, the youngest of seven children (four girls followed by three boys). His parents, Cordelia and James, with Philip's six siblings, had recently moved to Wales from Scotland. In 1888, shortly before his twelfth birthday, Philip along with his brothers Fergus and Herbert, entered Christ College.

Although only at school for a relatively short time, Philip, like his brothers, seems to have been involved in Athletics. Soon after joining the school, Philip was recorded as taking first place in the Under 12 100 yards race at the Athletic Sports held on Saturday 7th April 1888. The Breconian recalled this as "a very tight and amusing race". At the following year's Athletic Sports on Saturday 30th March 1889, Philip managed second place in the 150 yards race, despite the "miserable weather".

After leaving school, Philip, 5 feet 10 inches tall with a fair complexion, brown hair and blue eyes, decided on a seagoing life and soon found himself on his first voyage. In 1895 he gained his Board of Trade Certificate as Second Mate on Square Rigged ships. He then sailed on the 'Dunstaffnage', a four-masted steel barque. He spent nearly 16 months as Third Mate and then Second Mate in the Indian Ocean between 1895 and 1897. He was 'paid off' from the ship on 28th March 1897 and on 30th June 1897 joined the SS 'Heliades' for nearly nine months, in trade between England and the River Plate (South America).

In December 1897 he took ten days out to sit his First Mate (Square Rigged) examination but, unfortunately, failed on the Navigation section. However, he was successful at his second attempt at Liverpool on 25th April 1898 and was awarded an impressive looking 'Certificate of Competency as First Mate of a Foreign-Going Ship'. At the same time, he was commissioned in the Royal Naval Reserve as a Sub-Lieutenant.

With very little time at home between voyages, Philip served as Second Mate on the SS 'Heliades'. He undertook six voyages, totaling nearly 17 months at sea between April 1898 (when the ship was purchased by the British and South American Steam Navigation Company Limited) and November 1899.

On 12th February 1900 Philip sat his examination for 'Master of a Foreign-Going Ship' and again, the Navigation section defeated him. Undeterred, he retook the examination on 2nd March and passed. His address at this time was Hill House, South Weald, Essex.

At the 1901 Census held on 31st March, Philip was undergoing his Royal Naval Reserve training and was part of the 484 crew of the Orlando class cruiser HMS 'Galatea' under the Command of Arthur de Winton Kitcat. From there Philip moved out to Uganda and joined the Uganda Railways Lake Marine Service. Now Commander Kell, he was in charge of various ships crossing Lake Victoria. Several of these were known as 'Knock down' ships as the ships were made in the United Kingdom, all the parts numbered, disassembled and then transported in kit form by sea and rail, to be rebuilt on Lake Victoria.

Commander Kell returned home after several years. In late summer 1912, the 36 year old Philip married 27 year old Belissa Beresford at her home in Ireland. Belissa had just finished training as a Norland nanny in London where children and babies were always resident, not least to help with the training. The oldest boarder at the 1911 Census was 8 and the youngest, 2 months.

Two years after the marriage, war was declared and experienced naval personnel were quickly mobilized. As such, the now Lieutenant Commander Philip Kell RNR joined HMS 'Cressy'. He became the first Old Breconian to die in the 1914-1918 conflict when his ship was torpedoed by German U-boat U9 on Tuesday 22nd September 1914. HMS 'Cressy' was one of three armoured cruisers assigned to stop German surface vessels entering the Eastern end of the English Channel. The first, HMS 'Aboukir', was torpedoed at 6.20am and the assumption was made that she had hit a mine. HMS 'Hogue' and HMS 'Cressy' approached to rescue sailors from the sinking ship. However, at 6.55am 'Hogue' was torpedoed and at 7.20am 'Cressy' suffered a similar fate. For this and later significant action, the German U-boat, U9, received the Iron Cross in the First World War - one of only two U-boats to do so.

The news of the sinking of the three cruisers was announced by *The Brecon County Times* on 24th September 1914. Despite it being called "the worst naval news of the war", the report was rather too upbeat in stating that it was believed that the bulk of the sailors had been saved and that two German submarines had been sunk. This was far from the case and 1459 sailors and cadets, including Lieutenant Kell, died in the action.

Lieutenant Philip Arthur Graham Kell is remembered at the Chatham War Memorial in Kent and on the Christ College War Memorial.

Captain Edward William Lawrence
Royal Army Medical Corps attached 13th Royal Welsh Fusiliers

10TH JULY 1916 ~ AGE 28
Hostel 1900-1903

Edward William Lawrence was born on 20th January 1888 in the mining village of Pontycymmer, Mid Glamorgan. His father, Abraham, was a Colliery Clerk who rose to become Company Secretary and the family lived in Oxford Place, Llangeinor, a few miles north of Bridgend. Edward was the oldest of six children.

Edward entered the Hostel, Christ College, in September 1900 and left at Easter 1903. Although making little impression in sport, Edward received a Mathematics and Arithmetic prize at Speech Day on Tuesday 29th July 1902.

After leaving school Edward became a clerk at a water company and then studied Medicine at Edinburgh University from 1905 to 1910. He returned to his native area and commenced a practice in Bridgend. He was Medical Officer to the Board of Guardians and thus to the Bridgend Workhouse and Cottage Homes. Edward's grandfather had been a member of the same Board and was well remembered.

After the outbreak of war Dr. Edward William Lawrence MB, ChB volunteered for a commission in October 1914. At that time he was living in Park Street, Bridgend. His application to the Royal Army Medical Corps asked such questions as "Are you of pure European descent" as well as a range of general questions such as education and previous military experience.

Edward joined the 10th Service Battalion, The Welsh Regiment (1st Rhondda). The Battalion had been formed in the Rhondda Valley by D. Watts Morgan MP. The Battalion was based at Rhyl when Edward joined them and in August 1915 they moved to Winchester for final training, as did the 13th Service Battalion, Royal Welsh Fusiliers (1st North Wales). Both battalions entered France in December 1915 and Edward transferred into the 13th Battalion.

The 13th Battalion entered the trenches at Laventie on 11th December 1915. On 20th January they witnessed the German celebrations of the Kaiser's birthday through heavy shelling. They also suffered their first casualties when three men died in a grenade training accident.

The Battle of the Somme commenced on 1st July 1916 and Edward's Battalion was in the thick of it. Starting with the slaughter of over 20,000 men and decimating the new 'Pals' battalions, fierce fighting ensued over the coming days. Edward was last seen on 10th July, in the midst of the fighting. He was tending to five wounded men, who later reported that Edward was there one minute but then they lost sight of him. Quite possibly he had moved away to fetch more supplies. His body was never found.

A silence was held at the first Board of Guardian's meeting after news reached Bridgend of Edward's death. On Sunday 6th August a memorial service was held for Edward at the Hermon Calvinistic Methodist Church at Bridgend. The text was "Greater love has no man than this that a man lay down his life for his friends" and the large congregation heard the preacher, the Reverend James Llewellyn, say that the last time Edward was home he talked of the responsibility he felt: "a personal responsibility - his responsibility to God and man - his responsibility to his county; and his responsibility in the field of influence. He felt he had to give an account of his stewardship - that his time and talents were held in stewardship".

In a eulogy that brought tears to many, the Reverend Llewellyn said that Edward was a God-fearing and God-centred man, dependable and courageous who loved man and was loved by all in return. The people "mourned and grieved, and yet were not afraid. They had seen 'The coming of the glory of the Lord', which would keep them until the time came for them to go to him. The Cross must triumph over evil. Love must cast out hate. In the end character would always tell".

Captain Edward William Lawrence is remembered on the Thiepval Memorial and on the Christ College War Memorial.

Major Cecil Hallowes Lewis

1st Divisional Train, Royal Army Service Corps

28TH MAY 1915 ~ AGED 46

1881-1886

Cecil Hallowes Lewis was born in Derbyshire on 9th March 1869, the son of the Reverend David Phillips Lewis and his wife, Louisa. David and Louisa Hallowes married in late summer 1853. Cecil was the fifth of six children and bore his mother's maiden name, as was very much the custom of the time.

His father David was the Vicar of Guilsfield, Welshpool from 1863 to 1881 and then Rector of Llandrino, Montgomeryshire from 1881 until his death on 17th April 1892. Cecil's older brother, Charles Edward Llewellyn Lewis (School House 1879-1884), was already well-established when Cecil joined Christ College in 1881. Charles was not only in the 1st Rugby Football XV and 1st Cricket XI but was also a noted singer and member of the Debating Society. After leaving school he went up to Merton College, Oxford.

Both boys were excellent sportsmen and achieved their colours in the 1st Cricket XI. At the end of his only season with the Cricket XI, the critique of Cecil in *The Breconian* described him in the following terms: "A new member of the XI (who) showed that there was material for a good bat in him, as he shaped well and played freely: fielded well, with but few exceptions, throughout the season".

After leaving school, Cecil eventually joined the Army. He was thus a professional soldier who, after service with the Militia (commissioned Second Lieutenant in the 4th Battalion, South Wales Borderers on 7th January 1888), was commissioned on 18th February 1891 into the Dorsetshire Regiment. He was promoted to Lieutenant on 11th January 1893 and on 1st October that year transferred to the Army Service Corps. Promoted to Captain on 2nd February 1898, he was seconded to the Uganda Rifles as Company Transport Officer between 10th August 1898 and 22nd October 1902.

During his time in the Uganda Protectorate he was awarded the medal for the Nandi (East Africa) Expedition in 1900, the first of three twentieth century military expeditions to subdue the Nandi tribe who, until they submitted to British authority in 1905, were regarded as the most serious opposition to the British in Kenya.

Cecil was promoted to Major on 20th September 1904 and continued to serve in Africa. The 1911 Census reveals him commanding a number of troops there.

At the outbreak of the First World War he was part of the 1st Division Train of the Army Service Corps. The 1st Division was one of the first British Formations to move to France and was to remain on the Western Front for the entire war. Often considered to be the unsung heroes of the war, their role was logistical support. In short, anything that was needed by the troops had to be in the right place at the right time and getting everything in place and in time was a skilled job. Major Lewis' 'train' in 1914 consisted of 26 officers, 402 other ranks, 378 horses, 17 carts, 125 wagons and 30 bicycles.

As the train was the 'workhorse' of the Division, Major Lewis was heavily involved in most of the major battles in the early part of the war. In 1914 these were the Battle of Mons (and the subsequent retreat), the Battle of Marne, the Battle of the Aisne and the First Battle of Ypres (during which the Divisional Headquarters at Hooge was shelled, severely wounding the Divisional Commander and killing the senior staff officer). Cecil was also involved at the Battle of Aubers when, on 9th May 1915, the British sustained a loss of over 11,000 killed or wounded in what was, mile upon mile and division upon division, one of the bloodiest days of the war.

In a month of particularly bitter fighting, Major Cecil Hallowes Lewis was killed on 28th May 1915. It was always a dangerous work, resupplying front line units. Men and animals were often caught out in the open by shelling and thus Cecil lost his life in this crucial task. A dedicated soldier, he never married.

Major Cecil Hallowes Lewis is buried at St Sever Cemetery, Rouen and is remembered on the War Memorial in Christ College.

Second Lieutenant Leonard Glynne 'Siwel' Lewis MC
18th Battalion Welsh Regiment

24TH NOVEMBER 1917 ~ AGED 23
Hostel 1907-1912

Leonard Glynne Lewis was born on 27th July 1894 in Pontypridd where his father and mother, Oliver and Edith, were Master and Matron of the Local Workhouse. He joined the Hostel, Christ College as a scholar from Pontypridd Grammar School in September 1907 and left in July 1912.

Recalling his qualities after his death, *The Breconian* offers a very clear impression of 'Siwel' (as he was always known) - "a gallant and cheerful soul" and a popular and amiable friend:

> *At first his quiet, reserved manner kept him somewhat in the background, but as one got to know him better he revealed a genial and quaint sense of humour that made him generally popular. "Siwel" he was nicknamed to distinguish him for the numerous other Lewises, and as "Siwel" he was known for the remainder of his school career.*

On the last day of the summer term, 28th July 1908, he was presented with a Form III Prize and, along with Walter Bomford Davies, Frank Harrington Best and Basil Biggerton-Evans, shook hands with the Headmaster upon collection of the prize. Two years later, at the end of the summer term 1910 and shortly before his 16th birthday, he passed his Lower Certificate (Latin, Greek, French, Arithmetic, Mathematics and Scripture).

Clearly interested in sport, he participated in the athletic sports and played, at one time or another, for all the main sports teams. On Saturday April 3rd 1909 he took part in the Athletics Sports and came equal third in the Half-Mile Open Handicap. On 29th September of the same year, playing for Reverend A.E. Donaldson's XV in a rugby football match against the Christ College XV, 'Siwel' noted as being "most conscientious".

In the following term, on Saturday 12th February 1910, he was drafted in to represent the School at hockey and played forward in a team led by Harold Blakeney Davies, which won (3-1) in a match against Brecon Sports Club. That autumn he played for the Hostel in the House rugby football match and, although the Hostel lost, it was noted that he had "played well for the losers". The spring of 1911 saw him again playing hockey, this time regularly representing the School including against a somewhat aggressive Depot side. In the Senior Steeplechase of Wednesday 25th March, Harold Blakeney Davies came first with 'Siwel' coming a creditable sixth, just ahead of Geoffrey Boothby. On Saturday 11th April at the Athletics Sports, he was just beaten by Davies in the 220 yards Handicap, and again beaten by him in the Quarter-Mile, this time coming third to Davies' first.

By all accounts an enthusiastic player, he played 2nd XI cricket in the 1911 season. On 7th June he played against Brecon Sports Club 2nd XI, scoring 6 but bowling well. On Wednesday 24th June he played for Reverend A.E. Donaldson's XI against the Christ College XI, although he was unfortunately out for 0. In several further matches, his most successful outing was when playing for the 3rd XI and taking 10 wickets for 17 runs against Brecon County School 2nd XI. Thus in the 1911 cricket season, he had the distinction of occasionally playing against the 1st XI, playing mainly for the 2nd XI and also occasionally for the 3rd XI.

Noted for entering "into all games with skill and zest", 'Siwel' also organized a rugby football team of his own, the 'Heracleans', during the school holidays, which "added to the gaiety of the Pontypridd district". Back at school for the autumn term, he played right-centre for the 1st Rugby Football XV. The end of season critique in *The Breconian* reads: "Runs smoothly and straight, but is inclined to neglect his wing. A splendid kick, and greatly improved in his defensive play".

In the annual Llandovery Match, which was played at Swansea on Thursday 30th November 1911, he had a tremendous match and put pressure on Llandovery with some fine punts. *The Breconian* noted, "Just before the interval, Lewis made a thrilling run, in which he swung through the defence a scorer all over. The Llandovery back, however, just saved his side and Lewis' pass failed to reach the forwards who had backed up cleverly. It was a lucky escape for Llandovery". This was clearly an excellent game, not least for 'Siwel', and "Friend and foe alike admitted that it was one of the finest games of a long and famous series".

Despite his fine playing and being "conspicuous", the Hostel again lost in the rugby football House matches of 1911. Unusually a rugby football match was played in the spring and, on Saturday 2nd March the 1st XV beat Ystradgynlais in a well contested match, in which 'Siwel' played alongside Basil Biggerton-Evans and David Cuthbert Thomas. As the term's sport turned from rugby football to track events, he again came sixth in the Senior Steeplechase on Saturday 16th March, and second in the Quarter-Mile and third in the Mile at the Athletic Sports later in the month. He capped off the term by helping the Hostel win the House matches in hockey.

In the first cricket match of his final term at Christ College, he scored 39 runs against the Reverend Donaldson's XI and, in a match against Swansea 2nd XI, he "excelled himself by getting the hat trick". Unfortunately, the long anticipated match against Llandovery on Saturday 29th June was first of all postponed due to 36 hours of continuous rain. Scheduled to be played at Builth Wells on Wednesday 3rd July, the match was then cancelled due to illness. The Hostel, though, succeeded in winning the House matches.

In addition to his colours for playing rugby football, hockey and cricket for the School, Leonard Glynne Lewis gained his London Matriculation in July 1912 and also an annual scholarship for £20 to St David's College, Lampeter. He joined St David's College from his home at 17 Court House Street, Pontypridd, in October 1912 and immediately set about combining academic study with excelling at rugby football, playing for the St David's XV. He remained a valued member of the team the following year and also played for the St David's Cricket XI in the summer of 1914. He visited Christ College to play cricket for the Old Boys in the summer of 1913 and again in a two day match on 7th and 8th July 1914. That summer he was also awarded 2nd Class Honours, Classical Moderations from Lampeter.

He seems to have had no hesitation in enlisting and, just a few weeks after the cricket match for the Old Boys, he joined the 4th Public Schools Battalion, Royal Fusiliers. This battalion, known formally as 21st (Service) Battalion (4th Public Schools) The Royal Fusiliers (City of London Regiment), was one of four Public Schools Battalions known respectively as the 1st, 2nd, 3rd and 4th, to be formed at Epsom on 11st September 1914 by the 'Public Schools and University Men's Force'. With the Battalion, he trained near Epsom and then on 26th June they were formally attached to 98th Brigade, 33rd Division. The following month the Division gathered at Clipstone Camp, near Mansfield, moving to Salisbury Plain for final preparation with live ammunition in August. They landed in France in November 1915 and, by 21st November, the Division was at Morbecque, a little outside Hazebrouck. The 21st Battalion was attached to the General Headquarters. Although the Division did not begin to see major action until the Battle of Albert, which commenced on 1st July 1916 as part of the major Somme offensive, smaller actions took place before this and it was in one of these during the winter of 1916 that Leonard Glynne was wounded.

On 24th April 1916 the Regiment was formally disbanded with many of the soldiers taking commissions. Leonard Glynne, like other colleagues, had been undergoing officer training in the preceding few weeks and was commissioned Second Lieutenant on 26th April 1917 and attached to the 18th Battalion (2nd Glamorgan) Royal Welsh Regiment, joining them the following month. The 18th were attached to the 119th Brigade, 40th (Bantam) Division. (The word 'bantam' was Army slang for a soldier below the original 1914 Army height restriction of 5 feet 3 inches. Many strong men, particularly miners, were at first denied the opportunity to fight but such were the protests that the Government relented in November 1914 and the height restriction was dropped to 4 feet, 10 inches). The 18th Battalion, newly arrived in France, spent some time acclimatizing to fighting. They moved up to Cambrai, whose famous and initially highly successful battle commenced on 20th November 1917. This battle saw tanks prove their worth and the Hindenburg Line breached. However, prior to the battle, Leonard Glynne was in an action that was to see him awarded the Military Cross for great gallantry. The citation, published in *The London Gazette* of 19th March 1918, reads:

> *For conspicuous gallantry and devotion to duty. He guided a raiding party to the assembly position, and thence to a gap in the enemy's wire, a distance of 800 yards. With his sergeant he was the first of his party to enter the enemy trenches. Although stunned by a bomb on entering, he led forward with courage and determination, and with a small group of men continued the clearing of the trench until time for the withdrawal.*

When the Battle of Cambrai commenced, the 18th Battalion was in reserve around Graincourt. On 23rd November 1917, the 119th Infantry Brigade attacked Bourlon Wood; Leonard Glynne, along with the 18th Battalion, was soon called to reinforce the flowing battle lines. The next day, in the forefront of the fighting which was costing hundreds of lives each hour, Leonard Glynne Lewis was killed. His body was never found.

Second Lieutenant Leonard Glynne Lewis MC ('Siwel') is remembered on the Cambrai Memorial, Louverval as well as on the Christ College War Memorial.

Sergeant Observer Sydney Edward Lewis

55th Squadron Royal Air Force

13TH AUGUST 1918 ~ AGED 19

Hostel 1911-1916

Sydney Edward Lewis was born on 18th January 1899. He entered the Hostel in September 1911 from Pontrhydyfen. It seems that "the little, active, dark-eyed lad from near Port Talbot" was a general favourite from the time of his arrival.

"He was not great at his books, but he was at home in every branch of athletics" said *The Breconian* after his death. He certainly took an active part in sport, though the records of his early sporting achievements are modest. He came eighth in the Junior Steeplechase on Saturday 16th March 1912. At the Athletic Sports later in the month, he came third in the Quarter-Mile Under 16 Handicap but came first in the Under 15 150 yards Consolation Race. In the following year he took second place (and a silver medal) to Trevor Akrill Jones' first in the Junior Steeplechase. In the spring of 1913 he also took part in the Open Singles Fives Competition but was beaten in the first round. In the summer term he played for the 2nd Cricket XI (alongside Frank Harrington Best and Trevor Akrill Jones), including against the Sketty 2nd XI on 31st May in a match where the school's "bowling and fielding were wretched"!

In the autumn of 1913, though a small boy, he began to come into his own and it was said that "he played 'Rugger' with the judgement and skill of a veteran". In early 1914 Sydney won the first three rounds of the Fives Competition and on 25th March, he won the Handicap prize in the Golf Competition in very wet conditions. Three days later he played for the school golf team against the Masters and won his match against the Reverend Donaldson. That term he was also awarded the 'Football Cup' for the 2nd Rugby Football XV. In the summer term of 1914 Sydney played for the 2nd Cricket XI. He and Euan Arnott were described as two of the "most promising players". During the season he played a match for Mr. Munn's XI and then for the Masters XI against the 1st XI. There then followed a number of matches where he batted alongside Euan Arnott, Trevor Akrill Jones and David Cuthbert Thomas.

That autumn Sydney "won his Colours in the splendid XV of 1915, playing centre three-quarter in one of the fastest and best attacking lines we ever turned out". It is recorded that he had "capital notion of outside play" and was "particularly sound in defensive work". In the Llandovery match, in heavy rain, three nil down and with a player knocked out, Sydney and his Christ College team mates, led by David John Thomas, fought bravely to a 3-3 draw.

Playing outside left for the 1st Hockey XI in the spring of 1916, Sydney, whose "uncanny cleverness with the stick was a theme of general admiration" was also described as "a very clever player" with "an uncanny control over the ball and marked agility in the use of his stick". That summer the Hostel were awarded the House Fives Cup on account of the success in the matches of Sydney and E.J. Morgan (Hostel 1910-1916). Sydney rounded off his school sporting career by playing for the 1st Cricket XI and also making appearances for the 2nd XI. In his work for the 1st XI he was described as "A quick and accurate field anywhere" and "An erratic but occasionally useful change bowler".

Sydney left school in July 1916 and joined the Royal Flying Corps as a Cadet where he seemed to have found "a vocation well suitable to his alert and agile characteristics". He joined 55 Squadron which had been formed on 27th April 1916. The Squadron was originally a training squadron but in January 1917 it was given the DH.4 day bomber, a wooden two seat biplane armed with a Lewis gun for defence, the first unit to be so equipped in preparation for moving to France. The attrition rate for aircrew at the Front, particularly pilots, was high, as indeed were losses in training back home. In the First Battle of the Somme (1st July-18th November 1916), 308 pilots out of 426 were killed, wounded or missing.

55 Squadron moved to France in March 1917 and immediately began reconnaissance and bombing raids. Its role increased in strategic bombing ever further behind lines, the squadron being one of the earliest involved in this developing type of warfare. As the role increased, so did the dangers. August 1918 was a particularly busy month for the squadron, which had become part of the Royal Air Force on 1st April 1918, and it was augmented by American pilots from the 'American Air Service Units with the British Expeditionary Force' as well as Canadian pilots. When not flying, the flyers would take advantage of what transport there was to drive around the area of their base at Azelot, exploring north eastern France.

In the month of August 1918 the Squadron flew a dozen bombing raids as well as making a significant number of reconnaissance sorties (Strasbourg, Morhange, Boulay and Hagenau). 55 Squadron was hit hard in terms of casualties: seven pilots and observers went missing, one pilot and observer were killed, one pilot and two observers were wounded, and two observers died of wounds. One of these was the by now extremely experienced Sergeant Observer Sydney Lewis. His aircraft had been hit over German lines and he was wounded. Despite aid back at base, Sydney succumbed to the wounds on 13th August 1918.

"His personal qualities also made him a most jolly and likeable companion, whom many were glad to call their friend" recorded *The Breconian*.

Sergeant Observer Sydney Edward Lewis is buried at Charmes Military Cemetery, Essegney, and is remembered on the Christ College War Memorial.

Corporal Edward James Leyshon
Royal Army Pay Corps
27TH JULY 1918 ~ AGED 40
School House 1891-1896

Edward James Leyshon was born in Llantwit Fadre, Pontypridd in 1878. His father David was a brewer employing six men. Edward was educated at Cowbridge Grammar School and then at Christ College from 1891 until 1896. Whilst there, Edward was presented with a Science prize at Speech Day, 1st August 1893. He also won his rugby football Colours.

After leaving school, Edward followed his father into the brewing trade. He was also honorary secretary of the Glamorgan Cricket League from its foundation in 1897 until war service intervened. Edward married soon after his 20th Birthday and in 1901 lived with his wife Katie and two young children at Ty-Graig, Pontypridd.

Perhaps not surprisingly, Edward sent both his sons to Christ College. David Gwilym Edmund Leyshon (School House 1914-1916) and Howard Morgan Edward Leyshon (School House 1915-1917). D.G.E. Leyshon joined up as a Private in the Middlesex Regiment immediately he left school in 1916.

Ironically both sons, who each saw service in the Army, survived the war but Edward, who was a Sergeant in the Royal Army Pay Corps, died of pneumonia on 27th July 1918 at Shrewsbury.

Corporal Edward James Leyshon was buried in his home town of Pontypridd, and is remembered on the Pontypridd War Memorial as well as on the Christ College War Memorial.

Private Evan David Lloyd

6th Dragoon Guards (Carabiniers) attached Army Veterinary Corps

1ST FEBRUARY 1915 ~ AGED 37

Hostel 1892-1895

Evan David Lloyd was born in 1878 in Ferndale, South Glamorgan. Shortly after, his family moved to 7 Station Street, Aberdare where his father was a grocer/baker. By 1891 the family had moved to live over the shop in 15-17 Commercial Street, next door to the Eagle Inn, and the family remained living in Commercial Street for many years.

Evan entered the Hostel, Christ College in 1892 and left in 1895 to assist in the family business. He subsequently joined the Army, becoming first a trooper in the 6th Dragoon Guards; much later he was attached to the Army Veterinary Corps.

With the Dragoons he served in different parts of the Empire, including two years at Mhow, India. He was present during the Grand Durbar when the Prince and Princess of Wales visited Bangalore in 1906, the Prince presenting a new standard to the 6th Dragoons. When his time was completed, Evan returned home to Aberdare and, as was usual, he was placed in the Reserve. However, the moment war was declared, he left Aberdare for Aldershot, even "before the call arrived, bidding goodbye to his parents and brother and sisters, and adding 'I will do my duty whatever comes'".

Evan was attached to No. 2 Veterinary Hospital which moved to Marseilles in the opening weeks of the war. The Army Veterinary Corps was responsible for all the animals used in the war, primarily mules, horses (for cavalry, artillery and general purposes, including mounts for officers), pigeons, canaries (the latter to detect the presence of gas, at first underground but later also above ground), and even the occasional falcon (used to bring down carrier pigeons).

The winter of 1914 to 1915 was not particularly kind to the Army, with frequent bouts of cold and wet. On 29th January 1915 Evan wrote from France to two of his uncles. To one he wrote that "The weather here is bitterly cold but thank goodness we have had two dry days". To the other, he wrote:

Dear Uncle, I received your letter and tobacco quite safely. I think the tobacco was about the finest I have ever smoked, and I have used a few different kinds. I should like some more if you could manage to send me some. Please let me know the name when you send. I have a most awful cold, and keep coughing continually, especially at night, which keeps me awake, and I get very little rest. I shall be very glad when the summer comes, so that it may be a little better for us. Don't think we are downhearted. The Kaiser has got to go under, there's not the slightest doubt about that. We are out to win and we are going to win. The sooner the better for everybody.

Evan had been complaining about the cold in his chest for a few days and may well have been in hospital in Le Havre when he wrote these letters. Not wishing to worry his family, he made no mention of where he was writing from. He died of pneumonia on 1st February 1915.

Evan's Commanding Officer, Captain K.M.L. McKenzie, wrote to his parents on 4th February 1915 from No. 2 Veterinary Hospital that Evan was "popular, conscientious, and a very good soldier." He wrote too that "His many friends miss him very much. He was buried today at St Marie Cemetery, Havre. All his comrades attended the funeral, and three wreaths were placed on the grave. I am arranging for a tombstone to be erected". Another soldier wrote to his Evan's family that Evan "was held in the highest respect by his comrades . . . who have all liberally subscribed towards four beautiful wreaths".

Private Evan David Lloyd is buried in the Ste Marie Cemetery, Le Havre. One of the 222 men from the Parish of Aberdare who gave their lives, he is remembered on the Memorial at St Elvan's Church, Aberdare as well as on the Christ College War Memorial.

Captain Charles George Lyall

1st Lincolnshire Regiment

18TH OCTOBER 1914 ~ AGED 43

School House 1882-1884

Charles George Lyall was born on 28th February 1871 in West Hartlepool, County Durham. His father David (MD, Aberdeen; Licentiate of Royal College of Surgeons, Edinburgh) was a Royal Navy Staff Surgeon. During his career, Dr. Lyall had been a member of expeditions to both the Arctic and Antarctic, where he collected flora and fauna with the famous botanist Joseph Hooker. He had plants and a gastropod named after his discoveries, and surveyed the coast of New Zealand.

By 1881 Dr. David Lyall had retired, having reached the post of RN Deputy Inspector General of Hospitals and Fleets. The family moved to Chippenham and the following year Charles entered School House, Christ College where he stayed until 1884. The only extant record of his time at school is of his performance at the Athletic Sports in 1884. Originally scheduled for Wednesday 2nd April, two days of continuous rain meant that the 17 events did not take place until the Friday. Charles gained second place in the 150 yards race and this remains the only mention of him in *The Breconian* while at school. After leaving Christ College, Charles returned home and attended Cheltenham College as a day boy until 1888.

In 1891 the 20 year old Charles entered the Royal Military College at Sandhurst, passing out the following year as an officer in the 1st Lincolnshire Regiment. From 13th July 1892 until 31st January 1895 Charles served within the United Kingdom. He was then transferred to Malta where he served from 1st February 1895 until 4th June 1896. Returning with the 1st Lincolnshire Regiment to Home Service between 5th June 1896 and 2nd August 1898, he married Marjorie Burton at the Church of St Peter's in Eastgate, Lincoln on 20th April 1898. Four months later Charles was sent to Egypt as part of the Nile Campaign and remained there for three months (3rd August 1898 until 9th November 1898) before returning home. On 4th January 1900 he was deployed to fight in South Africa where he took part in a number of military actions.

Charles retired from the Lincolnshire Regiment in 1907 and was placed on the Reserves of officers List. In

1911, he and Marjorie were living with their 7 year old son and 6 year old daughter (and a governess and two servants) at Yew Tree Cottage in the small village of Tangley, near Andover. Later, during the war, Marjorie and the family moved to live at 'The Laurels', Alton Road, Roehampton, London.

At the outbreak of war Charles was recalled to 1st Battalion Lincolnshire Regiment. He joined them in France on 10th October 1914, the first day of the Battle of La Bassée. This battle, taking place in the Herties area of France, was one of several in what is generally known as 'The Race for the Sea'. After the First Battle of the Marne in September had stopped the retreat of the allied forces, it was decided to move the British Expeditionary north to Flanders which would allow easier supply from the Channel Ports; in addition, Flanders was supposedly a good area for cavalry fighting. Once at Abbeville, it was decided to move towards La Bassée. In fact this advance failed but not before heavy casualties were inflicted on the British forces with one Battalion, the 2nd Royal Irish, losing two thirds of its men on 19th October.

As part of the professional elite, who like many officers in the British Army had seen battle at first hand, Charles was expected to lead the men in this supposedly short European War. On Sunday 18th 1914, just eight days after arriving in France, he was killed in action during the Battle of La Bassée. He was the second Old Breconian to die in the First World War. His body was never recovered.

Captain Charles George Lyall is remembered on Le Touret Memorial and the Cheltenham College Roll of Honour as well as on the Christ College War Memorial.

Second Lieutenant Bruce Wallace Macaulay
2nd Battalion, Seaforth Highlanders

3RD MAY 1917 ~ AGED 27
School House 1905-1907

Bruce Wallace Macaulay was born on 26th July 1890 at Wavertree, Lancashire. The elder son of John and Janet Macaulay, he was baptised at St Bridget's Church in the Parish of Holy Trinity, Wavertree later that year on 7th September. His Scottish father, John, was a Railway Agent. By early 1901 the family had moved to Llanfrechfa Lower, Pontypool, where John was Railway and Dock Manager. He was also to be the General Manager of Alexandra Docks, Newport. John and his wife, Janet, had five daughters and then two sons, Bruce and Horace.

Bruce joined School House at Easter 1905, along with his younger brother Horace. The boys left at Christmas 1907. Bruce was described as a skilful musician and "one of the most charming boys Brecon has known; quiet, friendly, attractive, a boy of striking character and delightful manners". At Speech Day held on Wednesday 12th September 1906 he was awarded the From III Science prize.

Bruce entered the legal profession and became a law student and solicitor's articled clerk. Making good progress through the profession, by 1916 he was a partner in the stockbroking firm of Messrs F.P. Robjent and Co. in Newport. Later that year he enlisted. His obituary in *The Breconian* reflected on his willingness to join up:

> *Not, says one who knew him, a fighter by nature: but there is no fire until the flint is struck, and he left a quiet calling at home deliberately and cheerfully, to face known hardships and unknown perils on the battlefield. He girded himself for the struggle, believing that the best place in the world is the place where a man can add to the world's helpfulness.*

In 1916 Bruce became a Cadet in the Inns of Court Officers Training Corps. From there he joined the 3rd Battalion, Seaforth Highlanders as a Second Lieutenant. He then went on to the 2nd Battalion, entering France on 10th January 1917. Bruce and two fellow Second Lieutenants reached the Battalion on a cold, snowy and wet day on 13th January and were attached to D Company. On the night of 16th/17th January, the Battalion moved up to front line trenches at Bouchauesnes, taking over from the 3rd Battalion, 77th French Infantry Regiment and completing their operation by 2am. Hard frost and snow were reported and German aircraft and artillery were active but D Company held the right front line. The trench was described as being in a poor state and fallen in at places. The British troops set to, improving the trenches. However, German snipers took their toll and the Battalion Diary recorded for 20th January that two were killed and two wounded - two of these four having gone to rescue their Sergeant who had been shot in both legs.

On 23rd January 1917 the Battalion was relieved and Bruce and his men marched back to Camp 18, known as 'Suzanne'. The next day they marched to Camp 112. That night a German aircraft dropped six bombs on the camp killing and wounded several men, including the Drum Major (dead) and a Pipe Major (wounded). On 27th January 1917 the Battalion moved to Camp 13 for Company Training. Sickness, though, was taking its toll on the Battalion and during January the 'Wastage' report showed 127 other ranks and two officers sick in Hospital as well as 16 men and one officer having been killed.

On 29th January 1917 Bruce was attached to 4th Division Works Battalion and on 22nd February, moved to the Household Company, though still remaining on the books of D Company. During that time, on 13th February, the Battalion was ordered to Camp 18 to be isolated owing to an outbreak of German measles. Company training continued and on 14th March 1917 the Battalion was given the all clear and marched to Camp 12 via 'Suzanna, Bray'. Here, as is often recorded in the Battalion Diaries, they found the state of the camp to be "very dirty". From there, the Battalion seemed to be constantly on the move and, on occasion, no billets had been fixed up. By the end of the month the Battalion was billeted in Ourton, seven miles north-east of St Pol in northern France.

On 3rd April 1917 deep snow was reported but that did not stop the presentation in the afternoon of medal ribbons. Next day was recorded the final Divisional conference before the next 'big push'. On the 5th April, with all men paraded in fighting order, the news came that movements were postponed for 24 hours. On 7th April the Battalion was finally on the march, first to Brulin and on the next day - a beautiful Easter Sunday - to Savy. This was 'Y day' and a big offensive was due to open on the following morning. Thus, on the morning of 9th April 1917, with zero hour fixed for 5.30am, the Second Battle of Arras began.

The Battalion was not in the first wave of the attack which, again according to the Battalion Diary, captured the first, second and third German trench lines "according to the programme". The Battalion moved up to the front line area, arriving at 8.30am after passing, in the last half-mile, "a constant stream of walking wounded ... including a few Germans". Whilst waiting, larger batches of Germans were marched past in groups of 50 to 100 men, and were apparently "a poor looking lot, there being a noted difference from those met with on the Somme area last year". Later that afternoon, the Battalion moved up to front line trenches. An enemy aircraft spotted D Company and dropped several "whizz-bangs". Near the trenches a British 'tank' had broken down before even crossing the start line.

The Battalion then moved in to the captured German trench system. Enemy artillery was active, though, and a slow advance continued over the next few days with the Battalion often in the thick of the fighting. Between

9th and 20th April, when the Battalion finally reached safety having been relieved in their forward positions, 14 officers and 407 men were killed or wounded. The majority of these casualties were suffered on 11th April 1917 when the Battalion attempted to take the Hyderabad Redoubt. Just over 400 men and officers, strung along 1,100 yards, were ordered to cover the ground in the face of intense enemy machine guns. 12 officers and 363 other ranks out of 12 officers and 420 other ranks were killed or wounded.

On the morning of 3rd May 1917 the Battalion took their part in the 3rd Army's attack on the German Fresnes-Montabin-Plouvain line. The Battalion was to attack in two waves, with zero hour being 3.45am and troops moving behind a creeping barrage. The Household Company led the attack. The 27 year old Bruce was seen "revolver in hand fighting to the end, brave and undaunted in the face of the enemy who surrounded his men in overwhelming numbers." He was subsequently reported as Missing in Action. His body was never found.

The Breconian records "Clearly he met a hero's death: it is a splendid picture of the man, with no animal love of fighting for its own sake, yet dying with his back to the wall 'incapable of his own distress' . . . We shall not readily find a better type of character among Breconians of his or any generation".

Second Lieutenant Bruce Wallace Macaulay is remembered on the Arras Memorial as well as on the Christ College War Memorial.

Lieutenant Horace Macaulay
7th Battalion, Seaforth Highlanders

25TH APRIL 1918 ~ AGED 23
School House 1905-1907

Horace was born on 4th May 1894, the younger son of John and Janet Macaulay and brother of Bruce Wallace Macaulay. Horace arrived at School House at the same time as his brother at Easter 1905 and also left at the same time, Christmas 1907.

Joining the Honourable Artillery Company on 8th September 1914, Horace quickly rose through the ranks to become a Lance-Sergeant. He then attended officer training at the same time and place as Trevor Akrill Jones (both boys are listed in The London Gazette of 9th September 1915). Horace was commissioned Second Lieutenant in the 3rd Seaforth Highlanders on 10th September 1915. He later joined the 7th Battalion, Seaforth Highlanders as a full Lieutenant, entering France on 26th July 1916 aged 22.

Horace just missed out on the initial bloody engagements that marked the first three weeks start of the Battle of the Somme but he saw several months of intense action including the October Battle of Transloy towards the end of this major Somme offensive. Fast becoming a seasoned officer, in 1917 he and the Battalion fought through the First (9th-14th April) and Second (23rd-24th April) Battles of the Scarpe during the indecisive Arras offensive. The First Battle of Passchendaele took place on 12th October and most likely due to wounds or illness, Horace returned to England until April 1918.

Suddenly, in the fierce German Ludendorff offensive of March and April 1918, the 7th Battalion, now in the DammStrasse area of Ypres, had been caught in the midst of German gas and gunnery. The French, having lost control of Mount Kemmel and Kemmel Village, had made it impossible to hold the Vierstraat line. 23 year old Horace returned to the battalion on 24th April and immediately assumed command of D Company which was in the thick of the German advance. In an effort to hold on, Horace and his men were holding a defensive line which, according to the War Diary, "described almost a right angle at Piccadilly Farm". It seems as if D Company were, managing to delay the enemy by maintaining this position at Wytschaete, despite three heavy bombardments. Within hours of assuming command, Horace was "killed by a bullet through his brain" as the Battalion withdrew on 25th April 1918, a few days before his 24th birthday. His body was never recovered.

Horace's Commanding Officer wrote to his parents that "We were all so pleased to see your son back from his six months at home. He was most popular with everyone, and will be greatly missed". His Captain wrote "Your son was, I think, one of the best-known and most popular officers in the battalion, always cheerful and willing to help a fellow in any circumstances. He was very considerate of his men, and one of the straightest fellows I've met".

The boys' father, John Macaulay, applied for the medals of both his dead sons on the same day, 27th September 1921.

Lieutenant Horace Macaulay is remembered on the Tyne Cot Memorial as well as on the Christ College War Memorial.

Lieutenant Hopkin Thomas Maddock MC
Machine Gun Corps

15TH DECEMBER 1921 ~ AGE 40
Hostel 1894-1898

Hopkin Thomas Maddock was born on 1st January 1881 in Pontycymmer. His father, Jonathan Maddock, owned a colliery there. He entered the Hostel, Christ College in 1894 and left at the end of December 1898. Though known by the surname of Maddocks, including in his later rugby football career, there was no final 's' on his birth certificate.

He showed a little sporting promise in his early years at school and, in the Athletic Sports of April 1896, took third place in the 220 yards Under 15 Handicap. He again took part in the Athletic Sports in the following year and came second in the Under 16 Long Jump. In the summer of 1897 he was selected for the 2nd Cricket XI but it was in the following term, when he was selected to play for the 1st XV, that he showed his skills in rugby football.

The annual Llandovery Match of 1897 was postponed in the autumn and finally took place on Saturday 5th March 1898 with the Christ College team travelling by train to Llandovery. There were few supporters at first but "as the game progressed they were further augmented by the arrival of belated cyclists". Although Christ College lost the match by 10 points to nil, they made "a creditable fight of it". Hopkin had plenty of play. In the first half, when receiving the ball, he "put in a characteristic punt, and finished up by grassing the full-back before he could kick". In the second half it was noted that "Maddocks kicked well", also that "At three-quarters the only one to show any form was Maddocks, who tackled and kicked in a praiseworthy manner". Reports from other 1st XV matches mention some fine playing and his end of season critique was characteristically direct: "Maddocks (centre) a splendid tackler; kicks with good judgment, knows the centre three-quarter game, but would play it better if he learnt to pass; with unselfishness and more weight will develop into a first class centre".

In the summer term of 1898 he played occasionally for the 1st Cricket XI, where he took several good catches in various games, and also played regularly for the 2nd XI. The latter included the 2nd XI match against Llandovery held on Wednesday 6th July 1898. It was an exciting but not very high scoring match which Christ

College won. Hopkin took one wicket for six runs. He scored two runs in his first innings before being caught, and nine in the second innings before being run out.

In the autumn of 1898 he was again playing for the 1st XV. In the first match of the season, a win at home against Brecon Town on 15th October, he was reported as playing a "sound game". However, in the return match, a few weeks later, which Christ College lost, he was not on top form and "was too deliberate, and often muffed the ball". On Saturday 26th November, though, the team played their "old rivals" Monmouth Grammar School and Maddocks "dropped a good goal" to help the win. Then on Saturday 3rd December 1898 came the great annual contest against Llandovery. Christ College won by a goal and two tries (11 points) to a goal (5 points). "Maddocks once or twice was in very tight corners, but extricated himself". Llandovery kept up the pressure and would have scored a try except that Hopkin kicked "dead in the nick of time".

His end of season critique reads "H.T. MADDOCKS (back) - A sound player, tackles brilliantly considering his weight, and an accurate kick who always finds touch. Cool to a fault . . ." Such was his skill that, after he had left school, the Editorial in *The Breconian* noted that the team found it hard to fill his place. In the same Editorial, the introduction of hockey was complained about as "a further advance in the destructive appliances of this institution" and the editors went on to lament the "present craze among irresponsible people for golf"!

After leaving school, Hopkin returned to Pontycymmer but very soon after moved to London where he worked as a Tax Officer. He played for the London Welsh in the 1900/01 season. He continued to play for them and was later made captain after his performances in the 1908/09 season where a magnificent few weeks in the early months of 1909 saw Hopkin (or 'Hop' as he became known) steer the team from weakness to great strength. In particular, he oversaw the defeat (39 to 9) of the mighty and previously unbeatable Oxford University side on 5th February 1909. 'Hop' was made captain for the following (1909/10) season and again for the 1911/12 season. In total, 'Hop' made 275 appearances for the London Welsh, scoring 610 points. His total of 170 tries has never been beaten. During this time 'Hop' also played for Middlesex and Glamorgan.

In the 1906 Home Nations Championship he was called up for Wales in a match against England. He played alongside fellow London Welsh winger and Old Breconian, E. ("Teddy") Morgan (Morton's 1892-1899), and scored a try. He played further international matches in 1906 and 1907 and then took a break from international fame. However, 'Hop' was called up for the opening match of the 1910 Five Nations Championship held on 1st January at Swansea, a match against France which Wales won 49 to 14. It was his last international, despite the fact that he scored two of the ten Welsh tries. He gained 6 Welsh caps in all and, such was his fame, he was No. 23 in a set of 50 cigarette cards of 'Famous Footballers' issued by Ogden's Cigarettes in 1908.

At the outbreak of war he enlisted on 15th September 1914. Four Public Schools Battalions had been founded at Epsom on 11th September by the 'Public Schools and University Men's Force' and it was one of these battalions that he joined. They trained in England for over a year before landing in France in November 1915 and, during the training, 'Hop' captained the Public Schools Battalion rugby football team. In April 1916, whilst serving with the 10th Battalion, the Royal Fusiliers in France, he was sent back to England for officer training. He received his commission on 25th September 1916 and soon after joined the Machine Gun Corps. Towards the end of the year, he was wounded by shell fire, severely damaging his shoulder.

After recovering, 'Hop' returned to the Front and was promoted to Lieutenant on 26th April 1918. It was during this month, which saw desperate fighting to halt the German Ludendorff Offensive, that he was dangerously wounded in the neck and thigh while covering the retreat of his unit from Les Mesnil in Northern France. He held off the enemy, who were converging on three sides until all his men had crossed a bridge, and managed to reach the other side even though he was badly wounded. For his actions, he was awarded the Military Cross.

The injury he received in 1916 continued to trouble him and these latest wounds saw him being returned home to convalesce. However, he never fully recovered and died on 15th December 1921 from his injuries. The London Welsh played their last match of the year wearing Black Armbands as a mark of respect.

Lieutenant Hopkin Thomas ('Hop') Maddock MC died from wounds sustained in action after August 31st 1921, the date used as the cut-off point for recording the deaths of military personnel as First World War fatalities. He is therefore not included in the Commonwealth War Graves Commission records or on the Christ College War Memorial. In November 2013 his name was permanently added to the Roll of Honour read on Remembrance Sunday at Christ College.

Lieutenant Harold Madoc Jones MID (2)
C Company 17th Battalion, Royal Welsh Fusiliers

31ST JULY 1917 ~ AGED 38
Hostel 1890-1892

Harold Madoc Jones was born on 1st September 1878 at Llangynhafal, Denbigh to Eunice Martha and John Robert Jones JP, a local solicitor. The family later moved to Bodfeirig, Anglesey. Harold entered the Hostel in 1890 as "a small shock-headed freckled boy". Known as a scholar and athlete, he gained the nickname 'Silent' for his calm and resilient character.

He was awarded the Form V Classics prize at Speech Day on 25th July 1892 and left at the end of the term with a Scholarship to University College of Wales, Aberystwyth. After graduating with Honours in Classics, he became a schoolmaster and taught Classics at Llandudno, Llangefni in Angelsey, Porth, and Cardigan County School. In the Census of 1911 Harold, a 32 year old schoolmaster, was living as a 'boarder' at 2 Park Terrace, Cardigan.

At the outbreak of war he left Cardigan School and enlisted as a Private in the Royal Welsh Fusiliers at Llandudno. He was commissioned Second Lieutenant in February 1915, joining the 19th Service Battalion, Royal Welsh Fusiliers (a bantam battalion) as they were being formed by the Welsh National Executive Committee. Harold then transferred on 7th May 1915 into the 17th Service Battalion, (2nd North Wales) Royal Welsh Fusiliers, entering France on 2th December 1915.

The Battalion, which was part of 115 Brigade, 28th (Welsh) Division, moved to the Fleurbais area and here Harold became experienced in trench warfare. He saw service at Neuve Chapelle, Laventie, Festhubert and on the Somme. Harold was promoted to Lieutenant and for a second time Mentioned in Despatches "for his share of the good work at Mametz" which the Battalion had attacked on 7th July 1917 as part of the Somme Offensive. A fellow officer described him as "the calmest soldier I ever met in the face of danger; No Man's Land had no terrors to disturb the tranquility of his mind".

After the failure of the first attack on 7th July, a second was mounted on 10th July. Two days of bitter hand-to-hand fighting saw the Germans retreat and the Battalion move forward, halting at the Yser canal. On 31st July 1917 the Battalion was ordered to take Pilckem Ridge. Harold, a "tall, handsome man of commanding presence", was on patrol when a corporal was badly wounded. With total disregard for his own safety, Harold tried to save him, only to be shot dead by an enemy sniper. He was buried on the battlefield, close by Langemarck.

A senior officer wrote "A more gallant gentleman I have never seen. Had he lived he would have had a decoration. No soldier faced battle so calmly and so bravely." Another officer wrote "Never have men been led by a more gallant soldier. He was loved by everybody, and his men would do anything for him."

Harold's father had predeceased him and his widowed mother lived at Bryn Cadnant, Menai Bridge. Harold had family connections with Wraysbury, Buckinghamshire (and certainly his maiden sister Miss Eunice Mary Wood Jones lived there after the war). He is remembered at the Wraysbury Baptist Chapel, along with his cousin Gordon Doulton East. Both men were killed on the same day in the same battle.

Lieutenant Harold Madoc Jones is also remembered on the Ypres (Menin Gate) Memorial as well as on the Christ College War Memorial.

Second Mate Lewis William Marles Thomas
Merchant Service, Admiralty Transport
29TH APRIL 1917 ~ AGED 38
School House 1888-1890

Lewis William Marles Thomas was born in Llandyssul, Cardinganshire in 1879, the son of the Reverend William Thomas and his wife, Mary Marles Thomas. Mary was the daughter of the great Welsh radical, writer, schoolmaster and Unitarian leader the Reverend William Thomas. Better known by his bardic name, 'Gwilym Marles', he died the same year as Lewis was born. He was also the great-uncle of Dylan Thomas, who was given his middle name 'Marlais' in his honour. Dylan Thomas is thought to have created the *Under Milk Wood* character of Reverend Eli Jenkins in honour of 'Gwilym Marles'.

Lewis entered School House in 1888 and was at Christ College until 1890. After school he embarked on a sea going career, serving in the Mercantile Marine (later renamed the Merchant Navy by King George V in recognition of its service in the First World War). When war broke out Lewis "came home from China to offer his services to the Government". Admiralty Transport commandeered and directed a large number of civilian ships and Lewis was employed as Second Mate on the SS 'Daleby', registered in West Hartlepool. On 5th April the 'Daleby' left Huelva in south western Spain with a cargo of copper and silver ore bound for Garston, Merseyside.

At 3pm on a clear afternoon on 29th April 1917, the 'Daleby' was torpedoed without warning by the German submarine U-70, about 150 miles south east of Cape Clear (Ireland). A second torpedo blew up the lifeboats and sank the ship immediately. The submarine surfaced but ignored the survivors before moving on. The only two survivors found a dinghy and were at sea for 24 hours before being picked up. Lewis was one of the 26 crewmen to die in the attack.

The Breconian quotes a letter from someone who knew Lewis: "He always spoke of his old school with deep affection, though he did not shine as a scholar. But he had the mind of a poet, the vision of a seer, and the great heart of a patriot". Clearly the latter was a family trait, reminiscent of both his grandfather and Dylan Thomas.

Lewis' mother Mary, despite losing her youngest and only surviving son, continued her efforts for the Welsh Serbian Hospital Unit. The initial appeal, launched in April 1915, raised 100 guineas which "enabled Aberystwyth to equip and endow four beds for six months". She continued to raise money throughout the war for this cause.

Second Mate Lewis William Marles Thomas is remembered on the Tower Hill Memorial and the Aberystwyth War Memorial as well as on the Christ College War Memorial.

Private Francis Alfred Ismay Musk
2nd Battalion, Coldstream Guards

27TH AUGUST 1918 ~ AGED 20
Day Boy 1912-1915

Francis Musk was born on 13th March 1898 in Brecon and joined Christ College as a Day Boy at Easter 1912. At the time he and his parents, Richard William and Agnes Mary Musk (née Summers), lived at 6 Bowen Terrace, Brecon. His father, Richard, was an organist and teacher of music who had pupils at both Brecon County School and Christ College. Francis attended both schools.

A notable event took place when Francis was 8. On Friday 29th June 1906, an earthquake struck Brecon. Despite there being little damage, his father Richard was severely shaken. Although the organist at St Mary's Church, he had been practising music in the Roman Catholic Church when the rumbling caused him to rush into the street.

As with many day boys, Francis did not take a particularly active part in sports. The only reference to him at school is in the autumn of 1914 when he took part in the Fives Open Doubles Competition. In the following year Francis (sometimes referred to as Frank) left school to enter the banking profession in Bath. Soon, though, he was caught up in the bloody carnage of the war.

When he had reached 18 he joined the 2nd Battalion, Coldstream Guards early in 1916. He was at the Battle of Flers-Courcelette in September 1916 which was followed almost immediately by the Battle of Morval later the same month (both battles were part of the Battle of the Somme). In June 1917 Francis took part in pursuing the Germans during their retreat to the Hindenburg Line (14th March to 5th April 1917), and the Battle of Pilkem Ridge (31st July to 2nd August). The first day of this particular battle saw the death of fellow old Breconian Lieutenant Harold Madoc Jones.

A little over a year after joining up, Francis was killed on 27th August 1918. It was a terrible day for the 2nd Battalion. The Second Battle of Bapaume had started on 21st August and the 2nd Battalion had seen fierce fighting around Bapaume. On that day they were to attack German positions through a wood (known as St Leger Wood) of thick undergrowth and fallen trees. Attacking at 7am on 27th August 1918, the Battalion was soon hard hit by heavy, sustained and deadly German machine gun fire. At about 10am the Germans counter-attacked from roads south of Croisilles forcing the Guards to withdraw. During this time fierce hand-to-hand fighting took place in and around the wood. Francis was one of 310 men of the 2nd Battalion to die or be wounded in that fight.

Francis was at first reported as missing but his body was later recovered. His mother immediately wrote to his unit asking for information. In reply, a Captain C.P. Blacker wrote:

> Dear Mrs Musk, It is with the deepest regret - especially so after the receipt of your letter - that I write to inform you that you son, after all, was killed in the action of August 27th. He was found after the ground was recaptured and given a good burial in the cemetery near - by an Army Chaplain. He was not in the least disfigured by his wound, which was such that he could not have suffered a moment's pain. His loss was most deeply felt by all who knew him. He was a company runner and always fulfilled his duties most efficiently, cheerfully and willingly. Please accept my warmest and most heartfelt sympathy in your terrible bereavement.

A few weeks later the Chaplain, the Reverend L.M. Hodge, wrote to Mr. Musk about Francis' death "It may be some comfort to you and Mrs Musk to know that he met his death with the greatest bravery, and that it was instantaneous and caused by machine gun fire. His body has been buried and a cross erected."

A tribute published in *The Breconian* reads "He was one of those boys who had more in him than appeared on the surface, and his war record and final sacrifice are the best tribute to his character. He had few opportunities of distinguishing himself at school: but he did his part in winning victory for us, and Brecon pays a grateful tribute to his memory".

In October 1918, two months after Francis' death, his mother Agnes was appointed to Brecon County Girls' School to assist with needlework, at 10/6 per week. (Interestingly former Christ College teacher Mr. Le Brocq was appointed temporary master to the Boys' School at the same time, on £4 per week or £50 per term). Both Mr. and Mrs Musk had worked hard from the very start of the War in raising money and making items for the troops. His mother was a tireless worker for the YMCA as well as other organisations, such as the Red Cross, and serving on various committees.

One of these was the Central Committee of the Brecon Women's' Working Party which had been brought into being by the Mayor of Brecon on 14th August 1914. During that meeting, a message was read out from "Mrs Fawcett, on behalf of the National Union of Women's Suffrage Societies (Nonmilitant) ... expressing the hope that political work would be suspended for the present, and that local suffrage committees would devote their energies to relief war work".

In addition to the Central Committee, of which both Mrs Best and Mrs Musk were members, there were sub-committees for cutting out cloth, hospital supplies, stewarding, and knitting. In June 1917 Francis' father was contributing to the War Effort by raising money through an organ recital at the Plough Chapel in Brecon in aid of the Breconshire YMCA Hut Week Campaign. This was just one of many such recitals and both parents were involved in a range of other events and activities.

On Thursday 20th March 1919 Francis' parents placed an *In Memoriam* notice in *The Brecon County Times*.

Francis would have celebrated his 21st birthday on the previous Thursday. The notice read:

> *In loving memory of Frank Musk, Coldstream Guards, only son of Mr. and Mrs R.W. Musk, The Cottage, Brecon, killed in action Aug. 27th, 1918, in his 21st year. Born March 13th, 1898.*

The notice was followed by Rupert Brooke's poem *The Soldier* which commences "If I should die, think only this of me: That there's some corner of a foreign field, That is forever England".

On the afternoon of Sunday 10th August 1919, a memorial service was held at St David's Church, Llanfaes. The former Vicar of St David's, the Reverend D. Saunders Jones, whose son Henry St John Saunders Jones had been killed in action in East Africa almost exactly two years earlier, read the lesson. The Vicar, the Reverend J. Simon, after reading the names of the fallen, told the congregation to see "death was only a change in life, not an end . . . a higher calling" and that their loved ones died for "Righteousness, liberty, honour, equity and true brotherhood". He quoted the lines of a poem "For still for him high service waits, though earth's last fight is fought, God did not give that martial soul to end at last in nought".

A year after his death, on 28th August 1919, Francis' parents again placed an *In Memoriam* notice in the *Brecon County Times*: "MUSK - In affectionate remembrance of Frank Musk, Coldstream Guards, who fell fighting for his Country in France, August 27th, 1918, in his 21st year. How goes the day? They died and never knew, Ill or well, England! They died for you".

On 25th September 1921, in memory of their only child, Agnes Musk presented a framed Roll of Honour to St Mary's Church Brecon, where her husband was also sometime organist. The Roll remains on the south isle of the Church, in a dark wood frame. It has the following dedication: "In honoured memory of the following who gave their lives in the cause of freedom and right in the Great War 1914-1918." Handwritten in fine copperplate, it records in three columns the names of fifty-one local men followed by the words "In sure and certain hope of the resurrection to eternal life".

Private Francis Alfred Ismay Musk is buried at the Croisilles British Cemetery. He is remembered on the Roll of Honour in St Mary's Church, Brecon as well as on the Christ College War Memorial.

Captain Benjamin Ethlebert Nicholls (Leeder) MC (and bar)

20th Battalion, Canadian Infantry

8TH MAY 1918 ~ AGED 26

Hostel 1903-1904 and 1906-1908

Benjamin Ethlebert Nicholls was born on 15th February 1892, the youngest son of Frederick E. Nicholls and Emma Nicholls of 19 Waterloo Street, Swansea. He arrived at Christ College in September 1903 joining his older brother, Harry Nicholls (Hostel 1894-1899).

Ben took his stepfather's name of Leeder but was known in school as 'Inky'. His contemporaries found him witty and humorous and he certainly developed into a fine athlete. He was not at Christ College between ages of 12 and 14 but returned in September 1906. Though only 16 years old, Ben was made a School Prefect. Even more notably, he participated in the Llandovery cricket and rugby football matches of 1908 where he is recorded as taking an active part. In the Llandovery cricket match he put up a sterling defence and in the rugby football, he made several gallant tackles. Both matches were a hard fought draw that year. His rugby football critique was very promising: "B.E. Leeder (Left Centre Threequarter) - a neat dodgy runner and strong in defence . . . will probably turn out a more than useful Threequarter in a year or two".

His promising school career was cut short as in December 1908 he left Christ College and went to work at his stepfather's solicitors' office of Messrs Viner Leeder and Morris in Swansea. However, this work lasted only a few months because in 1909 he left Wales to "take up a ranch" in Canada. He returned home for a visit in 1911 and the Census of that year shows him living at Hinderwood Villa, Mumbles, Glamorgan with his family. On the death of his stepfather in 1912, Ben reverted to his original name of Nicholls.

Canadian record cards are detailed and well preserved. (Many of the British equivalents were destroyed by bombing in the Second World War.) Ben's records show that he joined up in Toronto on 14th December 1914; he was 5 feet 9 inches tall, of fair complexion, with blue eyes and fair coloured hair. He stated he was Church of England and a farmer by profession. Intriguingly, Ben indicated in the 'Next of Kin' section of his military record cards that in the event of his death, his sister and a young British girl, also living in Toronto, were to be notified.

He also stated that he was in the Militia at the time, thus indicating that he was in the Canadian Territorials.

57465 Private B.E. Nicholls was a member of the newly formed 20th Battalion (Central Ontario Regiment). Initial training in Canada was followed in May 1915 by further training in digging trenches, long-distance marches and weaponry at West Sandling, near Folkestone. By 1st September 1915, Ben had been promoted to full Sergeant and is listed as one of the NCO's of B Company.

On 14th September 1915, under cover of darkness and aboard the 'Duchess of Argyle', the 20th Battalion left Folkestone for France, arriving next day. On 5th January 1916 Sergeant Nicholls was wounded. The Battalion Diary, stating that there was fighting in the Dichiebusch Trenches (just outside Ypres), notes he was "hit but not badly . . . Enemy fire comes from direct line of Hollandschour Farm". However, the medical sheet from the Casualty Clearing Station records a rifle bullet wound that "entered his back right shoulder about the middle of his scapular, below the spine of the same and grazing the lower border of clavicle anteriorly. The bullet exited at the base of the neck, fracturing his clavicle". He also had a wound to his right knee. Being moved by ambulance back though the lines, he was repatriated to the Duchess of Connaught Canadian Red Cross Hospital at Cliveden, Taplow, Buckinghamshire arriving on 13th January for a three month stay.

Ben then briefly passed through several other convalescent hospitals before being declared fit for duty despite, stated the records, "some pain on throwing anything by hand". In order to further build up his strength, he acted as an instructor to the 35th Battalion who were at West Sandling, and it was whilst there that Ben was promoted to Temporary Lieutenant on 21st August 1916. He rejoined his own Battalion on 31st October 1916, one of many replacements for the heavily hit Canadians who had suffered severe casualties at the Somme. One in eleven Canadian servicemen were killed during the war; of the 60,000 Canadians killed, 855 were from the 20th Battalion.

On 17th January 1917, after two weeks of special training, 400 officers and men from the 20th Battalion raided the German lines in the Calonne sector with the aim to kill, take 'booty' and prisoners, and destroy dugouts. Lieutenant Nicholls had the special job of cutting gaps in the wire in front of each 'jumping off' (starting) point, leaving the wire in place but with ropes attached to enable it to be pulled quickly apart. This was to be done without alerting the enemy and it was done faultlessly. The raid was a great success with Ben capturing a number of prisoners and helping two fellow officers who were arguing in a captured enemy trench during the planned withdrawal about which way 'was home'!

Further trench fighting ensued and on 20th February Ben was promoted to Acting Captain. He was Mentioned in Despatches for actions on a snowy 9th April 1917 whilst in the front line in the Thelus Sector at Roclincourt, a little south of Vimy Ridge, where a thunderous battle was taking place. On 9th August 1917 Ben was one of a party of 72 men raiding German trenches. The attack started at 3.30am and the troops were preceded by a rolling artillery barrage. Wire in front of the German trenches caused problems as did enemy machine guns. The order to withdraw from the assault was given just over an hour later. 49 of the 72 men were casualties. Captain Nicholls then went out with a bearer party and brought back 14 wounded and 7 bodies. For this he was awarded the Military Cross. The citation reads:

> For conspicuous gallantry and devotion to duty. A number of men were lying badly
> wounded in 'No Man's Land' after a raid. He went to their rescue in broad daylight and

succeeded in bringing several of them in. After dark he went right up to the enemy's wire
and succeeded in bringing in men whom he had been unable to reach earlier in the day.
His courage and pluck were undoubtedly the means of saving many lives.

Six days later, on 15th August, Ben's Battalion was advancing at the start of the Battle for Hill 70, effectively a rise in the ground. There was only one strongly-held machine gun post in front of Ben's position and the Battalion Diary noted that he "gathered together a small party, rushed it, captured the two guns and putting the garrison out of action, he himself shooting four of them". For this he was awarded a second Military Cross". He was slightly wounded in the action but kept fighting.

In October 1917 the Battalion was sent to Passchendaele to take part in the Second Battle of Passchendaele. Shortly after and having seen little action, they were returned to the Ypres Salient. On 20th December 1917 Ben joined the 1st Army School as an Instructor but on 3rd February 1918 was given two weeks leave back in England before rejoining his Battalion as Officer Commanding D Company in France.

During this time he was contemplating joining the Royal Air Force (as it had become known on 1st April 1918), "in search of fresh opportunities". Before he could apply, though, Ben was killed on 8th May whilst in a front line trench at Mercatel, five miles south of Arras. A shell landed directly on top of the bay in which he was posted, killing him and three of his men. That evening their bodies were taken to Wailly Cemetery. The following day they were removed to Bellacourt Cemetery where, according to the Battalion Diary, "the funeral was held at 3.00pm. The Commanding Officer and all officers and other ranks in Bellacourt attended".

Ben's death was also mourned in Ascension Day, a poem written on 9th May 1918 by fellow officer and Canadian war poet, Captain T.A. Girling. In it he captures the moment of the burial of one "who loved earth's waking hours so well":

Mutely we mourned the spirit brave,
The bugles sounded o'er the grave,
The reverend last salute we gave,
In France so far away.

Ben was noted in *The Breconian* as a lovable boy who "was the soul of good temper, a faithful comrade with an overflowing supply of wit and humour" and as a man whose "sterling worth and patriotic spirit distinguished him in his military career". The obituary continues ". . . so passed a very gallant officer and gentleman, whom Christ College will long be proud to honour and remember".

In a book on the 20th Battalion published after the war in 1935, the author (Major D.J. Corrigall) wrote that Ben was "a keenly efficient officer and a great favourite: his death, at a time when experienced officers were becoming scarce, was a serious loss to the Battalion".

Captain Benjamin Ethelbert Nicholls, MC and Bar, is buried in Bellacourt Cemetery. He is remembered on the Christ College War Memorial as B.E. Leeder, his name while at school.

Private Thomas Parry
Royal Army Medical Corps

4TH MARCH 1919 ~ AGED 22
School House 1909-1913

Thomas Parry was born on 17th July 1896 to Dr. and Mrs C.P. Parry MD, JP of Castle Hill House, 1 Spilman Street, Carmarthen. Thomas and his brother, Charles Frederick Parry, entered School House together in 1909. They left in 1913.

Charles was something of an athlete and won a number of running prizes. Thomas, though permanently lame, competed at golf and, on Saturday 23rd March 1912, he won the Golf Handicap Prize on a very wet course. The Golfing prizes were given by the Reverend Donaldson and were awarded at the end of the Athletic Sports a week later. On Prize Day 1912 Thomas was awarded the Form IV Prize as well as the Division 2 Science Prize. He was also awarded his Lower Certificate in Latin, Mathematics, Chemistry, Arithmetic, Mechanics and Physics, Physics, and Chemistry - with distinctions in the last four.

In the spring of 1913 Thomas was again playing golf but was knocked out in the 3rd round of the Fives Open Singles by David Cuthbert Thomas. That summer Thomas picked up further Lower certificate examination successes, and both brothers, along with Geoffrey Boothby, passed the London Matriculation examination. Both Charles and Thomas were to follow their father into a medical career by enrolling as students to study Medicine. Charles successfully completed his studies at London University and became Dr. C.F. Parry MRCS, LRCP, LMSSA. Thomas decided not to join his brother in London and enrolled at Cardiff University College.

Their father, Dr. C.P. Parry, had become a Justice of the Peace in 1913 and, at the outbreak of war, he enrolled as a special constable in his home town. Thomas enlisted from home on 28th September 1914, joining the Royal Army Medical Corps. Given his lameness, it is interesting that he was able to enlist. However, his work as a Medical Student was enough to ensure that he was passed fit for Home Service. He was attached to the 3rd Western General Hospital in Neath, a military hospital where, according to his obituary in *The Carmarthen Journal*, "he served for two and a half years". He did not have a strong constitution and was eventually discharged from the Army. He died of tuberculosis at the family home early on Tuesday 4th March 1919. He was buried on 6th March in Carmarthen Cemetery.

Described in *The Carmarthen Journal* as being "of a genial disposition and was a promising student", *The Breconian* similarly recalls him as "a boy of charming disposition, never prominent at school owing to the handicap of permanent lameness, but much liked by all who knew him".

Perhaps because he died of illness at home, Private Thomas Parry is not included on the Christ College War Memorial but, as Private T. Parry 373158 of the Royal Army Medical Corps, he is on the records of the Commonwealth War Graves Commission. He is now also included on the Roll of Honour read on Remembrance Sunday at Christ College.

Second Lieutenant Howard Wynne Richards
1/1st Brecknockshire Battalion, South Wales Borderers

8TH AUGUST 1920 ~ AGED 32
Morton's 1901-1903

Howard Wynne Richards was born on 16th October 1887, the only son of the Reverend Thomas Charles and Mrs Richards. His father became Rector of Llanfihangel Talyllyn in 1894. Howard entered Morton's, Christ College, in 1901. Located at Ty'n y Coed, 16 Bridge Street (opposite the school gates) and named after its Housemaster, Percy Morton, Morton's usually accommodated a dozen boys. Howard remained at Christ College until 1903. There is no mention of his time at school in *The Breconian*, except for his second place in the 220 yards Under 15 Handicap in the 1902 Athletic Sports. After leaving school, Howard served his articles as a civil engineer in Brecon. Having completed his training, he became a member of the Land Valuation staff at Cardiff and Brecon.

On 7th October 1915 Howard was commissioned as a Second Lieutenant in the 1/1st Brecknockshire Battalion, South Wales Borderers. He entered the Indian Theatre of War on 27th March 1916, by which time the Battalion was in Mhow. Later that year, though, he was invalided home with "lung trouble" for an initial six month recuperation period. On arrival in England Howard went to the Hilltop Sanatorium, Wells where his condition deteriorated. He was later moved nearer home to The Villa, Llangorse. This Villa was also a refuge for other servicemen who had been invalided out of the Army. However, Howard died there suddenly on Sunday 8th August 1920.

His mother and father had pre-deceased him, having died within a very few days of each other in early March 1918. Mrs T.J. Parry of Brecon, his sister and the only remaining member of the family, looked after the funeral arrangements. Following a service at Llanfihangel Church, Howard was buried in the family vault at Cefn Coed Cemetery.

Second Lieutenant Howard Wynne Richards is remembered on the Christ College War Memorial.

Driver Thomas Ferrar Ricketts

Horse Transport, ASC attached 39th Field Ambulance

11TH JUNE 1916 ~ AGED 42

Day Boy 1887-1891

Thomas Ferrar Ricketts was born in Llandefalle, Bronllys in March 1874. He was the youngest of seven children (six of whom were boys, several of whom had the middle name Ferrar). His father was a farmer and the family lived at Trephillip Farm, Bronllys. There were various family members farming in the immediate area, such as at the neighbouring Trebarried Farm. One, Philip Williams Ricketts, had been at Christ College some thirty years earlier to Thomas and was a surveyor until his untimely death aged 32 in 1872. Thomas himself was a Day Boy from 1887 until 1891.

Thomas is recorded as playing rugby football matches for the 2nd XV, including against Llandovery 2nd XV on Wednesday 11th December 1889. In the 1890/91 season, Thomas again played matches for the 2nd XV where he is described as a forward doing "honest work". However, in that season he was also selected for the 1st XV and played in the eagerly awaited Llandovery College match on 6th December 1890 (a win again for the School). The report on the match stated that he "played well from start to finish". In the end of season critique Thomas was described as "a sturdy fellow, but does not use his great weight enough". It goes on to say: "Towards the end of last term he was plainly improving. He is at present slow in getting into the scrimmage".

After leaving school, Thomas went to work for the London and Provincial Bank, and was based at the Neath Branch. He continued to play rugby football and turned out regularly for the Neath 'A' Team. Thomas then went to South Africa where he worked for the Standard Bank of South Africa in both Pietermaritzburg and Greytown, KwaZulu-Natal Province. Whilst there, he was called out with the Natal Militia during the Native Rebellion of 1906.

After eleven years in South Africa, Thomas returned home to Wales but then moved again, this time to Canada. However, with thoughts of war in the air he returned home. On the 2nd September 1914 he wrote from the City Arms Hotel in Hereford to the Recruiting officer at the local Barracks:

Dear Sir,

I shall be glad to know if you will accept me in whatever Branch of His Majesties Service you think most suitable - I am 40 years of age, single, a Farmer's son, and during the South African War was with the Standard Bank of South Africa at Pietermaritzburg and subsequently at Greytown where I was called out with the Natal Militia during the Native rebellion of 1906. I can ride and shoot and am in good health generally, as far as I know. Unfortunately I have no proof of my statement but it can be substantiated.

Yours faithfully
T.F. Ricketts.

Thomas was medically examined on 5th September at Talgarth. Weighing 14st 4lbs and standing at 5 feet 10 inches, he was passed as in "perfect" health. On 7th September, the Officer Commanding the Hereford Regiment recommended him for Service as being "A strong, intelligent man. Keen on doing something for his Country". He further notes that Thomas served in the Natal Militia in the "Kaffer rising" and that he has "has shown me papers which prove that he held positions of trust".

On 8th September, the Officer Commanding the Hereford Recruiting Area stated that Thomas could be accepted. On 12th September, Thomas was formally attested at Hereford into the (now mobilized) Army Reserve "For a term of one year unless War last longer than one year, in which case you will be retained until War is over". He arrived at Aldershot the next day to join the Army Service Corps of the 1st New Army.

Thomas trained in England from 12th September 1914 until 5th November 1914. The next day he embarked at Southampton onto the SS 'Trafford' for the short hop across the Channel, disembarking at Le Havre later the same day. He served in France from 6th November 1914 until 5th April 1915. A month earlier, on 3rd March 1915, the Second Lieutenant in charge of the Document Clearing Station wrote to Thomas' brother Edward asking for information about the whereabouts of Thomas in order to send him some documents. Perhaps not unrelated to this uncertainty about where he was, Thomas received a Field Punishment on 29th March and was fined fourteen days' pay. Two days later, however, he was admitted to hospital with jaundice. Clearly ill, he was sent back to England on 5th April 1915 having been diagnosed with cholangitis, an infection affecting the liver.

Once recovered, Thomas was on Home Service in the United Kingdom (service reckoned from his arrival on 6th April 1915) until 20th January 1916, when he was sent to the Mediterranean Theatre. During this time he had heard, in the summer of 1915, of the death of his nephew Roger Jones, fighting with the Brecknocks in Aden. He had also been called upon to give evidence at the 27th December 1915 inquest on his brother Lloyd, a road surveyor for Hay District Council, who had died whilst being prepared for an operation on Christmas Eve.

Thomas left Devonport on 21st January aboard the 'Transylvania' and disembarked ten days later at Alexandria. From here he travelled to Basra, arriving on 9th February 1916. He was still in the Army Service Corps but was now attached to the 39th Field Ambulance. This was a field unit of 10 officers and 224 men. Like many so attached to the Field Ambulances in whatever role, he came into contact with sick as well as wounded soldiers. Perhaps also weakened by his earlier illnesses, Thomas was admitted to hospital on 30th March 1916 and was discharged after a week on 7th April. Two months later he was readmitted as seriously ill and died on 16th June 1916 of enteric fever at No. 3-A British General Hospital, Basra.

After his death, Thomas was remembered in *The Breconian* as "popular with his contemporaries". He was similarly described in *The Brecon and Radnor Express*, which referred to him having "a most interesting personality, having read much and travelled a great deal. His company was always congenial".

The Commonwealth War Graves records list his date of death as 11th June 1916, although his military records and newspaper reports record it as 16th June. His brothers, Edward and John Ferrar Ricketts were living at Trebarried Farm, Llandefalle, Talgarth along with a married sister. Another brother, William, was living close by in Trefecca, Talgarth. Edward was notified of his brother's death on 27th June 1916. Thomas' medals were sent to Edward at Trebarried Farm in December 1919, and a memorial scroll, plaque and King's letter in June 1920.

Driver Thomas Ferrar Ricketts is buried at Basra War Cemetery, and is remembered on the Christ College War Memorial.

Lieutenant John Stanley Robinson
HMS 'Royal Oak', Royal Navy

13TH NOVEMBER 1918 ~ AGED 30
Master 1911-1915

John Stanley Robinson was one of two former masters to die in the First World War. Educated at Sidney Sussex College, Cambridge, he arrived to live and teach Mathematics at Christ College in September 1911. He immediately began playing a full and active part in school life. At the time, masters could play for school teams against club sides and on 12th October 1911 he played for the School, alongside Basil Biggerton-Evans, in a rugby football match against 'Newport Thursdays'. In the following term's hockey matches he was one of four masters playing regularly for the team, Messrs Munns, Donaldson and Hill being the other three.

At the Athletic Sports on Saturday 30th March 1912, he had given the Under 16 Half-Mile second prize which was won by Trevor Akrill Jones - both were to die six years later in 1918. Clearly something of an all-round sportsman, John Robinson coached cricket throughout the 1912 season. He also played the occasional match such as on Saturday 11th May 1912 for the Reverend A.E. Donaldson's XI against the 1st XI, in which he scored two runs. In the autumn he kept up his interest in rugby football, not least in playing for the Old Boys on Tuesday 17th December against the 1st XV. Also playing for the Old Boys' team was David Harold Davies; playing for 1st XV were David Cuthbert Thomas, Frank Best and Geoffrey Boothby.

Apart from his academic work and school duties, John Robinson worked hard in hockey coaching alongside the Reverend Donaldson and Mr. Isitt as *The Breconian* of April 1913 recorded. On Saturday 5th April he acted as an official timekeeper at the Athletic Sports and in a repeat of the previous year, he gave second prize in the Under 16 Half-Mile, which was again won by Trevor Akrill Jones. Throughout the rest of 1913, John Robinson played cricket and then rugby football, both for and against the 1st XV. In fact on 13th December 1913 in a match against Crickhowell, he was one of the forwards alongside David Cuthbert Thomas and David Harold Davies. Behind them was Gordon Yendoll. At the end of the season *The Breconian* again thanked "Messrs. Lance, Donaldson, Robinson and Cryer, who have been indefatigable in their coaching and help during the past season".

John Robinson lived in College Hall, opposite the school gates (now the Llanfaes Diary) and seems to have enjoyed taking part in Old Boys events. He attended the Old Breconian Dinner held at Brecon on Friday 19th December 1913 where "By no means disheartened by the knowledge that the O.B. XV had been soundly trounced by the School earlier in the day, a good attendance sat down in the Castle Hotel and thoroughly enjoyed themselves." 45 Old Breconians attended the dinner, with "older and younger generations" well represented.

As is the life of a schoolmaster, 1914 saw the same round of assisting in games. Almost unbelievably, he repeated the giving of the second prize in the Under 16 Half-Mile to Trevor Akrill Jones for the third year in succession. There is also a mention of John Robinson playing golf in Master v School Singles and Foursomes matches. The summer term saw him coaching the 2nd Cricket XI as well as playing occasionally such as on Wednesday 13th May 1914 when he was part of Mr. Munn's XI against the School XI. Although making the highest score for his side with 17 runs, the team were no match for the School who won 156 runs to 55. The win was not surprising as David Cuthbert Thomas had knocked up 55 runs, David Harold Davies then added 30 and Trevor Akrill Jones scored 8 until he was caught out by John Robinson. It is perhaps worth noting that Euan Arnott was also playing in Mr. Munn's XI. Of the 22 players on the pitch that day, five would die in the conflict that was about to begin.

The dedication of the masters to assist and run games was frequently noted. In the autumn of 1914 The Breconian recorded that "Thanks are due to Mr. Cryer for his assistance to the 1st Game and to Mr. Robinson for much useful "whistle work" with the Junior sides. Without his aid the 2nd Game would have fared ill". He continued to turn out regularly for the Games sessions and was elected to the Games Committee.

Masters were versatile and, although the War Office could not be persuaded to register the Cadet Corps as an Officers Training Corps, John Robinson was one of three masters thanked "for the keenness they have displayed". He had "done stout work in the ranks of the Corps". His notional rank in the Corps was as a private.

The round of school sporting life continued. He played golf and was again the timekeeper in the Athletic Sports held on 7th April 1915. The following month, on 15th May, he played cricket for the Reverend Donaldson's XI, scoring 13 before being bowled out. On Saturday 22nd May and Monday 24th there was a two day fixture, School v Masters. It was a tight match with the Reverend Donaldson and Mr. Isitt scoring well but John Robinson scored 0 in the first innings and 3 in the second. The following month, on 5th June, he acted as best man on the marriage of Captain (Master, 1904-1914) and Mrs G. Lance at St Mary's, Brecon. The Archdeacon of Brecon officiated and was assisted by the Reverend Donaldson.

In his final term at Christ College, in the autumn of 1915, he was again on the Games Committee as well as being active in coaching. In reference to the latter, The Breconian recorded "Mr. Robinson once more devoted himself to the welfare of this game, and deserves the thanks of the School for his unselfish work". In the 'Cambridge Letter' published in The Breconian after he left at the end of 1915, the Old Breconians wish him luck and, intriguingly, "desire to know what he intends doing with his collection of statues".

Conscription was introduced by the Military Service Act, passed in March 1916. Clergymen, the medically unfit, some groups of industrial workers, and members of the teaching profession were to be exempt from military service. However, not wanting exemption, John Robinson voluntarily enlisted and became an instructor in the Royal Navy in early 1916. He was assigned to the Revenge Class Battleship HMS 'Royal Oak' and most likely saw action at the only major battleship engagement of the War, the Battle of Jutland (31st May to 1st June 1916). On Llandovery Day 1917 he visited the school before returning for duty. Unfortunately the following year he contracted flu. The 'Royal Oak' was anchored at Burntisland on the Firth of Forth but, despite receiving excellent medical care on shore, he died at the Royal Naval Hospital, South Queensbury, Scotland on 13th November 1918. At the time of his death, his address was given as 21 Kenbourne Road, Sheffield.

The Breconian published a heartfelt In Memoriam:

> The sudden death of Mr. Robinson at the very hour of peace and victory seems to us a very real tragedy. He loved peace and the daily routine of quiet duty and all the pleasant intercourse of School life; he gave all this up for duty's sake, always looking forward to the time when he could conscientiously return to it again. But at the moment when it became possible that his heart's desire would be granted, he had to answer a new call. Everyone in Brecon held him in respect and affection, and he too seemed to have a love for every part of it. He was so gentle, so industrious, so utterly unselfish that few perhaps realised how much hard effort it took on his part to make himself the valuable master that he surely was when he left.

> And his heart turned back to Brecon at every occasion; he made long journeys from the North to spend among us brief hours snatched from his scanty leave. Only last summer on Llandovery day he was here; and as he lay on the threshold of death he was often thinking and speaking (so a relative tells us) 'of his beloved Brecon'. We can ill afford (to lose) so faithful and affectionate a teacher and friend; we shall not readily find his like again.

Lieutenant John Stanley Robinson is buried at Queensferry Cemetery, South Lothian, Scotland and is remembered on the Christ College War Memorial.

Lieutenant Henry St John Saunders Jones
30th Punjabis

3RD AUGUST 1917 ~ AGED 22
Day Boy 1906-1910

Henry St John Saunders Jones, born on 24th June 1895, was another son of the cloth. His father, the Reverend David Saunders Jones was the Vicar of St David's, Brecon and then Vicar of Cantref. Henry joined Christ College as a Day Boy in September 1906 and was a contemporary of Frank Harrington Best.

Henry left Christ College at the age of 15 in July 1910, having coincided for two terms at school with his younger brother, David Willoughby Saunders Jones (Day Boy and School House 1910-1916). David was quite a sportsman and played for both the 1st Rugby Football XV and the 1st Cricket XI while at school. He later joined the Colonial Civil Service and was awarded the OBE for his work.

Henry, although of somewhat delicate health, also developed an interest in cricket and athletics and seems to have enjoyed both sports. In the summer of 1907 he is recorded as playing cricket and, although never gaining a permanent place in any of the teams, he was reported as a useful player in various matches. In athletics, he was an able runner and took a number of prizes over the years. At the Athletic Sports on Saturday 3rd April 1909 in the Under 14 150 yards race Henry took first prize, given by Mrs Morton, with a time of 20 and one-fifth seconds. The following year, on Monday 4th April 1910, he shared the winning of prizes with his younger brother, David: David took first place in the Under 12 100 yards and Henry took second place in the Under 15 100 yards; in the Under 16 High Jump, Henry came an equal third, whilst in the final heat of the Under 13 100 yards, David took second place.

When Henry left Christ College in the summer 1910 he had just turned 15. As it had become clear that "his interests lay in the workshop rather than the classroom", it is not surprising that he immediately started work training as a motor car engineer. He lived at home with his parents, two school teacher sisters (Elspeth Mary and Dulce Myfanwy) and his brother, David.

In September 1914, soon after the outbreak of war, 19 year old Henry joined the Brecknocks (The Brecknockshire Territorial Force Battalion of the South Wales Borderers) as a Private and went to India the following month along with Second Lieutenants Frank Best and Stephen Best. Henry served with them in Aden and India "where his skill as a motorist attracted his C.O.'s attention". Henry then took an officer training course and obtained a commission in the Indian Reserve of Officers, 15th November 1915. On 2nd February 1916 he resigned as Second Lieutenant, Indian Army Reserve of Officers in order to undergo a course of training at the Quetta Cadet College, passing out successfully. On 2nd July 1916 he was again commissioned as Second Lieutenant and attached to the 21st Punjabis on 2nd July 1916. On 29th June 1917 Henry, who was attached to the Duke of Cambridge's Own Infantry (Brownlow's Punjabis), was promoted to Lieutenant.

Henry had been sent to German East Africa to join the 30th Punjabis in December 1916. Here he saw action during the British Advance to Rufigi, when the 30th Punjabis acquitted themselves extremely well. From there, the Regiment went the 120 miles to Dar-es-Salem. On Monday July 23rd 1917 the 30th Punjabi Regiment left Dar-es-Salem. They encamped at Lindi on 25th July. On 29th July Henry left the camp to reconnoitre the land around and in front of the enemy lines. He returned having "got to know the ground well". On 3rd August Henry was killed whilst leading a column of troops to attack the enemy.

On Friday 10th August the Reverend and Mrs Saunders Jones received a telegram from the India Office announcing that their son Henry was missing in action. However, his death was confirmed very shortly afterwards. Some weeks later, the Reverend Saunders Jones received two letters. In the first, Colonel Murphy, Commander of the Regiment, wrote that Brigadier General O'Grady, commanding the Lindi Column, had asked for a "few picked scouts under a British Officer to go on a reconnaissance". Colonel Murphy continued:

> . . . I selected your son . . . during the night of 2nd/3rd August the regiment, guided by your son, who by this time had got to know the ground, marched to attack the enemy. On August 1st I had to go to hospital with sciatica, so I handed over the command temporarily to Captain Wilson. The enemy apparently heard our fellows coming their way through the dense bush, and collected around them in force, suddenly opening fire on them at a distance of only a few yards. As your son was guiding the battalion, and was therefore well up in the Front, it is probable he was among the first killed . . . in a short time, every single British officer who was with the regiment that day, except one who got separated, was either killed or wounded. Shortly after the fight your son's body was recovered and buried. I think it is certain that he was killed outright, and that the report that he died of wounds was a mistake on the part of the A.G.'s office at General Headquarters.

> I saw a great deal of your boy during my brief period of command and thought very highly of him. He was a very clever mechanic amongst other things, and most valuable to the regiment in explaining the mechanics of Lewis guns, machine guns, to the men. If he had lived I think he and I would have been great friends. These few details will, I am sure will be of great interest to you, though but poor consolation. Still, had he been my son I would feel as much pride as sorrow over his death, and I hope you will try and feel the same.

The second letter, dated 5th October, was from Colonel Ward, temporarily commanding the 30th Punjabis.

He wrote from hospital reiterating the build up to the surprise attack and added:

> It appears that the enemy became aware of our plans to attack on the 3rd, and owing to
> the extreme difficulty in reconnoitring in the dense bush we were unaware of their change
> of disposition of their troops; and they were able to concentrate on the point where my
> regiment was to operate and brought fire to bear on it from three sides . . . owing to the
> density of the bush it was difficult to keep up communication readily, and when all the
> officers, nearly, had been put out of action and the enemy were pressing heavily on three
> sides of us, it was found to be impossible to do anything else but retire . . . Your son was
> seen by some men to be wounded and immediately afterwards the enemy charged down,
> and it was impossible to help him. The German officers treated our wounded kindly, and
> you may be sure they did whatever was possible for your son . . . From what I can gather,
> your son was mortally wounded and nothing could have saved him, and he appears to
> have passed away within half an hour of receiving his wound. He was buried close to where
> he had fallen under a tree and a mark was put up to show whose grave was there. The
> Curator of military graves has been informed . . . Your son was one of the best officers I
> have had and I always felt that any work he was given to do would be done thoroughly
> well and conscientiously. He was always cheerful and happy, even during the very trying
> time we had in January and February last in the Rufiji area . . . hoping that this letter may
> bring you some little relief in your anxiety to know what occurred.

A third letter was received from the Reverend A.M. Jenkins, Chaplain to the Forces in East Africa. He revealed that in the surprise attack by overwhelming numbers Henry had been seen "fighting to the last with his revolver . . . (he was) wounded; but when he saw that the position was hopeless he gave orders for his men to retire, and to send out for him as soon as possible. He was last seen fighting gallantly though surrounded by the enemy . . . he died in a noble manner, giving his men the opportunity of saving themselves, though he could not get away himself." Another fellow officer wrote "His brother officers all deeply regret the loss of a gallant comrade, who was highly respected and loved by officers and men. By his coolness and pluck under fire he set a splendid example to his men, and at all times was a perfect example of a brave and fearless leader. His absence is very much felt by everyone, as he was most capable in the field and at all times displayed the spirit of a true gentleman".

The Breconian reported that Henry "was not one of the learned or distinguished among Breconians, but his war service and war sacrifice was no whit less than the greatest of them. He is another happy instance of how the call of duty finds all Brecon boys, without distinction, 'Ready, aye. Ready'!" The Breconian notes that Henry was killed on 12th August and a letter published in The Brecon County Times refers to the death on 13th August. Military records however confirm the death as killed in action in the Lindi District on 3rd August.

When the bodies of the fallen were being gathered into more formal cemeteries in the years after the war, relatives were given the opportunity to pay for more informal words to be added to the name, rank, regiment and regimental badge that was inscribed on all known graves. The Reverend and Mrs Saunders Jones had the following put on the headstone "Diligent in Business, Fervent in Spirit, Serving the Lord, Faithful unto Death".

Lieutenant Henry St John Saunders Jones is buried at Mookambika-Lindi and is remembered on the Christ College War Memorial.

Lieutenant Geoffrey Bernard Penberthy Shapland
17th Battalion Manchester Regiment
15TH NOVEMBER 1924 ~ AGED 26
Day Boy 1910-1912

Geoffrey Bernard Penberthy Shapland was born on 5th March 1898, the eldest son of Albert Henry and Jessie Shapland (née Dillow). His sister, Constance Frances, was born in 1900 and his younger brother, Eric Albert Penberthy, was born in 1912. Geoffrey Shapland joined Christ College in 1910 as a Day Boy and left school in 1912 at the age of 14 to join his father's tailoring business. His young brother later joined Christ College as a Day Boy (1922-1929).

A.H. Shapland was a well-known businessman in Brecon who employed a staff of tailors and dressmakers. From his premises at 5 The Struet he supplied tailored garments to the local gentry and tailored uniforms to the South Wales Borderers, the regiment which Geoffrey originally joined in 1914 and with which his brother served in the Second World War.

As is so often the case for those who left school before the Sixth Form, there is no record of Geoffrey in *The Breconian* and the first mention of him is in the list of Old Breconians 'Serving with the Colours' published in December 1914. One of 137 men who were already with the colours by Christmas 1914, Geoffrey had enlisted on 3rd September 1914. Adding a year to his age on his attestation papers, he was two days short of 16 years and 6 months old. Though there are anecdotal reports of other Old Breconians being younger when they signed up, Geoffrey B.P. Shapland is almost certainly the youngest Old Breconian to have enlisted. He joined the 'Brecknocks', the Brecknockshire Territorial Force Battalion of the South Wales Borderers, from which he obtained a commission into the 10th Reserve South Staffords in 1915.

Later gazetted Temporary Second Lieutenant to the 17th Battalion Manchester Regiment on 21st September 1915 at the age of 17, he entered France in July 1916 at the age of 18. The 17th Battalion Manchester Regiment was originally a Pals Battalion (2nd City) and its numbers were much depleted in the first few days of the Battle of the Somme. By 3rd July 1916, 350 of the 900 soldiers in the Battalion who had begun the attack were killed, wounded or missing. Within days of their heavy losses, the Battalion was ordered to the Front again, with assaults on Trones Wood on 10th July 1916, then Guillemont on the 30th July 1916.

After a period of rest followed by quieter service in the front lines, the 17th Battalion took part in an assault on German positions north of the village of Flerson 12th October 1916. Very little ground was gained in the attack and progress had to be conceded in the face of relentless German machine gun fire. Casualties were high and the Battalion lost 213 men; only a few of those who survived managed to reach their own trenches before nightfall and those who did not had to seek shelter in shell holes until cover of darkness.

For the rest of the year the Battalion remained in one of the quieter sectors around Bellacourt. Having already been wounded in September 1916 but still with his Battalion, Geoffrey was concussed by the impact of a shell early in December 1916 at Blairville. The shell had burst in a communication trench and Geoffrey was struck by shrapnel, which cut through his tunic jacket and shirt. "Shaking and trembling", he was later accompanied by another Officer to Headquarters where he was severely affected by the impact of another shell attack after which he suffered palpitations, headaches and sleeplessness.

Despite his physical injuries and apparent mental trauma, Geoffrey continued on duty for over three months but was forced to leave France at the end of February 1917 on Special Leave. He was ordered to attend a Medical Board in Brecon on 31st March1917, where it was recognised that he was showing neurasthenic symptoms that required "indoor hospital treatment". A later Medical Board found that he was unfit for active duty, caused by "shell shock" and, "in need of a long rest", he was sent to the Officers' Convalescent Hospital in Chester.

Although eligible for the Silver War Badge in July 1917, Geoffrey was gazetted Temporary Lieutenant in September 1917 and served with 3rd (Reserve) Battalion Manchester Regiment at Cleethorpes. While there, he applied for transfer to the Royal Flying Corps, clearly hopeful of re-joining active service in a different capacity. This never came about and following another Medical Board in February 1918 he was admitted to Wellesley House for further convalescence. He was declared permanently unfit with a diagnosis of 'DAH' - Disordered Action of the Heart – a term that was commonly chosen to give the impression of a physical abnormality that would explain the palpitations experienced by soldiers, like Geoffrey, who presented with neurasthenic symptoms.

The Medical Board at Wellesley House judged that his disability was contracted before war service, as a result of a history of rheumatic fever, and that his condition was aggravated by but not attributable to military service conditions. With affecting irony, the Medical Board report of 11th March 1918 mistakenly records his age as 27 but he had, in fact, turned 20 just a few days before. As a result of the Board's findings, Temporary Lieutenant Geoffrey Shapland was officially "discharged through wounds". *The London Gazette* recorded that he had relinquished his commission on account of ill-health contracted on active service and was granted the honorary rank of Lieutenant. However, the judgement of the Wellesley House Medical Board that his disability was not attributable to military service had a significant impact on his pension.

He returned home and married Gertrude Rees and they had three children. He continued to work in his father's business, though suffering bouts of illness. Later newspaper reports refer to blood poisoning as well as to a head wound but he had also undergone operations for "nasal trouble", which were believed to be a result of his war injuries. A further operation was expected but pain and depression continued to affect his health, aggravated by the injustice of receiving a very limited pension.

On 15th November 1924 Geoffrey was found dead in the cutting room of his father's tailoring workshop. Details of his death and the subsequent inquest were published in the local newspaper. The "sad story of a young man's sufferings as a result of his war experience" was revealed, with his parents telling the inquest of his repeated mental breakdowns. The inquest jury returned a verdict of "Suicide during a fit of temporary insanity," and added that "in their opinion deceased's condition was due to the injuries received in the war".

The findings of the various Medical Boards were frustratingly indecisive and inconclusive but the local community accepted the effect of war on one of their young men. Genuine sympathy for the family's loss is recorded in the inquest report, and is equally apparent in the messages attached to the many floral tributes received and printed in the funeral report. Geoffrey's younger brother, Eric, was a pupil in Christ College at the time and *The Breconian* published an obituary which similarly expressed "deepest sympathy to his parents and his young brother, also a Breconian, on the sad effect of war injuries which led to his tragic death".

The service in the church at Brecon Cemetery was conducted by the Christ College Chaplain, the Reverend Donaldson, who would have known Geoffrey as a schoolboy. The account of his funeral in the local paper, *The Brecon and Radnor Express*, describes the large attendance of businessmen and personal friends, and that "along the route to the Cemetery blinds were drawn or shutters erected" as a mark of respect. Though much public sympathy is evident in these reports, the family was profoundly affected by Geoffrey's death. Partly to alleviate its financial effects, the children were sent to board at the Warehousemen, Clerks and Drapers Schools in Surrey from the age of 6. The impact of being sent away to school after the death of their father was devastating, and it was recalled with much sadness by the children in later years.

In many respects the life of Lieutenant Geoffrey B.P. Shapland encompasses much of the mythology of the First World War - enthusiastic enlistment while underage, action in the muddy trenches of the Somme, injury, convalescence, and a return home to marry a local girl. His tragic death is also a reminder that many young men returned home deeply scarred by their experiences, and that their war and the effects of war experienced by their families did not end with the Armistice.

Lieutenant Geoffrey Bernard Penberthy Shapland is buried at Brecon Cemetery. In 2015 his name was permanently added to the Roll of Honour read on Remembrance Sunday at Christ College.

Captain Charles Owen Spencer Smith
1/16th Battalion, London Regiment
(Queen's Westminster Rifles)
attached 21st Battalion, King's Royal Rifle Corps
(Yeoman Rifles)

3RD AUGUST 1917 ~ AGED 37
Hostel 1893-1898

Charles Owen Spencer Smith was born in 1880 in Norwich, the oldest of six children (four boys and two girls). His father, also called Charles, was the Secretary Receiver of five endowed schools: United Westminster Schools and Grey Coat Hospital School. His mother was Charlotte Owen Spencer Smith (née Gaze). In 1891 the family were living at 17 Cheriton Place, Folkestone, although very shortly after they moved to London. Just before the war they were living at 51 Palace Street, Westminster. During the war the family moved to The Dower House, Woldhurstlea, Ifield, Sussex.

Charles joined the Hostel in 1893 and stayed at Christ College until 1898. His brother, Philip, was in the Hostel from 1896 until 1901. Their younger brother, Martin, joined the Hostel in 1904 until 1909. As well as attending the same school, the three 'Hostelites' were all commissioned into the same regiment. From this trio, only Philip survived. Their brother, Arnold Patrick ('A.P.') Spencer Smith, did not attend Christ College.

At the Speech Day of Saturday 25th July 1895, held in "the Big Schoolroom", 'C.O.' as Charles became known was awarded the Form III Prize for English and Science. That Christmas his brother, Philip, took a significant part in the "new Serio-comico-magico-historical burlesque opera entitled 'Alfred and the Grate' (which) certainly deviated far enough from the sober paths of history to deserve this Aristophanic Appellation". Penned by Messrs W.S. Borrow (Master 1894-1899) and R.B. Lattimer (Master 1895-1904), the 'opera' was a huge success and much enjoyed by players and audience alike.

Philip clearly had a great singing voice and also performed solos in Chapel as well as in various entertainments and at Christmas in 1897, he was joined by Charles as part of the 'Chorus of Jurymen' in *Trial by Jury*. Charles was also a member of the School Choir and, like his brother, seemed to enjoy singing.

Though "not physically strong" and not permitted to "take violent exercise", Charles was a member of the Cadet Force and had been promoted from Private to Corporal in May 1896. In the autumn term, he was made up to Sergeant. Despite his ill-health, he "more or less surreptitiously entered" the Putting the (16lb) Weight at the Athletic Sports of 1897 and came equal first. The Cadet Corps Annual Inspection, by Colonel Browne V.C., took place on 16th July 1897. The Colonel "was very well pleased with the smart turn out of the corps ... He wished the Cadet Corps, as well as the Volunteer movement in general, to be taken more seriously, with a view to greater usefulness in defence of Queen and country". The Senior Sergeant was Charles Spencer Smith who was congratulated on doing "his evolutions very creditably". Charles rounded off the year by becoming a School Prefect.

Early in the summer term of 1898, Charles was promoted to Lieutenant in the Cadet Corps. At the same time, Philip was promoted from Private to Lance Corporal (reaching Sergeant rank in the autumn of 1899). Unfortunately, the Cadets were told they could not go to Annual Camp with the Volunteers as their camp was in the middle of examinations, and the Public School Camp was full. Neither could a proper Field Day be arranged so the Cadet Corps organised their own mini Field Day. Thus on 3rd June Lieutenant Spencer Smith successfully defended the School Buildings "against an attack over the cricket field ... the defending force were excellently posted under cover of the walls, with an outpost in the open and a detachment occupying the Hostel".

At Speech Day 1897 Charles had received his Lower Certificate in English and Science (the latter First Class). He also gained First Class (as did Philip) in Additional Mathematics. At Speech Day, held on Tuesday 26th July 1898, both Charles and Philip received Science Prizes. Charles also received his Higher Certificate in what the Headmaster described as the "best lists we have had since 1891". During this final term Charles also played for the 2nd XI cricket team and won the Open Diving Competition held in Newton Pool as part of the Swimming Sports.

On leaving school Charles, who at school had displayed "more than an ordinary capacity for drawing", started his training in Architecture by becoming an articled pupil. On Wednesday 17th December 1906 he and (as a guest) his brother, Arnold Patrick ('A.P.') attended the Old Boys' Dinner at the Gaiety Theatre, London. He also maintained his military connections after leaving Christ College and the Cadet Corps, obtaining a commission as Second Lieutenant in the 13th Middlesex (Queen's Westminster) Volunteer Rifle Corps on 6th December 1899. In the 1908 Volunteer Army reforms, the 13th Middlesex were renamed the 16th Battalion London Regiment (Queen's Westminster Rifles).

In 1911 Charles was working in a surveyor's office and still living at home. On 14th March 1914, a practice mobilization of the Regiment had occurred. When war was declared for real, Charles, Martin and Philip, all in the same Regiment, were mobilized. The Regiment moved to Leverstock Green, near Hemel Hempstead, and landed in France on 3rd November 1914. In February 1915 they were in the Hallencourt area south of Abbeville (Somme). The Regiment was involved in trench warfare as well as a number of battles. On 1st July 1916 they took part in the attack on Gommecourt, which aimed to remove a German salient and draw German reserves away from the main area of action. In this action Philip, who was the 1st Battalion's Bombing officer, was severely wounded and taken prisoner. There then followed the Battles of Ginchy (9th September), Fleurs-Courcelette (15th-22nd September), Morval (25th-28th September), and Transloy Ridges (1st-8th October).

However, Charles had some time earlier been attached to the 21st Battalion King Royal Rifle Corps (Yeoman Rifles) and was operating with them near the Belgium border when he died on 3rd August 1917. He had entrusted to a clergyman a message to his father that he was "not dangerously ill". Unhappily, the message ultimately conveyed by the Clergyman was rather different. He wrote to Charles' parents:

> *I know you will be glad to hear how splendidly your son did before he was wounded. I was*
> *at another dressing station that night, and an officer came in there and almost the first*
> *words he said were 'Padre, old Spencer Smith was splendid, quite magnificent.*

The Breconian, in recounting the above, continued "When our time comes to go, may we all go out with a record as good as that! To his family we offer our respectful sympathy, while we hope his school may be allowed to share with them the pride they must feel for one who did his duty so nobly and well.

Charles, "A singularly gentle and amiable fellow" who was "a good influence wherever he went", was the third of the sons to die. 'A.P' had died of scurvy while attached to Shackleton's Imperial Trans-Antarctic Expedition of 1914 to 1917 as Chaplain and photographer. Deployed in putting in supply depots across the Great Ice Barrier, he was part of the ill-fated Ross Sea Party and died on 9th March 1916. His youngest brother, Martin Spencer Smith, had been killed in action on 10th September 1916. Philip survived the war after being taken prisoner at Gommencourt in July 1916.

Charles Owen Spencer Smith is buried in Godewaersvelde British Cemetery, France. He is remembered on the Althorne War Memorial, Essex as well as on the Christ College War Memorial.

Second Lieutenant Martin Spencer Smith
1/16th Battalion, London Regiment
(Queen's Westminster Rifles)

10TH SEPTEMBER 1916 ~ AGED 25
Hostel 1904-1909

Martin was born on 27th June 1891 in Westminster, the youngest of the four brothers. He was the last of the three brothers to attend Christ College and joined the Hostel at Easter 1904. He stayed until July 1909. Following the lead of his brothers, Martin was clearly a singer and in the autumn he arrived, is noted as singing a song on 12th November in the Hostel social evening. On Thursday 19th December 1905 *HMS Pinafore* was "put on the boards of King Henry's Theatre, Christ College". Martin played Josephine, the daughter of Captain Corcoran, played by Cecil Broadbent. His duet, with a fellow actor, "brought down the house". The reviewer stated that the young actor

> *… shone as a star of great brilliancy, both in acting and singing. He has a very sweet treble voice of considerable power and compass, perhaps the best treble voice we have had at Christ College for some time. He was delightfully distinct in his enunciation, and his singing all through was clear and full of verve. His best effort was his rendering of the recitative and aria, The hours creep on apace. These he gave with much dramatic effect and with correct musical intonation, the solo being received with the greatest enthusiasm.*

Being also something of a keen sportsman, as was his brother Philip, Martin entered the Athletic Sports on Monday 2nd April 1906 and came second in the 220 yards Under 15 Handicap, having shown "good form" in the race. On Tuesday 18th December 1906 he again took to the boards, this time in Sheridan's *Trip to Scarborough*. In this comedy Martin played, in the words of the reviewer, "a bouncing Miss Hoyden". Charles Piper Hazard played 'the Jeweller'.

At the Athletic Sports 1907 Martin ran in the 220 yards Open Handicap and won. He also won the Under

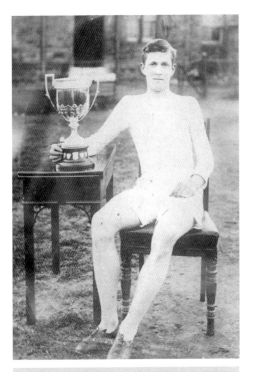

M. Spencer Smith: Winner of the Challenge Cup 1908

16 High Jump as well as coming third in the Half-Mile Open Handicap, second in the Under 16 Long Jump, and first in the Quarter-Mile Under 16 Handicap with a time of 65 and 4/5ths seconds. In the summer term he played cricket and was one of the Reverend Donaldson's XI in a match against the 1st XI on 11th May; though his side lost, the Reverend Donaldson managed to take five wickets for 19 runs. Martin also turned out for the 2nd XI.

In the autumn of 1907 Martin proved himself to be a good shot on the Cadet Rifle Course, coming first in the scores. In the following Easter he was promoted from Corporal to Sergeant in the newly restyled Christ College Cadets ("Mr. Haldane's new Territorial Army came into existence (and we) have ceased to be any longer 1 CC IVB SWB.").

In the Athletic Sports on Monday 6th April 1908 Martin secured a close run victory for the Challenge Cup, which was in the balance for quite some time during the day:

Spencer Smith, by his splendid victory in the Quarter, secured a decided advantage in the morning, an advantage which he followed up by winning the High Jump in the afternoon, after a breathlessly exciting struggle. The two points which put him ahead were picked up in the Hurdle race. The closeness of the fight may easily be seen from the fact that only eight points separated the winner and the fourth competitor.

Martin had achieved the Cup by winning the 220 yards Open Handicap, coming second in the Long Jump (Open), third in the Hurdle Race (Open), first in the High Jump (Open) and first in the Quarter-Mile (Open) - a race where the last part was "fought out inch by inch". The Cup was presented that afternoon in the Big Schoolroom.

In the summer term of 1908 Martin also continued to play for the 2nd XI, and achieved his highest score of 15 on 27th June - his 17th birthday - in a match against Brecon Sports Club 2nd XI. The much anticipated 2nd XI match against Llandovery on Saturday 11th July was not played due to bad weather.

The autumn of 1908 saw Martin selected for the 1st XV, and his end of term critique must have been reassuring and pleasing: "After varied experiences among the backs (he) settled down to capital work in the scrum. Follows up fast, tackles well, and is good in the throw out from touch". He and fellow team mate Benjamin Leeder played a number of matches against such teams as 'Merthyr Thursdays' and 'Cynthlais Rovers' as well as against Monmouth Grammar School. The annual Llandovery Match on Wednesday 18th November ended in a well earned draw (3-3) with each side scoring a try. The final match of the term, against the Old Breconians, was played on the last day of term, December 22nd. Martin was also appointed School Prefect and won the Glanusk Challenge Shooting Cup. The year ended in the usual way, with Martin treading the boards in the Christmas Theatricals. The play chosen was Coleman's *Heir-at-Law* and Martin played Henry Morland ("with due decorum") alongside David Mansel Griffiths who played Kenrick.

In the following spring Martin played for the 1st Hockey XI. On one occasion, in a match against Brecon Sports Club, it was noted that Martin "occasionally adopted somewhat unsafe fancy tactics". Thus his end of season critique reads "Hits hard and well, and has plenty of pace and dash. Must beware of unsound fancy strokes; but has done good service in defence". He also ran in the Steeplechase in March, and came "a fairly distant fourth". He played in the Fives Doubles and Singles Competitions, and was knocked out only in the semi-final of the latter. At the Athletic Sports of 3rd April 1909, Martin narrowly lost the Challenge Cup. He came first in the Long Jump (Open) with a jump of 17 feet 5½ inches, first in the Quarter-Mile (Open), first in the High Jump (Open) and third in the One Mile (Open), where he "did well ... after a tiring day".

In the summer term, Martin was selected for the 1st Cricket XI. The team played a number of matches, including against Hereford Cathedral School, where the somewhat humorous match report included the comment that a player "placed his leg in front of the wicket and forgot that he possessed a bat!" In the annual Llandovery match, played on Saturday 3rd July 1909, the Christ College XI won a "very substantial victory". Martin's end of season critique reads "A better bat than his scores suggest. His defence is good, and he can cut; but does not deal faithfully with the over-pitched ball. Much improved in the field". Martin also played for the 2nd XI as well as in House Matches. In the latter competition it was noted that now the Day Boys, who were for the first time a separate team, did not have the help of Mr. Morton's boys, so they would have "to fight their own battles ... (and) the prospect of doing so will urge some of them to take part more regularly in School games!"

After leaving Christ College, Martin went on to study Agriculture. His aunt, Mrs H.D. Hunter, lived in Donavan, Saskatchewan, and Martin emigrated to become a farmer in that part of Canada. After war was declared, Martin joined the Canadian Forces on 17th April 1915, being attached to the 46th Battalion (South Saskatchewan). On his attestation papers he claimed six years with the OTC attached to the South Wales Borderers, a clear reference to Christ College's Cadet Force. The 46th Battalion had been formed on 1st February 1915. On 28th May 1915 the Battalion moved to Camp Sewell, Manitoba and left Halifax bound for England on 18th October, arriving at Plymouth on 30th October.

On arrival in England, Corporal Martin Spencer Smith requested a transfer to enable him to join his brothers as an officer in the Queen's Westminster Rifles. Thus, on 9th January 1916, Martin was commissioned as Second Lieutenant and joined them in the Somme where he spent time in training and trench warfare. A few months after arriving, Martin survived the attack on Gommecourt on 1st July 1916 which saw 11 officers and just over 700 men killed or wounded (out of a total of 44 officers and 922 other ranks), and in which his brother, Philip (Hostel 1896-1901) was severely wounded and taken prisoner. During August, having received considerable reinforcements, the Regiment found itself having to contend with "A certain amount of hostile whizz-bangs ... and Bosch machine-guns" whilst in the Bienvillers area.

At the end of the month several days training were followed by a Brigade march to Happy Valley, just outside

Bray. On 9th September 1916 the Brigade attacked into Bouleaux Wood, as part of the Battle of the Somme. Fierce fighting ensued at 1am on 10th September and orders were received to clear an enemy trench on the south east side of the wood before dawn. However, the night was very dark, shells were pouring in and communications could only be made by runner - an hour each way. As "the maps (were) known not to be accurate", the attack did not take place until 7am. Fierce gun and shell fire resulted in Martin and four fellow officers, all second Lieutenants, being killed and 303 other ranks dead, wounded or missing. The Battalion Diary records "From start to finish we had, as it turned out, no chance". Martin's body was never recovered.

Second Lieutenant Martin Spencer Smith is remembered on the Thiepval Memorial and on the Althorne War Memorial, Essex as well as on the Christ College War Memorial.

Second Lieutenant David Cuthbert Thomas
3rd Battalion, Royal Welsh Fusiliers

18TH MARCH 1916 ~ AGED 20
Hostel 1906-1914

David Cuthbert Thomas was born on 16th June 1895 in the small village of Llanedi, Carmarthenshire where his father, The Reverend Evan Thomas, was the local Vicar. David joined the Hostel in September 1906 along with Henry St John Saunders Jones and Benjamin Leeder (who was rejoining the school).

The first record of David appears in the summer of 1910 and, not surprisingly given his later passion for the game, the 15 year old played "with some success" for the 4th XI. He is also noted as having scored 24 runs in the House Match against School House N-Z. His academic start was less successful though as David fell one short of achieving the requisite five passes to obtain his Lower Certificate in the examinations of 1910.

In early 1911 David played for the Hostel in the House Fives Cup and the team beat the Day Boys in the final. In the Singles, David made it through to the third round before being beaten. In the following term he played cricket for the 2nd XI, often opening the batting. In one match, played on 5th July 1911 against Brecon Sports Club 2nd XI, David "went in first and was out last", batting "very prettily for 31" - helping Christ College to win by 18 runs. He also played occasionally for the 3rd XI, as did Basil Biggerton-Evans, and finished the year by achieving his Lower Certificate with five passes in Latin, Greek, Arithmetic, Scripture and History in the summer examinations.

In the autumn of 1911 the 16 year old David was selected to play for the 1st XV. Alongside him again in the team was Basil Biggerton-Evans. Though still relatively young, David was a useful player. In the second match of the season against 'Newport Extras' on Saturday 7th October, David had to leave the field with an injured shoulder and, from this point to the end, "Newport had all their own way". The result was that the School XV was "hopelessly beaten".

He played in the Fives Competition again in spring 1912 but was knocked out of the semi-final. He was selected for the 1st Cricket XI in the summer term and made a number of "useful scores". He was, his end of term critique reported, "a most promising bat... (with) a nice style and an excellent back-stroke." In the autumn of 1912 David again played for the 1st XV, alongside Geoffrey Boothby, in what was described as a most disappointing season. His end of term critique noted that he had not "learnt to shove straight in the scrum" but, at 9st 7lbs, he was a "very light forward" and "excellent tackler". In the same term David was made House Prefect and Editor of *The Breconian*.

1913 saw the usual round of sports, starting with the Fives Competitions in which he and his partner came second in the House Cup. The summer cricket season saw David again playing "some useful innings" for the 1st XI. He opened the batting for the team which resoundingly defeated Llandovery on Wednesday 25th June 1913. The Llandovery match of 1913 was a great occasion. The Headmaster had granted a day's holiday on the day of the match in recognition of the "elevation to the Bench" of Old Breconian J.R. Atkin (School House 1879-1885). The holiday meant that boys of all ages were able to travel to Llandovery "by brake, motor and bicycle" and a large number went to watch the match. The occasion was most opportune as Judge Atkin still held the record for the highest individual score in a Llandovery match (94 runs made in 1895).

That autumn David played as a forward for the 1st XV alongside Gordon Yendoll and David Harold Davies. He was still relatively light but a "fair player", and clearly getting taller. His end of season critique reports that he made "the most of his height in the line-out" and refers again to his tackling skills, though the annual Llandovery

1913 Rugby Football XV including D.C. Thomas (seated far right) and D.H. Davies (middle row standing second from right) and J.G. Yendoll (seated on ground left)

THE TOLL OF WAR

match was a disappointing loss to Christ College. In the same term he went up to Oxford "Schol. Hunting" - visiting Colleges to prepare for a later application for a Scholarship. He remained an Editor of *The Breconian* and was, by now, a School Prefect.

In the spring of 1914 David was again School Prefect and Editor. He also played left-back for the 1st Hockey XI and was described as "A much improved player who uses his stick with great skill. Tackles well, but is apt to foul. Rather inclined to overdo dribbling". He also entered the Fives Competition, though the Hostel missed out on winning the House Cup. At the Athletic Sports on Monday 6th April, he gained a very creditable third place in the Open High Jump. On Friday 6th June 1914 Judge Atkin, whose elevation to the Bench had been celebrated the year before, made his first official visit to Brecon for the Summer Assizes. An illuminated address, signed by the three School prefects including David, was presented to him by his old school.

During that summer term, his final term at School, David played for the 1st XI again, alongside Trevor Akrill Jones. In one notable match against Mr. Munns' XI on Wednesday 13th May, David scored 55 runs in a 91 opening partnership. In that match he also bowled 12 overs, taking 4 wickets. In a House Match against the Day Boys, David scored 113. When the 1st XI played the Masters later in May, David scored 42 runs before being caught by Mr. Lance from a ball by Mr. Munns. In his end of term critique he was reported as "A sound rather than a brilliant bat" and "an erratic bowler". The same report notes his "brilliant" fielding but another account wryly observes that he was "rather more showy than a real good fieldsman needs to be"!

At the end of the summer term David successfully gained his Higher Certificate and left school on the eve of the declaration of war. He immediately volunteered and joined the 4th Public Schools Battalion, Royal Fusiliers, one of four battalions raised on 11th September 1914. David joined them at Epsom for training and, early in 1915, he was sent to Cambridge for officer training. It was there that David, who had just turned 19, shared rooms with a fellow cadet, the 28 year old Siegfried Sassoon. David had penned some light verses whilst at school and Siegfried showed David some of his already privately printed work. On 20th May 1915 David was promoted to Second Lieutenant and attached to 3rd Battalion, Royal Welsh Fusiliers, a training unit that had just moved to Litherland, near Liverpool. Nine days later he was joined by his friend Second Lieutenant Siegfried Sassoon. In late August David went on leave to his home in Llanedi, Pontardulais.

Both David and Siegfried were then attached to the 1st Battalion, Royal Welsh Fusiliers in France. Robert von Ranke Graves was also an officer in the Royal Welsh Fusiliers and they all became firm friends. At Fricourt, twenty miles north-east of Amiens, the night of 18th/19th March 1916 was to be deadly for three of the officers in the Battalion, one of whom was David. Robert Graves later wrote about that night and remembered on 17th March 1916 five officers meeting at a trench junction and one saying that in all the many casualties recently, no officer had been hit. David then shouted "Touch wood" but only Graves had any on him, a pencil! David, apparently with a cold and rather fed up, was moving up with C Company the following night; he was overtaken by Robert Graves leading A Company, whose job it would be to pile 3,000 or so sandbags along the front of trench.

At around 10.30pm on the night of the 18th March 1916 David, who was in front of his trench repairing wire, was hit in the throat by a bullet. He was able to walk to the dressing station but, despite the doctor telling him not to raise his head, David attempted to give an orderly a letter for the young lady to whom he was engaged and, in doing so, suddenly choked. The doctor, who happened to be a throat specialist, performed an emergency operation but David died very quickly from his wounds. Within a few hours, two more of the five officers who had been talking to David Thomas and Robert Graves were killed.

Robert Graves and Siegfried Sassoon attended David's battlefield funeral, which took place amidst the chatter of a loud machine gun and a falling shell. Such was that the shock and anger at David's death that Siegfried 'Mad Jack' Sassoon (noted Graves) became committed to looking for Germans to kill. He also took dangerous risks as if daring death to kill him too. One such exploit in July 1916, in the same area as David died, saw Sassoon spending an hour and a half under shell and rifle fire bringing in wounded. The action earned Sassoon the Military Cross but there is little doubt that David's death contributed to Sassoon later putting pen to paper in the 'Declaration against the War' that led to him being sent to Craiglockhart Hospital.

Ten days before David's death, Sassoon had written a poem about him entitled *The Subaltern*. He appears again in The Last Meeting and A Letter Home. Robert Graves wrote several poems about David, including *Not Dead* and *David and Goliath*.

The Breconian published its own tribute to David in April 1916:

D.C.T.

Since you were here two years have sped,
But you're remembered still;
Your memory has never fled,
Nor yet it will.

You trod the muddy football-field
On many a hard fought day;
'Twas then you learned to scorn to yield
In grim affray

We've seen you batting, calm and cool,
When runs were coming fast;
In a greater game, for Country and School,
You fall at last.

Rememb'ring what you were and did,
To you, who fighting fell,
Breconians, past and present, bid
A last farewell.

David Cuthbert Thomas also reappears in later literary works, most notably as 'Dick Tiltwood' in Sassoon's *Memoirs of a Fox-Hunting Man*. Graves wrote about him in *Good-Bye to All That*. 'Thompson' in Bernard Adams'

Nothing of Importance: A Record of Eight Months at the Front with a Welsh Battalion is also most likely to be based on David.

Second Lieutenant David Cuthbert Thomas is buried in Point 110 New Military Cemetery, Fricourt. He is also remembered on the Pontardulais Memorial and the War Memorial at Llanedi as well as on the War Memorial at Christ College.

Private David John Thomas
2nd/5th Battalion, Loyal North Lancashire Regiment
26TH FEBRUARY 1917 ~ AGED 19
School House 1912-1916

David, or 'D.J.' as he was affectionately known, was born at Porth on 9th August 1897. His parents were John Rees and Mary Ann Thomas. He and his younger brothers, Michael Glanffrwd (School House 1912-1915) and Gwilym Caledfryn (School House 1912-1916), entered School House together in September 1912. At the time of entry, the boys' father ran the Eagle Hotel, Ynyshir in the Rhondda.

All three boys were noted athletes and David John was a 'distinguished' member of all three teams. He won his Rugby Football Colours in 1914/15 and his Hockey Colours in 1915. He was also a "useful" member of the 1st Cricket XI in 1915.

His sporting promise was evident early. In his first Athletics Sports on Saturday 5th April 1913, David John came equal first in the Under 16 100 yards in the morning and second in the Under 16 220 yards in the afternoon. Also gaining first place in the Under 16 Long Jump, he went on to win second place in the Under 16 Challenge Cup for the day's events. In the Athletics Sports in the following April, David John came third in the Long Jump held in the morning and equal second in the 100 yards Open in the afternoon. Throughout that long hot pre-war summer, he played cricket for the 3rd XI and, at the end of the summer term on Prize Day, he received the Division III Science Prize.

In the autumn of 1914 David John had several good rugby football games. His speed was clearly an asset to the team, though he seems to have been inconsistent in his performance. The report for the match against Monmouth Grammar School, played on 18th November, records David John making a "fast 30 yards dash". His quick running gave the Llandovery XV "some concern" later in the month, though the Llandovery side managed to win 0-7 away at Brecon. The end of season critique offers a fuller report: "Speedy and often resolute in his running, but not sufficiently resourceful. Owing to bad sight is terribly weak in taking a pass. Sound in defence and kicking".

In the spring of 1915 David John played on the outside right for the 1st Hockey XI. Described as "the best attacking player among the forwards", he was known to be "fast and dashing" on the hockey pitch. Renowned for his bursts of speed, it was not surprising that at the Athletic Sports on held on Wednesday 7th April 1915, he came second in the Long Jump (Open) and won the 100 yards (Open) with a time of 11 and 2/5ths seconds. It was a "distinctly good" time after "a splendidly contested struggle". The points he earned meant that he came second in the Senior Challenge Cup.

In the summer term of 1915 he played cricket for the 1st XI where he is recorded as having "little pretension to style but watches the ball closely and knows how to hit a bad one". Described as "hardworking in the field", he also played well for the 2nd XI, scoring 40 in a match against Brecon County School on Wednesday 19th May 1915.

In the autumn of 1915 David John was elected as Captain of Rugby Football and the XV of 1915 was regarded by the School as being one of the best ever. 'D.J.' was credited with much of this, owing to "his vigorous example and highly effective three-quarter play". At the end of the season he was congratulated by Reverend Donaldson for the "vigorous efficiency of his captaincy". The key match of the season took place on Wednesday 17th November when Christ College played against Monmouth. It was the first time the match had been played at the Christ College ground and 'D.J.' and his team won 25 to 6.

The Llandovery Match was played away under severe wet weather conditions on Wednesday 1st December and David John made many desperate attempts to score. The team fought hard to win, with one of the team being carried off with concussion after "being knocked out in checking a rush". The match was a draw and David John wrote a letter to *The Breconian* in December 1915 to thank the many who had sent letters and telegrams after the Llandovery draw as well as after the Monmouth victory. His end of season critique summarised his qualities as captain: "A good captain who inspires confidence, and set a splendid example to the side". The captaincy brought with it a seat on the prestigious Games Committee and, as well as being captain of a successful side, he was also made a Prefect; the autumn of 1915 was undoubtedly a happy time for 'D.J.'

'D.J.' continued his sporting life throughout the spring of 1916. He played again for the 1st Hockey XI (in which he "Only falls short of real excellence by an obstinate indifference to the off-side rule") and continued too as a member of the Games Committee. The last mention of his sporting achievements are at the Athletic Sports on Monday 10th April 1916 when he gained second place in Putting the Weight and second in the Long Jump.

David John left Christ College shortly before his 19th birthday. Soon afterwards he enlisted with the Territorials (Loyal North Lancashire Regiment) at Brecon. He was deemed upon examination fit enough to join the Army and joined the 2nd/5th Battalion, Loyal North Lancashire Regiment. After training, the Battalion arrived in France on 9th February 1917.

David John reached the front line on 25th February but was killed the next day by a shell which landed on his trench.

The Breconian of April 1917 noted shock at the news that one so recently at school had been killed. A poem was published in his memory.

Can this be true?
Can he, who few short months ago we saw
Excelling all upon the field or track,
Can be swallowed up by Death's wide maw?
And will he ne'er come back?

Can this be true?
We scarce can credit the fell news that he
Who only lately shouldered soldiers' pack
Is now so soon from earthly cares set free,
And never will come back.

'Tis but too true,
His memory is with us still so clear;
Kind fate spared him, from torture of pain's wrack,
He lies out in that shell-strewn plain so drear,
He never will come back.

Of his fellow players in the 1913/14, 1914/15 and 1915/16 rugby football seasons, David Cuthbert Thomas (18th March 1916) and Euan Arnott (23rd September 1916) had already been killed in the trenches of Flanders. Three others (Trevor Akrill Jones, Frank James and Sydney Lewis) would die in the final months of the war.

Private David John Thomas is buried in the Rue-Petillon Military Cemetery, Fleuribaix in France and is remembered on the War Memorial at Christ College.

Lieutenant Theodore Gauntlett Thomas MID

47th Battalion, Canadian Infantry

12TH AUGUST 1918 ~ AGED 35

Hostel 1896-1901

Theodore Gauntlett Thomas was born on 18th July 1883 to the Reverend David and Una Gauntlett Thomas of Pwllcrochan, Pembrokeshire. Like so many sons of the cloth he was enrolled at Christ College, joining the Hostel at Easter 1896.

He seems to have made little impact on the games field but showed a preference for study. His studious approach saw him awarded a smattering of academic prizes from the start and, on Speech Day 22nd September 1896, he was awarded the Lower School Prize for his efforts in the first term. The following Speech Day on 26th July 1897 he received an Honorary Mention for his Greek as well as the Form Prize. A year later he was awarded the Mathematical Prize and in 1899 he was awarded a John Morgan scholarship. In 1901 Theo, as he was known, was made a Prefect. After what was described as a happy and successful career at school, he and W.H. Williams (Hostel 1894-1901) left later that year for St Catherine's College, Oxford.

As at school, Theo immediately made an impact. An 'Oxford Letter' to *The Breconian* of December 1901 refers amusingly to his activity on the river:

> *T.G. Thomas has fallen into the hands of the River-gods, commonly known as the boating men. No doubt there is some pleasure in toiling at the oar on a wintry afternoon from two to six, listening to the gratuitous and sarcastic comments of one's coach about 'rotters' in general, as the icy spray freezes upon the numbed fingers, and one realises that the sharpness of the seat will prevent one's sitting down upon a hard chair with any degree of comfort for some weeks to come. No doubt one thus becomes inured to the severest sufferings. No doubt the sweet satisfaction in the consciousness of self-martyrdom is "pleasing". No doubt! And we call ourselves a refined and civilized nation. A wise and prudent nation! No doubt!*

A year later the Oxford Letter reveals that Theo is still enjoying his rowing and is described as "…blossoming as a lily on the bosom of the Isis". In 1903 he was made vice-captain of the St Catherine's Boat Club and, during the spring of 1904, Theo was reported as "coaching his Torpid with marvellous results", a reference to preparing his team for the annual Oxford University inter-college boat races.

The records of the Oxford University Officers Training Corps show him as a Lance Corporal. On 21st November 1903 Theo and another Old Breconian, A.F. Sladden (Hostel 1895-1903), went with the Oxford University Officers Training Corps (Light Infantry) to Cambridge for a joint Field Day with the Cambridge University Officers Training Corps.

In the summer of 1904 Theo obtained a 3rd class BA from the School of Theology, Oxford and entered the teaching profession. He was appointed to the staff at the University College, Jamaica and then, in 1910, became a member of staff at the University School, Victoria, British Columbia, Canada. Whilst there, he held a commission in the 50th Gordon Highlanders (Canada). Theo was also noted as being an extremely conscientious teacher and a tremendous master of the shooting-range and the University School achieved great successes in the Dominion Shooting Competition.

In November 1914 Theo attended a medical examination prior to military service abroad. He passed the examination and his records show him as 5 feet 11 inches tall, of fair complexion with blue eyes and brown hair. His formal attestation took place on 4th December 1914. Theo was then commissioned into the 47th Battalion, Canadian Infantry (Western Ontario Regiment). He landed in England in March 1915 and is listed as a musketry instructor at Shorncliffe. *The Breconian* records that he "did much excellent work in training men in these early days" and the University School's Magazine, *Black and Red*, notes that several old boys visited him.

In September 1915 Theo married Miss Gertrude Cunliffe Marsh, daughter of Major-General and Mrs Marsh, of 8 Castle Hill Avenue, Folkestone at Christ Church, Folkestone. *The Folkestone Herald* of 25th September 1915 gave a report on the event, with photographs of the bride and groom. Their married home was at Acton Lodge, 12 Radnor Park West, Folkestone. Theo was recorded as being desperate to get to the Front; in September 1917 he achieved his wish and was sent to France. In a letter to his old school in Canada he wrote about the terrible slaughter and appalling conditions at Passchendaele.

In the early months of 1918 Theo was Mentioned in Despatches. On 12th August 1918, however, Theo was in the Menelars Trench which was being held by the 47th Battalion, consisting on that day of 30 officers and 559 other ranks. The Battalion Diary indicates "Orders were received for an enemy counter-attack which, however, did not materialize" and notes "some heavy artillery fire which caused a number of casualties". These amounted to one officer and three other ranks killed and six other ranks wounded. The officer killed was Theo.

After his death *The Breconian* noted that "Enthusiasm and loyal affection for his old School was characteristic of this keen Breconian". His Colonel, in writing to Theo's widow, refers to the loyal affection he engendered among his men: "… his conduct on all occasions was most gallant … he was a magnificent officer, and very popular with officers and men alike; while his Captain writes of him that his men would have followed him anywhere".

Lieutenant Theodore Gauntlett Thomas MID is buried at Rosières Communal Cemetery Extension, France. Theo's widow had inscribed on his headstone the words "And the spirit shall return unto God who gave it". He is remembered on the Christ College War Memorial.

Private Edwin Charles Trew MM

1st Battalion, The Buffs (East Kent Regiment)

3RD AUGUST 1918 ~ AGED 42

Day Boy 1890-1892

Edwin Charles Trew was born in 1876 and attended Christ College as a Day Boy from 1890 to 1892. He lived and grew up just over the bridge from Christ College at 13 Ship Street, Brecon. His father, Thomas, was a local butcher and JP. His mother, Martha, was Thomas' second wife, and the mother of three of his children. Edwin Charles was the sixth of eight children in total (three girls, five boys) although only he and one other brother, John, attended Christ College. He does not seem to have taken a particularly active part in games, in common with many day boys, and his name does not appear amongst the many sporting records recorded by *The Breconian*.

After leaving school, Edwin Charles began his working life as a bank clerk in Stafford where he lived with his uncle in the Parish of St Chad's, Tamworth. By 1915 he had moved back to Wales and enlisted whilst living at 34 Gwdyr Crescent, Swansea. According to his enlistment papers he was 39 years and 5 months old, his profession was 'bank cashier' and his religion was 'Baptist'. His first period of duty, from 10th December 1915, was on home service before being shipped to France on 21st September 1917.

Edwin Charles joined his regiment, the East Kent Regiment, in time for the Battle of Cambrai (20th November to 30th December 1917). He was twice wounded in battle, the second time 'copping a blighty' and thus needing evacuation back to England. After his recovery, he returned to France and was awarded the Military Medal on 19th March 1918 in the immediate build up to the Battle of St Quentin (which officially commenced on 21st March 1918). Less than five months later, on 3rd August 1918, Edwin Charles Trew was killed in action. His younger brother, Melville George Trew, a well-known musician in Brecon who had joined the South Wales Borderers, had been killed in Belgium just under a year earlier on 18th September 1917.

It took time to process Edwin's personal effects because of the number of war casualties but, on 14th March 1919, the officer in charge of records sent home his possessions to his mother, Martha. These included his wrist watch, razor, spectacles in their case, Income Tax papers, religious books and photographs.

Private Edwin Charles Trew is buried in the Esquelbecq Military Cemetery, France. His headstone bears the words chosen by mother: 'Peace Perfect Peace'. He is also remembered on the Christ College War Memorial.

Driver John Gordon Yendoll
Army Service Corps

27TH FEBRUARY 1921 ~ AGED 24
School House 1910-1913

John Gordon Yendoll was born on 30th January 1897 in the Bedwellty district of Monmouthshire. At the time of joining Christ College, his father, Bohannah Yendoll, ran the Duffryn Hotel in Aberbargoed, having moved from the Ivy Bush Hotel in Pengam some months earlier. The extended Yendoll family owned a number of hostelries, mainly in South and Mid Wales.

Gordon was the second of four brothers to join School House. His older brother Raymond Bohannah Yendoll (School House 1909-1912) gained a reputation for himself as an all-round sportsman. Gordon joined his brother in School House in September 1910 and, in turn, he was joined by his younger brother, Leslie Rees Yendoll (School House 1912-1917). The youngest of the four brothers, Leonard Godfrey Yendoll (School House 1915-1916) later became a Surgeon Commander in the Royal Navy. He served with distinction throughout the Second World War, and was twice Mentioned in Despatches.

Gordon enjoyed playing rugby football and on Wednesday 7th December 1910 played for School House N-Z against the Hostel in the House Matches. The Hostel won easily "by 8 goals 1 try (43 points) to nil" but the match report revealed that the "chief feature of the game was the good tackling of G. Yendoll at full-back". For his work in the back row in the autumn of 1911, Gordon was awarded a Junior Rugby Football Cup, presented at the Athletic Sports on Saturday 30th March by Mrs Evans of Ffrwdgrech.

In the summer of 1913 the 16 year old Gordon was made Captain of the 2nd Cricket XI and also played for both the 1st XI and the 'A' team on a number of occasions. He and Trevor Akrill Jones were chosen to play for Mr. Munns' XI against the 1st XI for the first match of the 1913 season. Although this took place on Saturday 10th May, recent flooding had left the ground wet and the wicket treacherous. This made runs hard to get and the 1st XI were dismissed for 47 runs. Mr. Munns' XI made a rather better 61 thanks to the work of the Reverend Donaldson, an excellent cricketer. These runs were made despite the best efforts of the 1st XI's superb bowler,

David Harold Davies. On the cricket field that term David Harold Davies and David Cuthbert Thomas played for the 1st XI, Trevor Akrill Jones for the 2nd XI, and Frank Harrington Best, John Gordon Yendoll and Harold Blakeney Davies played for both the 1st XI and the 2nd XI. Within a few years of playing together on the Christ College cricket squares, all six of these young lads would be dead.

In the autumn of 1913, his final term, Gordon was selected for the 1st Rugby Football XV and, alongside David Harold Davies and David Cuthbert Thomas, he played in his usual full-back position. In the end of season critique, *The Breconian* described him as "A very plucky player, never afraid to go down to a forward rush, and can kick a fairly long ball". Several plaudits were given in match reports to his work either as a three-quarter or as full-back - though he would probably want to forget one particular House Match that season when N-Z lost 84 points to 3 against A-M!

After leaving school Gordon returned to the family hostelry in Aberbargoed. However, in mid-1915 his address is recorded as 63 Carisbrooke Road, Walton, Liverpool. He intended going into banking and on Prize Day 1915, which was to be the last public prize-giving until 1921, it was announced that he had passed the necessary bank examinations to do so. Instead of taking up his chosen profession, Gordon voluntarily joined the Army Service Corps.

In 1917 Gordon was serving in Salonica and, while in the area of main fighting, Lake Dorian, he was seriously wounded. Although there was little hope of a recovery, he was sent home. He suffered greatly, particularly towards the end of his short life. *The Breconian* reported that his death on February 27th 1921 was "not unexpected". Gordon, who had been known at school as "a keen and painstaking boy and a plucky football player", died just a few weeks after his 24th birthday at Willesden, Middlesex where he was being nursed by his mother.

To be included on the Commonwealth War Graves list, the casualty had to have died between 4th August 1914 and 31st August 1921. Death also had to be attributable to resulting from an injury received or illness suffered during military service. Though both of these conditions were met at the time of his death, Driver John Gordon Yendoll is not yet included in War Graves List. He is, though, remembered on the Christ College War Memorial that was unveiled in 1922.

Reginald Somers Yorke

Government Driver

29TH JANUARY 1916 ~ AGED 59

Christ College 1865-1867

Reginald Somers Yorke was born on 10th June 1854, the ninth of twelve children. He entered Christ College from Newcastle Emlyn in 1865 and left two years later, moving to Tonbridge School (1867-1872) from where he won the Judd Exhibition Scholarship at St Catherine's College, Cambridge. He married Emmeline Crofton on 10th February 1886.

For many years Reginald served in the Chinese Imperial Customs Service but returned home to live at Scethrog around 1907. He took a great deal of interest in his old school and in December 1908 he presided as Senior Steward at the Old Breconians' Annual Dinner in Brecon in which he proposed the toast "The School: may it live long and prosper well".

Although too old for military service in the First World War, yet "being an ardent motorist", Reginald volunteered as a driver for "Government purposes". It was while engaged in this work that he contracted pneumonia. He died on 29th January 1916.

Reginald was a relation by birth to the Earl of Hardwicke, whose family name was Yorke. The male members of the Yorke family tended to be in government service of one form or other, and had been so for centuries. Given his family connections and impeccable record of service, Reginald's offer as a driver would have been readily accepted. Drivers of this calibre, and there were very few, were often required to carry highly sensitive material as well as important passengers who needed a degree of anonymity. By the nature of their service, hard information is very difficult to come by but Reginald Somers Yorke is included here because he died while in the service of his country.

Reginald Somers Yorke is not recorded on the Christ College War memorial but his name has been permanently added to the Roll of Honour read on Remembrance Sunday at Christ College.

Lieutenant Colonel George Udny Yule DSO MID
Royal Engineers
22ND DECEMBER 1918 ~ AGED 37
School House 1894-1895

George's father, also called George Udny Yule, married his mother, Maria Kipling Howard, in Kensington in 1879 before moving to India where George Senior had business interests. Their son, George, was born and baptised in Calcutta. He attended Ripley Court School in Surrey, from where he moved, with his two older brothers, to Christ College.

The three brothers entered School House in 1894, and then left together in the following year. Robert Abercrombie Yule was the oldest, born on the 4th November 1879, Harry Howard Yule was born on the 30th November 1880 and George Udny Yule was born on 17th November 1881. A fourth brother, Jack Seymour Yule, born in 1890, did not attend Christ College. The boys came from a distinguished military, business and political family and the family home at the time of entry was 41 Eaton Rise, Ealing.

George had gained a scholarship from Ripley Court but nothing is known of his academic progress while at Christ College. In the summer of 1895, though, George would have seen his brother, Robert, collect the Form IV Physics Prize at the prize-giving ceremony at Speech Day on Saturday 25th July. The next person in the line, this time to collect the Form III Science prize, was Charles Owen Spencer Smith; the following prize, this time for drawing, was collected by William Logie Lloyd Fitzwilliams who died during the Boer War. Both boys, like George Udny Yule, were to become Old Breconians who gave their lives in the service of their country.

After finishing formal education, George elected to go into the Army. On 18th August 1900 he was commissioned Second Lieutenant, Royal Engineers. At the time of the 1901 Census Second Lieutenant Yule was based at Gillingham, Kent. He was promoted to Lieutenant on 18th August 1903. George married Phoebe Chicheley Plowden at Rawalpindi, India on 31st October 1908 and their first son, Robert Chicheley Yule was born and baptised at Quetta in late 1909. In the following year on 18th August 1910, George was promoted to Captain and remained with the British Army in India for a number of years.

However, he entered France on 2nd February 1915. In the bitter fighting around Thiepval in September 1916 George was shell shocked when the roof of his dugout was blown in by a shell. He was sent via 22 Ambulance Train to No. 7 Stationary Hospital, Boulogne, arriving on 14th September after a journey that had taken five days. His medical report stated that he needed rest and, on the following day, George was moved to England on the Hospital Ship 'Newhaven'. From the ship, he was admitted to London General Hospital on 17th September 1915.

A Medical Board found him unfit for General Service for three months due to "shell shock and gassing" but, instead of taking sick leave, he was attached to the India Office. On 23rd November 1916 George was promoted to Major. On 1st January 1917 it was announced that George was to receive the Distinguished Service Order; another announcement the following day stated that he had been Mentioned in Despatches.

A further Medical Board, held on 12th January 1917, found George fit for light duties in India and on 26th January he sailed on the P&O ship 'Khyber', landing in Bombay on 24th February. On 21st May 1917 George was promoted to Temporary Lieutenant Colonel. He served the remainder of the War in India but in the closing weeks of 1918 he became ill and died of pneumonia at Colobar War Hospital, Bombay on 22nd December 1918.

Lieutenant Colonel George Udny Yule DSO, MID is buried in Bombay and commemorated on the Kirkee War Memorial in Poona, India. There is also a plaque to George and his wife, Maria, at Gullane Parish Churchyard, East Lothian, an area of Scotland where his family had strong roots.

Lieutenant Colonel Yule is not listed on the Christ College War Memorial because his death was not known at the time of its unveiling. However, in November 2013 his name was permanently added to the Roll of Honour read on Remembrance Sunday at Christ College.

Appendices

Cricket Pavilion

Appendix One

Words and Poetry from *The Breconian* 1914-1818

The strident patriotism that had been building in pre-war Britain spilt out when hostilities commenced in late summer 1914. Reading the school magazine a century later, a real sense of God and duty comes through. Although the idea of the British and Commonwealth fighting a tyranny is maintained through the years, there is perhaps a sense of weariness by 1918, with fewer militaristic and nationalistic sentiments overtly expressed. On the cessation of hostilities, there are comic poems pointing fun at the restrictions and a great sense of relief combined with satisfaction that school life has been maintained.

From The Editorial of *The Breconian*. December 1914:

> *"Deep graved in every Brecon heart,*
> *O never let those names depart"*

Everywhere we hear the bugle call to arms … we see some sign of death … we hear and read of the heroic deeds of England's glorious sons … Some old Breconians have laid down their lives for King and Country and many others have responded to the call to arms in a manner worthy of the name and traditions of Christ College … They have died; but let us not forget those who have bought such honour and glory to the old School.

The Breconian. December 1914:

An article entitled "From Louvain to Brecon" not only welcomes Belgium refugee Professor Adrien Henri van Emelen to Christ College as a teacher of French and Drawing but also relates his experiences in fleeing from the "burning, pillage and massacre" in his homeland by the Germans.

The Breconian. December 1914:

84 year old (General) Lord Roberts of Kandahar, a colossus of military leadership in Victorian and Edwardian England, died whilst visiting Allied troops in France on 14th November 1914.

Bobs

He is gone! For death a great nation bereaving
Has come with his silent tread.
We receive the message with ears unbelieving -
Lord Roberts is dead.

The soldier, than whom no other was dearer
To the men that he often led,
Than whom to their hearts no other was nearer -
Lord Roberts is dead.

All apprehensions and fear, as by magic,
Banished by hope, had fled;
Then came the news, in its suddenness tragic -
Lord Roberts is dead.

And our hopes of success on the morrow
Are veiled in this grief so dread;
For the loss of our hero the Empire's in sorrow -
Lord Roberts is dead.

The Breconian. December 1914: (Rugby) Football Season

"The War overshadows everything just now, and so (Rugby) Football, like much else, has taken a somewhat secondary position this winter. We acquiesced as in a thing but right and inevitable when a promising club fixture list was cut to ribbons: our thoughts generally have been preoccupied in a sterner and more deadly strife.

"Still, without encroaching on the new military duties, it was clear that we must continue to have exercise and recreation, and the problem has been to keep (Rugby) Football alive minus the usual incentive of foreign matches. The decision to retain the annual School fixtures helped a great deal, and the 1st Game has certainly risen to the occasion, and played and trained if anything more keenly than usual. They have shown an excellent spirit in that they played the game for the mere love of it".

The Breconian. **December 1914:**

The Rally

Since to refuse were shame
And worse than death,
With our last breath
To keep unsullied our fair name,
Belgium! We come; behold, we come, O France!
To share your cause, and with your urgent foe to break a lance.

Not with unseemly boast,
We, being few,
What we shall do
Assert in no prophetic boast;
Comrades in arms! - From Belfort to Tournay,
From Petrograd to Lodz - this we will do, what best we may.

Not with the lust of Hate
Of Man for Man,
Thy rushing van,
Thy serried legions we await,
O Germany! - but from our piece alight
To speak with thee of Honour written and unwritten Right.

And with a faith that saves
That proud and free
O'er yon North Sea
Britannia still shall rule the waves;
Jellicoe's fleet! man of the Nelson breed,
Our homes to you we leave to keep and succour at their need.

Yea, verily in this Day,
O peace from strife,
Thro' death, thro' life,
Since we now love as brothers may,
India! We call thee - Panthan, Gurkha, Sikh!
Say, will ye ride with us this Day? Shall your guns also speak?

And knowing as we know
Across the seas
That all of these
Come whence we came, go where we go;
North, South, East, West - ye younger Britains all!
We listen where your steps, unasked, unfalteringly fall.

Therefore, whatever Fate
Holds in her hands,
Here England stands,
Her soul unconquerably great,
Where Marlborough fought, where Wellington of yore,
To fight, to endure, to die; our trust in God: we can no more.

The Breconian. **December 1915:**

How Victories Are Won

The Kaiser was sitting in state on his chair,
Reading a list with a satisfied air
Of victories won bravely on land and on sea,
Provided that day by his Wolff's agency;
When in rushed a man, who for miles had been bunking,
Yelling, "Sir, I must tell you, your Prussians are funking.
From the battle I've come with the greatest of haste,
For I must say that fighting is not to my taste".
The Kaiser then rose with a loud explanation,
But calmed himself soon and wrote this proclamation:-
"Announce to my people that now without doubt
The Russians again are in one complete rout".
The people with joy these glad tidings receive,
And Wolff's some "Official News" very soon weave.
Then back goes the Kaiser triumphant to tea,
And thus has been gained one more great victory.

From The Editorial of *The Breconian*. April 1916:

"It would be impossible for us to conclude the Editorial without some reference to those Old Breconians, who, since our last issue, have sacrificed their lives upon the altar of duty in the World War…The example set by these heroes should be long remembered, and may the time be far distant, when mention of their names ceases to arouse feelings of pride in the mind of every Breconian".

The Breconian. December 1916:

Letters from the War

The Breconian regularly published letters from Old Breconians on war service. For censorship reasons the names of the writers were withheld although there are sometimes clues as to the author. The following was written by D. C. Thomas:

Your letter, with all its news, reached me a few days ago. The parcels, so kindly provided by the Hostelites, arrived en masse yesterday. I wish to thank you all very much indeed for your kindness and thoughtfulness; please thank the contributors for me and tell them how much the good things are being appreciated.

The 'footer' results make excellent reading. To beat Monmouth by such a score reminds me of my early days at Brecon: the Llandovery match must have been a very good one. I've had two games of Rugger since I came out. The second game wasn't at all bad fun, but my wind gave out early after half time. The men mostly play Soccer; we have a very good regimental side. Very few officers seem to know much about Rugger.

Christmas out here was a very merry festival. A burlesque Soccer Match, Officers v. Sergeants, came off in the morning. The sergeants showed great ingenuity in their 'makes-up,' some wearing gas-helmets, others women's clothing. The men quite enjoyed their Christmas and are all ready for work again this week.

I shall get my leave about March, I expect. If I get time, I should like to spend a few hours in Brecon. If I cannot do so, I must wait until I get a "Blighty packet" - i.e., a soft "cushy," wound, necessitating slack convalescence. I'm getting well up in T.A.'s expressions, several of which are mutilated French - e.g., "no pooh" (? il n'y a plus), which can mean countless things.

From France.

(We print this letter for its pathetic interest. The writer was killed, just at the very time when he speaks of expecting his leave. No "Blighty packet," alas! but the eternal discharge. Sit terra levis!)".

The Breconian. **December 1916:**

A Route March

What is this great martial throng,
Setting off with cheery song,
As they gaily march along?
The Cadet Corps.

Who are these with weary tread,
Many hours in marching sped,
Tramping on with drooping head?
The Cadet Corps.

Who are these that like a hearse
Homeward creep with mutter'd curse,
Stony roads their thoughts emerse?
The Cadet Corps.

Who are these at last at rest
Back at their collegiate nest?
Many of them have not bless'd
The Cadet Corps.

The Breconian. **December 1916:**

Occasional Notes

"J. V. Martyn (O.B.) has composed a March, "The Devil's Own," which was played at the annual concert of the Cymmer Colliery Military Band of which his father is conductor. He is attached to the Inns of Court, O.T.C. The March is described as "intensely forceful" and one of the audience remarked that "if the O.T.C. was imbued with the aggressive spirit of the Composer, the Germans would have much cause to fear them."

The Breconian. December 1916:

*Lord Kitchener was a well known soldier and imperialist, famous for victories in the Sudan
and in the Second Boer War. He became Secretary of State for War in 1914 and was one
of the few who foresaw a long war. His iconic image from the 'Your Country Needs You'
campaign encouraged tens of thousands of young men to enlist. He was on his way to meet
Tsar Nichols II of Russia when his ship hit a mine off the Orkney Islands.*

Lord Kitchener

Viscount Kitchener, Lord of Broome,
Known to fame by the fight at Khartoum,
Sirdar of Egypt, 'twas there your star shone;
By the stroke of a mine to your death you have gone.
By planning and scheming 'twas your great work
To baffle the German, th' Austrian and Turk,
And for this great purpose you went on your way
To meet with the Tsar on that fateful day.

Creator of armies, England's strong hand,
Directing our forces that fight on the land,
Little we thought that your death you should meet
Upon the great ocean where fights England's fleet.
The seas running high, the gale blowing strong,
The good ship "Hampshire" went steaming along;
Of her twenty-five knots she was making the most,
When she struck that stray mine off the grim Scottish coast.

Viscount Kitchener, Lord of Broome,
Doing your duty you went to your doom;
You found the soldier, Lloyd George found the gun,
Alas, you'll never see your great victory won.
"Lord Kitchener's dead, our strong hand no more,"
Your second great fight with our enemy o'er;
Mourned by all England you ever shall be,
Living for aye in the hearts of the free.

The Breconian. December 1916:

Occasional Notes

"Lieut. and Quarter-Master C.W. Price (O.B.) was in command of a Tank during the September fighting on the Somme". *He was thus one of the first in action in this new invention.*

"2nd Lieut. P.S. Lewis (O.B.), who was reported wounded and a prisoner after the fall of Kut, has been exchanged".

"Lieut. A.R. Evans (O.B.), R.E., did good work in France last year in supplying the troops with water. In view of the coming offensive at Loos, it was imperative that abundance of water should be available, while the only spring of any size near was the foot of a disused coal-mine. In the face of almost incredible difficulties, he succeeded in raising this water, though every tool and article of machinery had to be improvised".

From The Editorial of *The Breconian.* April 1917:

"One great change has come over school routine. On the issue of the new Government food restrictions, when their significance was demonstrated, many and loud and deep were the groans of the hungry. Still louder they became on the institution of ruthless parcel censorship".

War Rhymes

Ancre Song

When the Hun came to anchor on the Ancre,
In the fair land of France like a canker,
O, he thought he's come to stay
For ever and a day
You can bet the bottom dollar at your banker.
But a general named Gough,
He said to him, "Gee-off!"
And from Prince down to corporal and ranker,
The Hun slipped his anchor on the Ancre
And stole away.

Mesopota-mania

Wrote daughter Maude to father Maude-
"When you cut Kut,
We such a flag wave had, Dad.
Old Enver must be awfully bored;
He'll say 'Tut, tut!
Should you but bag Bagdad, Dad."

General Maude captured Baghdad on
11th March 1917.

From The Editorial of *The Breconian*. July 1917:

"The end of yet another term sees us still in the throes of this great struggle, of which "the beginning of the end," as did the waters from Tantalus, ever seem to recede from our grasp. Bit by bit the routine of our lives has been changed to suit the new conditions: such things as the enrolment of a corps of harvesters and watching the cricket team, plus umpire and scorer, going away in a magnificent chariot intended to hold eight, remind us that there is a war on. Still, though we may occasionally think of the "piping times of peace," yet we try to carry on, and keep up our pre-war fields of activity as far as is compatible with patriotism".

From The Editorial of *The Breconian*. December 1917:

"Despite every effort of the Hun, in air, land, or sea, we are still "Carrying on."… Finally, we would turn with sorrow, but also with admiration to our ever-growing Roll of Honour, and pay our humble token of respect to those, some of whom were even yesterday our schoolfellows, who have willingly answered the last summons. Whatever our pride in the minor successes of our school, it is but a puny thing beside this grander record, in which Breconians, past, present and future, will always glory".

From The Editorial of *The Breconian*. April 1918:

"It is once more our sad but glorious duty to mourn the loss of many schoolfellows in the service of their country. The lustre that our Roll of Honour sheds upon the School - though bought dearly by noble self-sacrifice - will live undimmed among coming generations of Breconians. Upon this note of nobility we would end with the hope that their successors may but add to its glory".

From The Editorial of *The Breconian*. December 1918:

"One or two events, quite unprecedented in the history of our School, have combined to make a term, never monotonous, one teeming with interest for us and for future Breconians.

"The conclusion of any war in which our country is involved, be it only a campaign, must of necessity be a "red-letter" day for us. What, then, have been our feelings upon November 11th at the termination of a conflict whose parallel the world has never known, in which Britain and her Allies fighting for Right against Might have triumphed?

"In our joy and thankfulness, however, we cannot lose sight of the fact that this was accomplished by great sacrifice of life, and that on the altar of that sacrifice many Old Breconians have died. We should feel we have been honoured in that "Alma Mater" has been granted the high privilege of helping to pay for that great Day with the lives of her sons."

The Breconian. **December 1918:**

The rather stringent Defence of the Realm Act (D.O.R.A.) was introduced on 8th August 1914 and was added to as the war progressed. Michael Drayton was a well known poet in the Elizabethan period whose sonnet 'Since There's No Help' was used as the basis of 'To D.O.R.A'.

To D.O.R.A.
(With apologies to Michael Drayton).

Since there's no war, come let us kiss and part-
Nay, I have done, you rule no more o'er me;
And I am glad, yea, glad with all my heart,
That thus completely I am rid of Thee.

Shake hands for ever, cancel every clause,
And if we meet at any time again,
Be it not legal under any laws
That you one jot of former power retain.

Now at the last gasp of Big Berth's breath,
When, her heart failing, proud Bellona stops,
And peace is kneeling at her bed of death,
And Winny closing up munition shops,

Now, when all me forever give thee over,
Never again thy sway shalt thou recover.

The Rational Anthem

We've beat the German powers,
Their submarines are ours
To sink no more;
We shall have more to eat,
Plenty of fat and meat,
Sugar to make things sweet,
And cakes "galore."

Coupons we shall not need
To get ourselves a feed;
Full plates away.
No longer I'll be thin;
To eat won't be a sin
Puddings with currants in
On Christmas Day.

The Breconian. July 1919:

*On 28th June 1919, five years exactly after the assassination of Archduke Franz Ferdinand,
the Treaty of Versailles was signed.*

The Twenty-Eighth of June

Hark! For the bells are ringing,
Ringing out over meadow and moor;
Listen, they bring us good tidings,
The news that all fighting is o'er!
It is peace, it is peace, come rejoice,
For today is the greatest of days,
Raise your heart, and your soul, and your voice,
While the nation re-echoes with praise.

Three cheers for our glorious allies,
In Europe and in the far west,
Three cheers for our soldiers and sailors
And the women who gave of their best!
And now let us bow down and worship,
For to-day is the greatest of days,
And-not unto us, O Lord,
But to Thy name give the praise.

Appendix Two
Date of Attendance at Christ College

Arrived	Name	Left School
1865	Yorke, R.S.	1867
1881	Lewis, C.H.	1886
1882	Lyall, C.G.	1884
1883	-	
1884	-	
1885	-	
1886	-	
1887	Ricketts, T. F.	1891
1888	Kell, H.J.G.	1890
	Kell, P.A.G.	1890
	Marles Thomas, L.W.	1890
1889	-	
1890	Madoc Jones, H.	1892
	Trew, E.C.	1892
1891	Leyshon, E.J.	1896
1892	Lloyd, E.D.	1895
1893	Spencer Smith, C.O.	1898
1894	Maddock, H.T.	1898
	Yule, G.U.	1895

Arrived	Name	Left School
1895	Aitken, G.T.	1898
	Bell, S.W.	1899
1896	Abbott, W.D.	1901
	Fitzwilliams, J.K.Ll.	1898
	Jones, P.B.	1898
	Thomas, T.G.	1901
1897	Best, A.S.M.	1901
	Jones. T.G.	1905
1898	-	
1899	Gibbon, W. St.M.	1906
1900	Best, S.W.	1906
	Cobb, J.C.	1900
	Hughes, L.	1902
	Lawrence, E.W.	1903
1901	Davies, W.B.	1908
	Harries, H.L.	1905
	Jenkins, D.R.	1903
	Richards, H.W.	1903
1902	-	
1903	Broadbent, C.H. (Master)	1906
	Nicholls (Leeder), B.E. (with gap)	1908
1904	Best, F.H.	1910
	Hazard, C.P.	1907

Arrived	Name	Left School
1904	Hincks, B.	1908
	Spencer Smith, M.	1909
1905	Macaulay, B.W.	1907
	Macaulay, H.	1907
1906	Saunders Jones	1910
	Thomas, D.C.	1914
1907	Biggerton-Evans, A.B.G.	1912
	Grant, H.N.	1909
	Griffiths, D.M.	1909
	Hunter, C.G.R.	1910
	Lewis, L.G.	1912
1908	Evans, F.W.	1910
1909	Akrill Jones, E.T.	1915
	Akrill Jones, R.R.	1910
	Boothby, C.G.	1913
	Davies, H.B.	1911
	Parry, T.	1913
1910	Shapland, G.B.P.	1912
	Yendoll, J.G.	1913
1911	Green, C.G.	1912
	Lewis, S.E.	1916
	Robinson, J.S. (Master)	1915
1912	Davies, D.H.	1914
	Musk, F.A.I.	1915
	Thomas, D.J.	1916

Arrived	Name	Left School
1913	Arnott, E.E.	1915
	Evans, N.V.	1916
	James, F.	1915

Appendix Three
Date of Death, Chronological Order

Date	Name	Rank	Age
1914			
September 22nd	Kell, P.A.G.	Lieutenant	38
October 18th	Lyall, C.J.	Captain	42
1915			
February 1st	Lloyd, E.D.	Private	37
April 24th	Hunter, C.G.R.	Lieutenant	21
May 28th	Lewis, C.H.	Major	46
August 3rd	Dempster, H.S.D.	Lance-Corporal	27
August 7th	Griffiths, D.M.	Trooper	22
September 28th	Jones. P.B.	Captain	34
1916			
January 29th	Yorke, R.S.	Government Driver	59
March 1st	Broadbent, C.H.	Second Lieutenant	34
March 18th	Thomas, D.C.	Second Lieutenant	20
April 21st	Hazard, C.P.	Second Lieutenant	28
April 23rd	Davies, H.B.	Second Lieutenant	25
April 28th	Boothby, C.G.	Second Lieutenant	21
June 11th	Ricketts, T.F.	Driver	42
June 14th	Bell, S.W.	Lieutenant	34
July 1st	Grant, H.N.	Second Lieutenant	23
July 10th	Lawrence, E.W.	Captain	28
September 10th	Spencer Smith, M.	Second Lieutenant	25
September 23rd	Arnott, E.E.	Second Lieutenant	19
October 28th	Evans, F.W.	Second Lieutenant	21
November 13th	Harries, H.L.	Second Lieutenant	28
December 18th	Hincks, B.	Second Lieutenant	26

Date	Name	Rank	Age
1917			
January 21st	Jenkins, D.R.	Captain	28
February 13th	Best, F.H.	Lieutenant	22
February 23rd	Best, A.S.M.	Lieutenant	30
February 26th	Thomas, D.J.	Private	19
March 11th	Green, C.N.	Driver	21
April 9th	Akrill Jones, R.R.	Second Lieutenant	22
April 20th	Jones, T.G.	Lieutenant	30
April 29th	Marles Thomas, L.	Second Mate	38
April 30th	Best, S.W.	Lieutenant	28
May 3rd	Macaulay, B.W.	Second Lieutenant	27
July 31st	Madoc Jones, H.	Lieutenant	38
August 3rd	Saunders Jones, H.	Lieutenant	22
August 3rd	Spencer Smith, C.O.	Captain	37
August 16th	Evans, N.V.	Second Lieutenant	19
November 6th	Hughes, L.	Private	32
November 24th	Lewis, L.G.	Second Lieutenant	23
1918			
March 18th	Akrill Jones, E.T.	Lieutenant	19
April 24th	Gibbon, W.St.M.	Lieutenant	29
April 25th	Macaulay, H.	Lieutenant	23
May 8th	Nicholls (Leeder) B.E.	Captain	26
June 26th	Kell, HJG	Master Mariner	44
July 27th	Leyshon, E.J.	Corporal	40
August 3rd	Trew, E.C.	Private	42
August 12th	Thomas, T.G.	Lieutenant	35
August 13th	Lewis, S.E.	Sgt. Observer	19
August 23rd	Cobb, C.C.	Lieutenant	33
August 27th	Musk, F.A.I.	Private	20
August 30th	Fitzwilliams, J.K.Ll.	Major	33

Date	Name	Rank	Age
October 10th	Aitken, G.T.	Sqd. Segt-Major	36
November 1st	James, F.	Lieutenant	22
November 13th	Robinson, J.S.	Lieutenant	30
November 18th	Davies, D.H.	Second Lieutenant	21
December 3rd	Abbott, W.D.	Chaplain the Rev.	35
December 3rd	Davies, W.B.	Second Lieutenant	28
December 22nd	Yule, G.U.	Lieutenant Colonel	37
1919			
March 4th	Parry, T.	Private	22
December 17th	Biggerton-Evans, A.	Captain	26
1920			
August 8th	Richards, H.W.	Second Lieutenant	32
1921			
February 27th	Yendoll, J.G.	Driver	24
December 15th	Maddock, H.T.	Lieutenant	40
1924			
November 15th	Shapland, G.B.P.	Lieutenant	26

Private C.A. Collins is not included in the above list as he survived the war.

Appendix Four
Grave or Memorial Location

Name	Grave Location	Plot/Panel
Abbott, William David	Janval Cemetery, Dieppe	II.A.1
Aitken, George Taylor	Drummond Cemetery, Raillencourt	I.C.7
Akrill Jones, Edward Trevor	Bolsover St. Mary's Old Churchyard	-
Akrill Jones, Robert Rowland	British Cemetery, St Martin-Sur-Cojeul	D.4.
Arnott, Euan Edward	Warlencourt British Cemetery	II.L.23
Bell, Sydney William	Ypres (Menin Gate) Memorial	24-6-8-30
Best, Arthur Stephen Middleton	Amara War Cemetery	XX1M20
Best, Frank Harrington	Basra Memorial	Pan.16/62
Best, Stephen Wriothesley	Basra Memorial	Pan.16/62
Biggerton-Evans, Arthur Basil George	Plovdiv Central Cemetery	F. 2
Boothby, Charles Geoffrey	R.E. Grave, Railway Wood	-
Broadbent, Cecil Hoyle	Warloy-Baillon Communal Cemetery	D. 5
Cobb, James Cassels	Dernancourt Communal Cemetery Extension	VIII. G. 5
Collins, Cecil Arthur		-
Davies, David Harold	Niederzwehren Cemetery	VII. B. 4
Davies, Harold Blakeney	Essex Farm Cemetery	1.A.30
Davies, Walter Bomford	At sea returning from India	
Dempster, Harold Skeel Duncan	Etaples Military Cemetery	II. A. 31
Evans, Frederick William	Lijssenthoek Military Cemetery	IX. B. 13
Evans, Neville Vernon	Artillery Wood Cemetery	V.A.1
Fitzwilliams, John Kenrick Lloyd	Vis-En-Artois British Cemetery, Haucourt	V.G.1
Gibbon, Wilfred St. Martin	Nowshera Military Cemetery	A.15
Grant, Henry Norman	Redan Ridge Cemetery No. 2, Beaumont- Hamel	C. 31
Green, Cyril Norman	Boulogne Eastern Cemetery	VIII. A. 190
Griffiths, David Mansel	Lone Pine Memorial	Panel 6
Harries, Howard Locke	Euston Road Cemetery, Colincamps	1.G.68
Hazard, Charles Piper	Essex Farm Cemetery	II.G.6
Hincks, Bertram	Delville Wood Cemetery, Longueval	XXIV.L 7
Hughes, Lewis	Passchendale New British Cemetery	XIII. E. 5
Hunter, Charles Gawain Raleigh	Ypres (Menin Gate) Memorial	Panel 47

James, Frank	Vaux-Andigny British Cemetery	C. 17
Jenkins, David Roy	Nolton (St. Mary) Churchyard	2.1
Jones, Percy Barrett	Loos Memorial	Pan. 99-100
Jones, Titho Glynne	Gaza War Cemetery	XVI. G. 4
Kell, Herbert James Graham	Tower Hill Memorial	
Kell, Philip Arthur Graham	Chatham Naval Memorial	Panel 7
Lawrence, Edward William	Thiepval Memorial	Pier/Face 4C
Lewis, Cecil Hallowes	St. Sever Cemetery, Rouen	Officer A1.8
Lewis, Leonard Glynne	Cambrai Memorial, Louverval	Panel 7
Lewis, Sydney Edward	Charmes Military Cemetery, Essegney	I. E. 13.
Leyshon, Edward James	Pontypridd (Glyntaff) Cemetery	FB. 535.
Lloyd, Evan David	Ste. Marie Cemetery, Le Havre	Div.14. K 6
Lyall, Charles George	Le Touret Memorial	Panel 8
Macaulay, Bruce Wallace	Arras Memorial	Bay 8
Macaulay, Horace	Tyne Cot Memorial	Panel 132-5
Maddock, Hopkin Thomas		
Madoc Jones, Harold	Ypres (Menin Gate) Memorial	Panel 22
Marles Thomas, Lewis William	Tower Hill Memorial	-
Nicholls (Leeder), Benjamin E.	Bellacourt Military Cemetery, Riviere	II. H. 6
Musk, Francis Alfred Ismay	Croisilles British Cemetery	III. A. 31
Parry, Thomas	Carmarthen Cemetery	B. 60
Richards, Howard Wynne	Cefn Coed Cemetery	
Ricketts, Thomas Ferrar	Basra War Cemetery	VI. M. 16
Robinson, John Stanley	Dalmeny and Queensferry Cemetery	445
Saunders Jones, Henry St. John	Dar-Es-Salaam War Cemetery	7.B.2
Shapland, Geoffrey Bernard Penberthy	Brecon Cemetery	
Spencer Smith, Charles Owen	Godewaersvelde British Cemetery	1.C.13
Spencer Smith, Martin	Thiepval Memorial	Face 13 C
Thomas, David Cuthbert	Point 101 New Military Cemetery, Fricourt	D. 3
Thomas, David John	Rue-Petillon Miltary Cemetery, Fleurbaix	I. L. 14
Thomas, Theodore Gauntlett	Rosières Communal Cemetery Extension	III.F.13
Trew, Edwin Charles	Esquelbecq Military Cemetery	III. D. 31
Yendoll, John Gordon		
Yorke, Reginald Somers		
Yule, George Udney	Kirkee 1914-1918 Memorial	Face B

Appendix Five
Location of Grave or Memorial by Country

Africa

Dar-Es-Salaam War Cemetery (Tanzania) — **Saunders Jones, Henry St. John**

Belgium

Artillery Wood Cemetery — **Evans, Neville Vernon**

Essex Farm Cemetery — **Davies, Harold Blakeney;**
Hazard, Charles Piper

Lijssenthoek Military Cemetery — **Evans, Frederick William**

Passchendale New British Cemetery — **Hughes, Lewis**

R.E. Grave, Railway Wood — **Boothby, Charles Geoffrey**

Tyne Cot Memorial — **Macaulay, Horace**

Ypres (Menin Gate) Memorial — **Bell, Sydney William;**
Hunter, Charles Gawain Raleigh;
Madoc Jones, Harold

Bulgaria

Plovdiv Central Cemetery — **Biggerton-Evans, Arthur Basil George**

France

Arras Memorial — **Macaulay, Bruce Wallace**

Bellacourt Military Cemetery, Riviere — **Nicholls, (Leeder), Benjamin E.**

Boulogne Eastern Cemetery — **Green, Cyril Norman**

British Cemetery, St. Martin-Sur-Cojeul — **Akrill Jones, Robert Rowland**

Cambrai Memorial, Louverval — **Lewis, Leonard Glynne**

Charmes Military Cemetery, Essegney — **Lewis, Sydney Edward**

Croisilles British Cemetery — **Musk, Francis Alfred Ismay**

Delville Wood Cemetary, Longueval — **Hincks, Bertram**

Dernancourt Communal Cemetery Extension — **Cobb, James Cassels**

Drummond Cemetery, Raillencourt — **Aitken, George Taylor**

Esquelbecq Military Cemetery — **Trew, Edwin Charles**

Etaples Military Cemetery — **Dempster, Harold Skeel Duncan**

Euston Road Cemetery, Colincamps — **Harries, Howard Locke**

Godewaersvelde British Cemetery — **Spencer Smith, Charles Owen**

Janval Cemetery, Dieppe — **Abbott, William David**

Le Touret Memorial — **Lyall, Charles George**

Loos Memorial — **Jones, Percy Barrett**

Point 101 New Military Cemetery, Fricourt — **Thomas, David Cuthbert**

Redan Ridge Cemetery No.2, Beaumont-Hamel — **Grant, Henry Norman**

Rosières Communal Cemetery Extension	**Thomas, Theodore Gauntlett**
Rue-Petillon Miltary Cemetery, Fleurbaix	**Thomas, David John**
St. Sever Cemetery, Rouen	**Lewis, Cecil Hallowes**
Ste. Marie Cemetery, Le Havre	**Lloyd, Evan David**
Thiepval Memorial	**Lawrence, Edward William;**
	Spencer Smith, Martin
Vaux-Andigny British Cemetery	**James, Frank**
Vis-En-Artois British Cemetery, Haucourt	**Fitzwilliams, John Kenrick Lloyd**
Warlencourt British Cemetery	**Arnott, Euan Edward**
Warloy-Baillon Communal Cemetery	**Broadbent, Cecil Hoyle**

Germany

Niederzwehren Cemetery	**Davies, David Harold**

India

Kirkee 1914-1918 Memorial	**Yule, George Udny**

Iraq

Amara War Cemetery	**Best, Arthur Stephen Middleton**
Basra Memorial	**Best, Frank Harrington;**
	Best, Stephen Wriothesley
Basra War Cemetery	**Ricketts, Thomas Ferrar**

Israel

Gaza War Cemetery	**Jones, Titho Glynne**

Pakistan

Nowshera Military Cemetery:	**Gibbon, Wilfred St. Martin**

Turkey

Lone Pine Memorial	**Griffiths, David Mansel**

United Kingdom

Bolsover St. Mary's Old Churchyard	**Akrill Jones, Edward Trevor**
Brecon Cemetery	**Shapland, Geoffrey Bernard Penberthy**
Cefn Coed	**Richards, Howard Wynne**
Carmarthen	**Parry, Thomas**
Chatham Naval Memorial	**Kell, Philip Arthur Graham**
Dalmeny and Queensferry Cemetery	**Robinson, John Stanley**
Nolton (St. Mary) Churchyard, Bridgend	**Jenkins, David Roy**
Pontypridd (Glyntaff) Cemetery	**Leyshon, Edward James**
Tower Hill Memorial	**Kell, Herbert James Graham;**
	Marles Thomas, Lewis William